THE ART OF MEDIEVAL FALCONRY

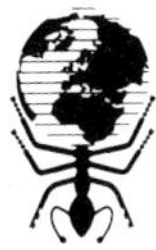

Covering one of the most fascinating yet misunderstood periods in history, the MEDIEVAL LIVES series presents medieval people, concepts and events, drawing on political and social history, philosophy, material culture (art, architecture and archaeology) and the history of science. These books are global and wide-ranging in scope, encompassing both Western and non-Western subjects, and span the fifth to the fifteenth centuries, tracing significant developments from the collapse of the Roman Empire onwards.

SERIES EDITOR: Deirdre Jackson

Albertus Magnus and the World of Nature *Irven M. Resnick and Kenneth F. Kitchell Jr*

Alle Thyng Hath Tyme: Time and Medieval Life *Gillian Adler and Paul Strohm*

Andrey Rublev: The Artist and His World *Robin Milner-Gulland*

The Art of Anatomy in Medieval Europe *Taylor McCall*

The Art of Medieval Falconry *Yannis Hadjinicolaou*

Bede and the Theory of Everything *Michelle P. Brown*

Christine de Pizan: Life, Work, Legacy *Charlotte Cooper-Davis*

Francis of Assisi: His Life, Vision and Companions *Michael F. Cusato*

Geoffrey Chaucer: Unveiling the Merry Bard *Mary Flannery*

Marco Polo and His World *Sharon Kinoshita*

Margery Kempe: A Mixed Life *Anthony Bale*

The Teutonic Knights: Rise and Fall of a Religious Corporation *Aleksander Pluskowski*

The Troubadours *Linda M. Paterson*

THE ART OF MEDIEVAL FALCONRY

YANNIS HADJINICOLAOU

REAKTION BOOKS

For N.A.N.A.

Published by Reaktion Books Ltd
Unit 32, Waterside
44–48 Wharf Road
London N1 7UX, UK
www.reaktionbooks.co.uk

First published 2024

Printed and bound in India by Replika Press Pvt. Ltd

A catalogue record for this book is available from the British Library

ISBN 978 1 78914 910 4

CONTENTS

Introduction 7

1 Global Beginnings 19

2 Human–Animal Interaction: Training and Tools 33

3 Power and Aristocracy 65

4 East and West Dimensions 97

5 Chivalry, Warfare, Religion 121

6 Diplomacy and Gifts 157

Coda: Falconry's Visual Legacy 173

REFERENCES 190

SELECT BIBLIOGRAPHY 220

ACKNOWLEDGEMENTS 223

PHOTO ACKNOWLEDGEMENTS 224

INDEX 226

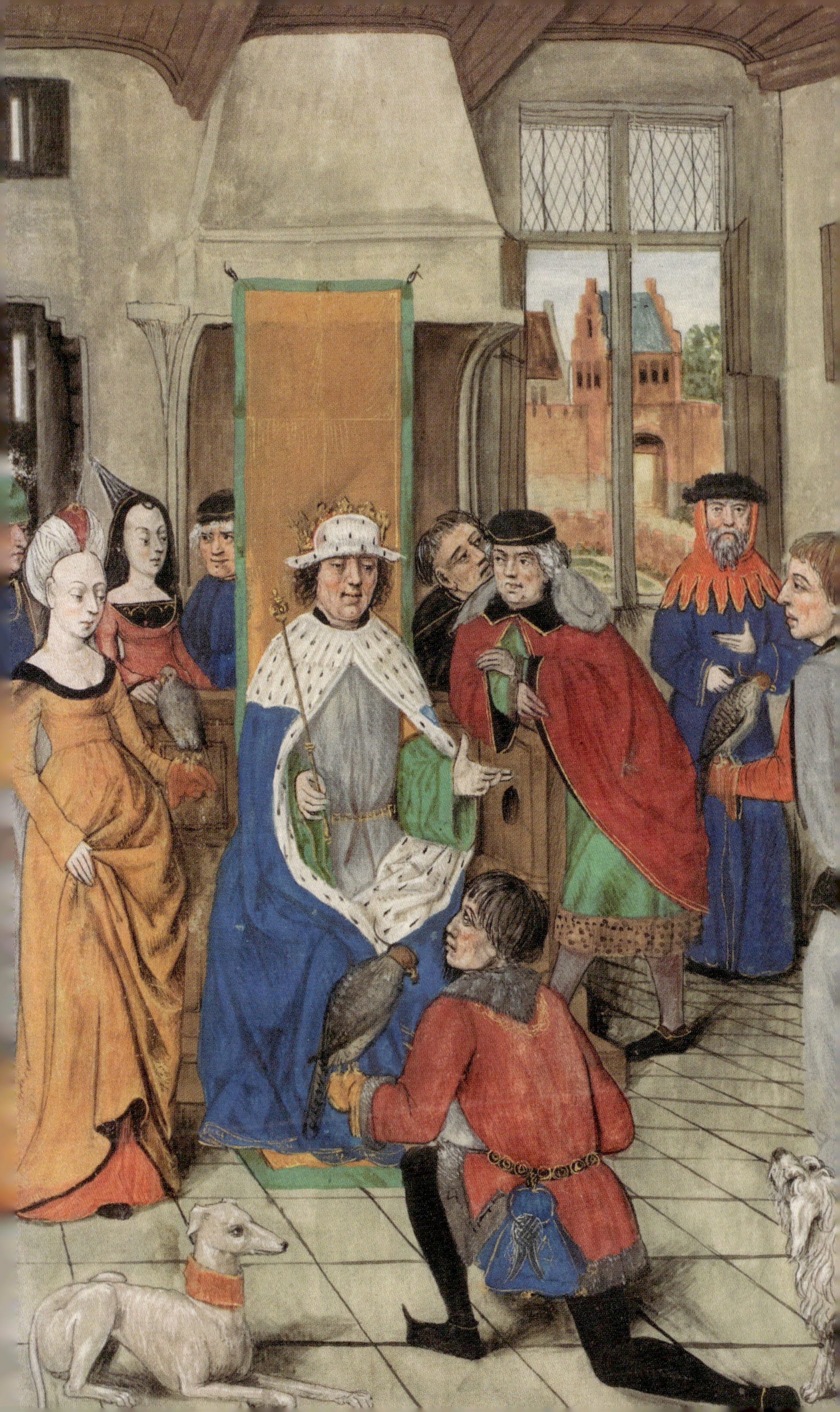

Introduction

During the medieval period, falconry held immense significance in various aspects of life. It was intertwined with court culture, employed in diplomatic endeavours and primarily valued as a recreational pursuit. The act of hunting with birds of prey encompassed more than a mere hunt; it was an artistic skill that had a profound aesthetic impact.

Depictions of falconry were never mere illustrations of the activity itself. Instead, they evoked visual associations and sparked ideas. Such images today serve as a means through which we may perceive and engage with the subject and its historical context. In fact, one could argue that our understanding of the Middle Ages largely derives from such representations, though modern-day art forms such as films and even comic books have also played a significant role in shaping our perception of this period.

It is in this sense that we will deal with the visual power of falconry. Two main issues go hand in hand here: visuality and power; in other words, the way in which falconry is also a matter of sovereignty and state theory manifested in, and through, images. There are analogies between handling a hawk and managing a state. The power of visuality refers to the agency of the

1 Detail from the frontispiece of *Livre de l'art de chasser au moyen des oiseaux* (On the Art of Hunting with Birds), a French copy of Frederick II's *De arte venandi cum avibus*, Bruges, c. 1482.

image and its ability to move us.[1] Although an image is a thing created from inorganic materials, it nevertheless possesses power over its beholders. Those viewers may even respond in extreme ways, such as with the destruction of images (iconoclasm) or their adoration (iconophilia). In eighth- and ninth-century Byzantium, violent conflicts took place between those who attacked and those who defended religious images.

In exploring this subject, one must differentiate between the practice of falconry itself, illustrated manuscripts or general texts about handling hawks, and images concerning human–animal interactions. We will deal primarily with this latter category, the visual manifestations of falconry. They are connected to the practice itself and its textual evidence, both dimensions that have been quite well studied. What has not so far been pursued, even if significant steps have recently been undertaken in this direction, is the consideration not only of falconry's visual representation in symbolic and practical terms but of falconry itself as an image practice.[2]

The hawk has a power that is related to the nature of the image, especially when the bird of prey becomes an image itself. There is an interactive, egalitarian relationship between hawk and falconer; indeed, one might even say that humans are more dependent on hawks than the latter are on people. The interchangeable relationship between passivity and activity characterizes both humans and hawks during the practice of falconry. One is passive when the other is active, and vice versa: for instance, when the hawk is on the wing and the human is watching from below (although the falconer might be moving as well to follow the flight or to flush quarry) or when the hawk is hooded and the falconer is in motion.

Vision is one of the most powerful instruments of the hawk and, especially, the falcon, beside their dazzling speed and perception of space. This does not mean, however, that the other senses are not important. Touch in particular is often manifested in images of the falconer carrying a hawk on his or her fist. We will bring this multisensorial aspect of falconry into focus later.

Falconry can be an excellent paradigm for looking at flying and movement in general from the viewpoint of visual culture; looking at the circulation of images (falconry images and objects) but also things (the hawks themselves, perceived as precious, even luxurious aesthetic 'objects'). In this sense falconry is visual and material culture on the move.

In this book the focus will rest on the notion of flying predatory birds and, hence, the way in which images of falconry play a crucial role in shaping certain associations relating to rulership, chivalry, religion and diplomacy, to name just a few areas. The transfer of visual tropes and pictorial traditions will be addressed. In this sense, the present endeavour might be seen as complementary to Helen Macdonald's seminal cultural history of the falcon, published in 2006, in which, on the subject of images and their formative power, she is remarkably silent, her focus lying more on biology and behaviour.[3] This book will show how images and techniques may be brought into a direct association with one another. These reveal the iconic power of falconry as a pragmatic as well as a symbolic pursuit.

Images of falconry have a specific aesthetic and visual quality, engaging simultaneously different, sometimes even conflicting, views and ideas that do not depend purely on practice. The artists are not necessarily falconers, and they may even get things 'wrong' from a practitioner's perspective, but this is not the point at all. What is at work in such images is not the illusion or simple representation of reality as such, which would be a tremendous simplification. Neither is it the simple materialization of historical processes in objects and texts relating to falconry.

The visual power of falconry has been neglected by art historians and cultural historians alike. We know from a contemporary source that in the thirteenth century, Emperor Frederick II hired falconers from different parts of the world to practise the art. He wrote:

> We, at great expense, summoned from the four quarters of the Earth masters in the practice of the art of falconry. We entertained these experts in our domains, meantime seeking their opinions, weighing the importance of their knowledge, and endeavouring to retain in memory the more valuable of their words and deeds.[4]

This bears witness both to Frederick's universalism and to the various culturally informed techniques that shaped medieval falconry and which still, in a certain sense, dominate falconry worldwide.[5]

There are several different types of treatises on medieval falconry, which may be classified into five categories: treatises containing ornithological information; treatises on the stages of manning as well as training birds; those covering hygiene issues such as diet and general care; those addressing veterinary information, especially concerning illnesses and cures; and, last, treatises on falconry's various cultural aspects.[6] We will focus our attention mostly on the second as well as the last categories by drawing our information primarily from the key medieval treatise *De arte venandi cum avibus* (The Art of Hunting with Birds), a text that covers all of the five above-mentioned categories.

De arte venandi cum avibus was composed around 1240–48 by Frederick II himself. It would prove to be deeply influential in the centuries to come, not only in terms of its written content but through the images that accompanied the author's impressive corpus of knowledge.[7] A passage from *De arte venandi cum avibus* makes his perspective clear: 'We have studied with the greatest detail all that relates to falconry, exercising both mind and body so that we might be qualified to interpret the fruits of knowledge acquired from our own experience or gleaned from others.'[8]

An iconic example from the so-called Manfred manuscript (a copy commissioned by the son of the emperor; the original is now lost), held in the Vatican Library, that brings together falconry, art and power is the famous image of Frederick posing on his throne with a falcon at his side (illus. 2). Frederick's left hand seems to point to his falcon, which is seen from the back with a hood covering its head, as if the animal is obeying him, like his other subjects. The falcon is simultaneously a potential weapon and a faithful companion. On the same page of the manuscript, directly below Frederick, another figure on a throne, perhaps Manfred, is presented with two falcons wearing red hoods and held up by two kneeling people. This falconry-related illustration became the monumentalized and definitive image of Frederick with his falcon, alone and without text or further image below him.

Even if *De arte venandi cum avibus* was not printed until the late sixteenth century, it was copied many times earlier in several manuscripts, especially in the fifteenth century, one of the peaks of the fashion for falconry during the Middle Ages and beyond. It is worth taking a look at another example that is also connected to the political aspect of falconry (illus. 3), a miniature from a French translation made in circa 1482. In a Burgundian court, a falconer, identified by his clothing as well as a falconer's bag, is holding a hawk. The bag, containing the hawk's food, is called a *carneria*, from the Italian word *carne*, meaning meat. The man is kneeling before Frederick II, who is clothed in contemporary costume and grants him audience. He presents the emperor with a hooded hawk (illus. 1). The kneeling figure has been identified as Frederick's son Manfred.[9] The idea and practice of succession is visually manifested through the vehicle of falconry.

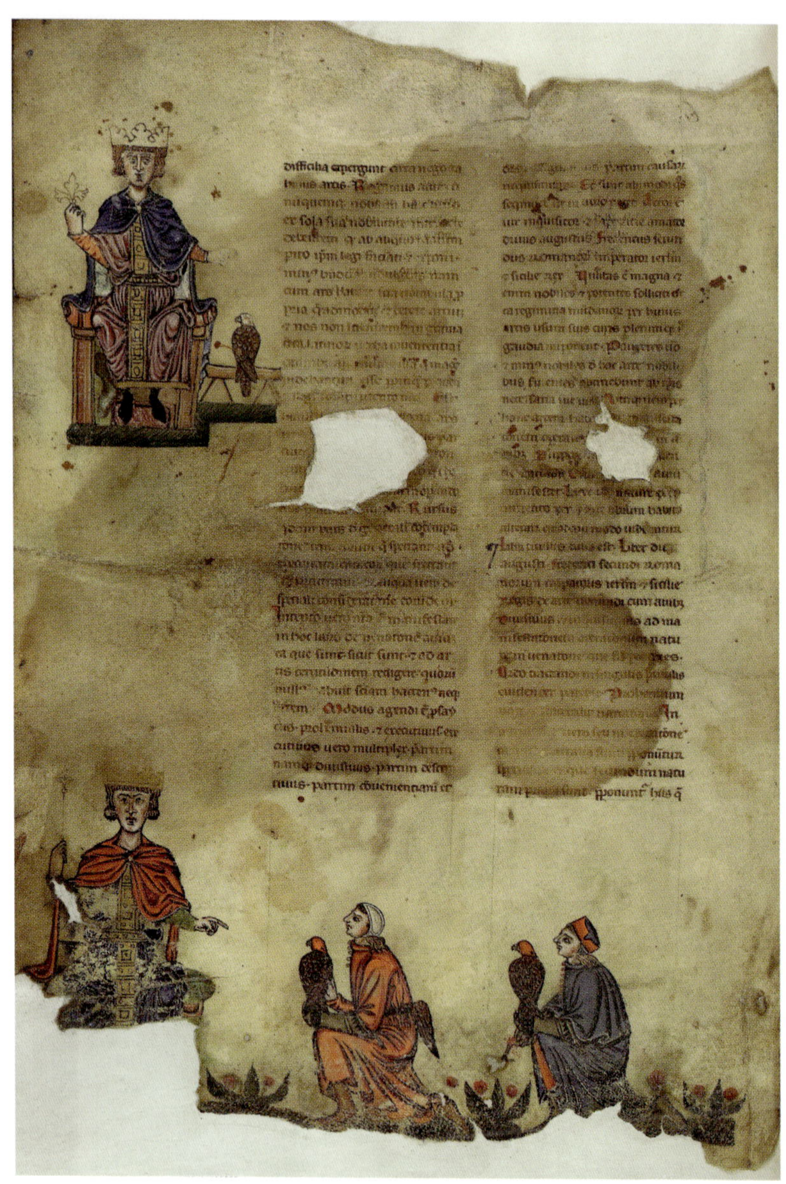

2 Frederick II, *De arte venandi cum avibus*, Manfred manuscript, southern Italy, c. 1258–66.

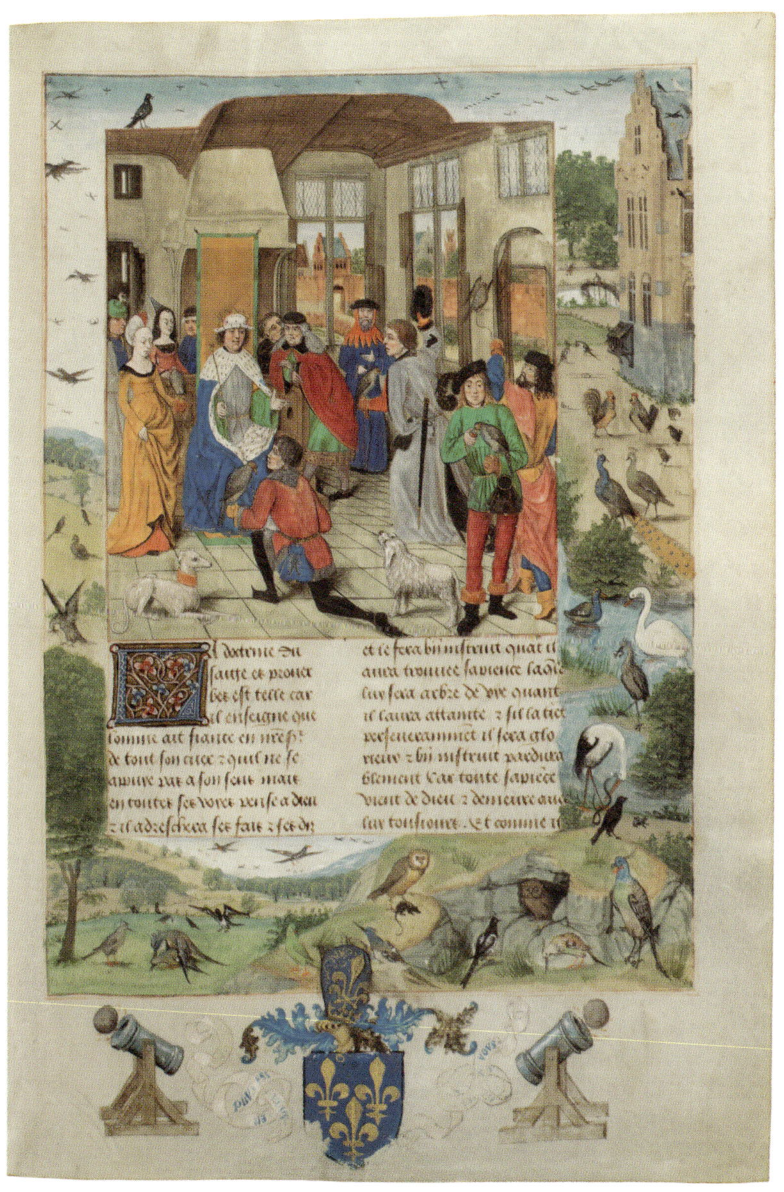

3 Frontispiece from *Livre de l'art de chasser au moyen des oiseaux* (On the Art of Hunting with Birds), a French copy of Frederick II's *De arte venandi cum avibus*, Bruges, c. 1482.

Every time period is, necessarily, perceived from one's own vantage point. The present case is no exception: the fifteenth century imagines the thirteenth in its idiosyncratic way. Next to Frederick one discerns a woman with a hawk, clearly representing the ladies at court (the sovereign's wife?). The image demonstrates the passion that aristocratic women had for falconry, a fascinating subject to which we will return.

Three more men around the kneeling figure handle hawks in various ways and underline the cultural technique of falconry and its practical dimensions. One seems to be feeding a hawk, or indeed he could be offering it water in a small glass, something generally thought of as a Central Asian practice involving eagles, but it would be eminently sensible to keep a hawk hydrated. Another man tries to gain the dispassionate falconer-sovereign's attention, while a further person's hawk is bating (flapping its wings and attempting to leave the perch) at the end of its leash, launching into the air. In this way the entire scene, which opens the treatise as a frontispiece, gains a symbolic aspect. The image sums up the content to follow in words; the impressive handwritten letters appear almost as subtitles, in today's vocabulary. In addition, from this perspective, images are condensed, powerful entities of knowledge.

Falconry appears as a political ritual and is an integral part of the court. However, this image is also framed through an additional one, in the sense of an image within an image. Here we find the dazzling colours of various birds, ranging from a cockerel to an owl, among myriad other species, used to illustrate the zoological remarks of the ruler in his book. This is based on an idiosyncratic, sometimes critical Aristotelian tradition drawing much from the Greek philosopher's work dedicated to the history of animals (*Historia animalium*, fourth century BC). The birds shown, which are partly in the wild, partly in the domesticated Burgundian landscape, are differentiated from culture, especially with regard to the hawks that appear in the interior. This is an analogy to falconry, a technique that moves precisely on the boundaries between nature (the wild hawk) and culture (the process of manning and training hawks, which can never be tamed in the same way as other animals, for example the horse).

We have not only the miniature within the image constellation on the sheet of paper, but an emblematic image. The foreground depicts the coat of arms, featuring two cannons, of Louis de Gruuthuse (1422–1492), the Flemish courtier who commissioned this copy of *De arte venandi*. Here another aspect is crucial: the techniques of war, depicted through the technologically advanced cannons, are in visual dialogue with the 'weapon' of falconry and its symbolic quality of making war (or chivalry, as we shall observe in a later chapter). The copy was later owned by Louis XII of France, demonstrating precisely the idea of royal power connected to falconry as an imperial gesture, revived in space and time.

Falconry is an art form, an *ars* or technique with deep parallels with the performing arts, in which context it is perceived as an aesthetic practice. Frederick's own descriptions are the aesthetic observations of a connoisseur, bearing much in common with someone who approaches an artwork. Falconry is a work of art in motion.

The iconic survival of falconry is a cross-cultural phenomenon that has taken new shapes and meanings throughout the centuries. The idea of falconry as the exercise of a ruler, and the pictorial life thereof, has a global dimension, as testified to by images deriving from or circulating throughout the Arab world, Europe, North Africa and Asia.[10]

Hardly tameable, the hawk might just fly away and never return. Similarly, the ruler had to learn early on how to handle unforeseen – indeed uncontrollable – situations, and hawking was one of the pedagogical tools used.[11] The interaction between nature and culture is reflected in that between falcon and falconer, undisciplined and disciplined. True sovereigns must learn how to discipline and, like the hawk, be disciplined themselves.

For instance, the so-called *Dancus Rex*, one of the first falconry treatises in the Western world (*c.* first half of the twelfth century), speaks of how a king named Gallacianus was instructed by the legendary Armenian king Dancus, the supposed author of the text:

> I come in my condition of King to see and hear if what people say is true meaning that you are a wise man, and that you know an art by which you have become even wiser, that is to say you have a bird catch another bird, whereby I want to be your disciple.[12]

It is clear from this passage that learning how to handle and train a falcon was thought to enhance the abilities of the king and so, at least implicitly, his own ruling.

An important question is how images trigger or even challenge certain views and ideas, and how they move their beholders, bodily as well as intellectually. The notion of political iconography is another thread used to capture the visual power of falconry.[13] The physical presence of a ruler, of sites of power such as castles and palaces, and of activities associated with the exercise of authority, among them hunting, are some of the elements of political iconography. In the case of falconry, political iconography means – among other things – the use of falconry as a visual tool in political representation (for instance in diplomacy or at the court, and of course during hawking itself).

Falconry was not exclusively connected to aristocracy in the Middle Ages, even if the surviving artefacts relate mostly to this segment of society. Falconry was used as a political weapon, but it was also pursued by commoners, though this has been much less frequently represented. Political iconography and iconology involve, in this sense, not only the oppressors but the oppressed. The absence of something is as important as its presence because this reveals a certain disposition for the specific subject.

What follows are six chapters that deal with central aspects characterizing falconry in the Middle Ages. We deal with issues such as the global beginnings of the practice (Chapter One), the human–animal interactions underlined through falconry tools and training (Chapter Two), and also with power and the aristocracy (Chapter Three). The geographical dimensions of transfer between East and West concerning the handling of hawks forms another important field (Chapter Four). Symbolic aspects linked to the practice, such as warfare, chivalry and religion, highlighting the cultural life of the times, are approached in Chapter Five, alongside falconry's role in diplomacy and gifting – how political relations were forged through the donation of precious falcons around the globe – in Chapter Six. Finally, in the Coda, the book will focus on the pictorial legacy of falconry, its visual agency. Multiple aspects of falconry survive today, and this visual legacy partly explains the subject's great fascination.

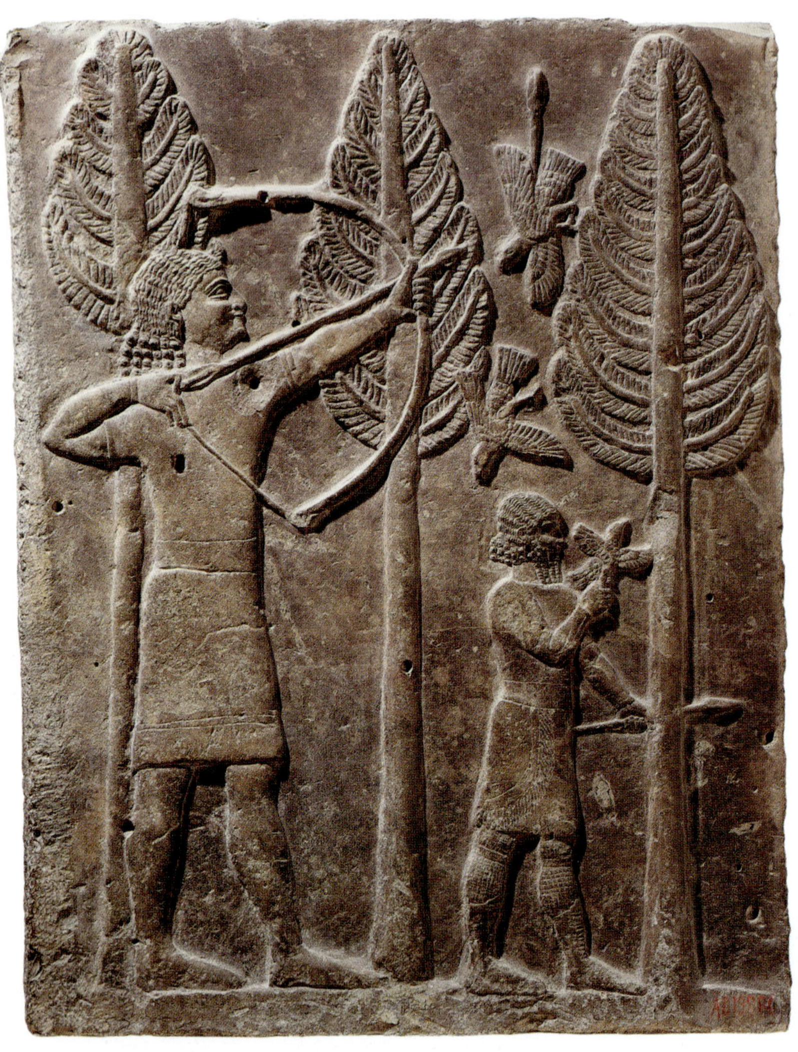

4 Falconer, bas relief from Nineveh, Mesopotamia, 8th century BC.

ONE

Global Beginnings

The definition of falconry is hunting quarry solely with the help of trained birds of prey (primarily falcons, hawks and eagles), either mounted or on foot, with no other aids aside from dogs (or ferrets) and the appropriate falconry furniture, like lures and hoods. This interaction between human and animal – that is, the training of the latter for catching quarry – was initially developed primarily because of the need to secure food.

Hawking emerged in disparate places around the globe, with parallel developments taking place in different geographical areas that contemporaries may have been more or less aware of.[1] Western forms of falconry did not exist before the late Greek and Roman periods – the fifth and sixth centuries AD. Frederick II 'imported' knowledge of this cultural practice from the Arab world.[2] When dealing with falconry's history and visual representation, therefore, one should take into consideration a broader, global antiquity rather than a narrower, European one.

Falconry was considered a barbaric practice during Graeco-Roman antiquity.[3] It was cultivated in the Roman provinces of Mesopotamia and North Africa, among others, and later in the Byzantine Empire, whence it was subsequently brought to Europe. Aristotle mentions falconry in his *Historia animalium*, where he indicates that the practice was common in Kedripolis

(Thrace); since it took place outside Greece, it was, to the Greek understanding, 'barbaric'.[4]

The Near and Middle East, China and India, and Central Asia in general, were, among other places, known for the practice of falconry.[5] As early as 15,000–17,000 years ago there are hints of the use of birds of prey in the social life of the Near East, documented through burials.[6] In the case of the Han dynasty in China, falconry was connected to imperial hunting and the state. For instance, the tombs of some wealthy commoners and officials are decorated with falconry scenes (c. AD 147–84).[7]

In Egypt, Horus, god of the sun and moon as well as of the pharaohs, took the shape of a falcon, as a half anthropomorphized, half animalized deity, typical of the Egyptian pantheon. Thousands of such depictions have survived to date, and this is the reason the Egyptians were characterized as the first falconers.[8] Such representations of Horus offer an example of the power that an image gains through manual reproduction on a massive scale. Today this idea of ancient Egyptian falconry is rather dismissed, since, as yet, no persuasive evidence has been found to support it. In this case, actual practice and its imagery follow totally different paths.

The presence of falcons in Egyptian art may be compared to the role of the eagle in Graeco-Roman mythology as well as heraldry. In Egypt, the falcon was a primarily religious symbol imbued with political implications that did not depend on human–animal interaction but was rather a god-given extension of the pharaoh's power. It was in itself divine and united both natures in one figure: animal and human, falcon and man. At the temple of Nectanebo II in Saqqara, which was dedicated to Isis, mother of Horus, 100,000 mummified votive falcons were kept.[9] In this way, even during eternal death falcons are precious and divine objects that live forever as images and bodies.

A second-century BC coin depicting Alexander the Great as Hercules on one side, a common theme of political iconography, features Zeus holding an eagle on the reverse.[10] This example indicates human–animal interaction on a visual level, albeit an interaction elevated to the mythological sphere (illus. 5).[11] Such images have certainly played an important role in the development of visual representations of a ruler or falconer holding a bird of prey, one of the most common iconographic renditions of falconry. Coins were per se vehicles of exchange, though not exclusively in monetary terms, and were found in distant places like the Arabian Peninsula, for instance. The coins put not only the image of Alexander into motion but that of Zeus holding the eagle, as if the latter might at any time, on command, fly from his fist to do the work of an avatar of the god and, at the same time, that of the ruler.[12]

The nineteenth-century Assyriologist Austen Henry Layard's classic publication *Discoveries among the Ruins of Nineveh and Babylon* (1853) mentions one of the oldest known depictions of falconry from the eighth century BC.[13] Layard's excavations in the ruins of Dur-Sharrukin, the former Assyrian capital, uncovered 'a falconer bearing a hawk on his wrist'.[14] This gesture is a fundamental one in the depiction of falconry and over the centuries became an emblematic representation of the practice.

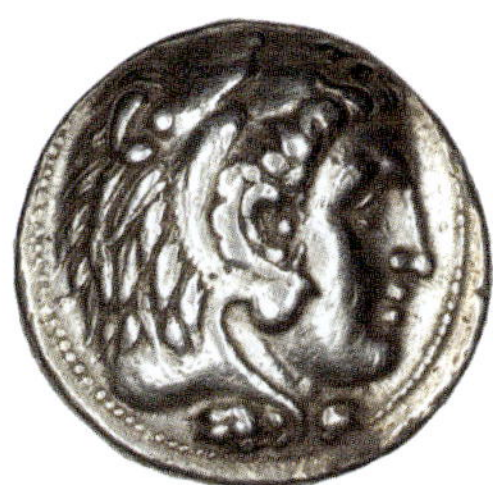

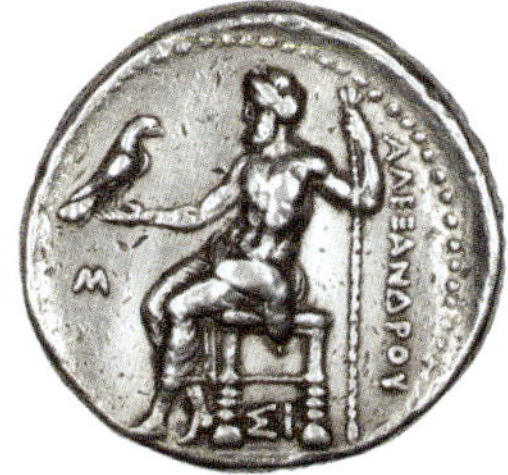

5 Tetradrachm (coin) portraying Alexander the Great on the obverse and Zeus holding an eagle on the reverse, 336–323 BC, silver.

One of the best-known and most ancient examples of falconry, similar to that described by Layard, appears in an eighth-century BC relief from Nineveh, present-day Mosul, about 20 kilometres (12 mi.) south of Dur-Sharrukin (present-day Khorsabad) (illus. 4). A man with a characteristic Assyrian beard and coiffure stands upright between two trees carrying a hawk upon his right hand. This bas relief is actually part of a larger hunting scene also depicting archery and the killing of quarry. As a trade hub for goods and artefacts, Mesopotamia played a crucial role in the transmission of falconry as a cultural technique between not only Europe and Asia but North Africa and the Arab world.[15]

Pictorial evidence for falconry has also been found from around the third millennium BC in today's Syria, and from the Hittite civilization (c. second and first millennium BC) in present-day Turkish Anatolia. Since there are no Western examples from that period, this is further visual proof suggesting the origin of the practice and its images are from the East.[16] One of the earliest depictions of a human holding a bird of prey, dated to the thirteenth century BC in the Louvre in Paris, comes from this area.[17] We know that Anatolia is one of the regions that attests to a very early practice of falconry, since excavations also found jesses (thin straps to retain the hawk on the fist), among other things.[18] Falconry as a practice is already documented in prehistoric times, but, as already mentioned, the practice is one thing and images of the practice another.[19]

Visual testimonies from classical European antiquity depicting falconry are scarce.[20] Some examples should be mentioned in this context to give an idea of the development of certain motifs and their legacy, or rather continuation, into the European Middle Ages that are here at the centre of our interest.

A mosaic from Argos in Greece dating from the late fifth to the early sixth century AD, during the Roman Empire, is one of the most iconic examples within an aristocratic or patrician context, since mosaic-decorated floors were commissioned within that segment of society. Two scenes clearly relate to the interaction between man and hawk in the process of hunting. In the first image, two young men are each holding a dog on a leash (illus. 6). On the forearm of the male figure with the seemingly more exuberant hound, on the right, one can discern a hawk, which quite likely denotes active falconry. The other mosaic piece shows the successful outcome of duck hawking, for many centuries one of the most common flights (that is, the actual pursuit for quarry) (illus. 7). The outstretched male hand, gloved as protection from the hawk's sharp claws, reaches towards the hawk, which sits triumphantly upon the duck, underlining

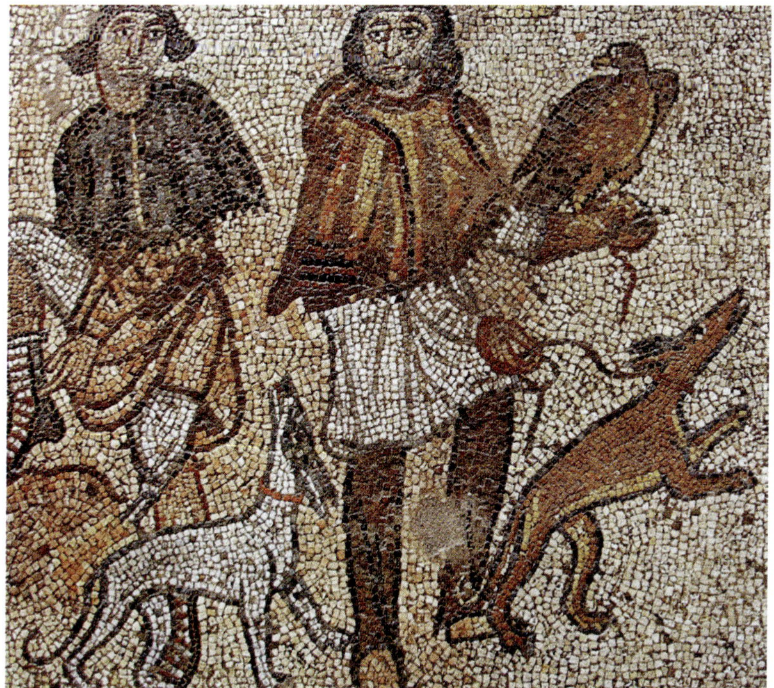

6 Departure for the hunt, mosaic from the Villa of the Falconer in Argos, Greece, late 5th–early 6th centuries.

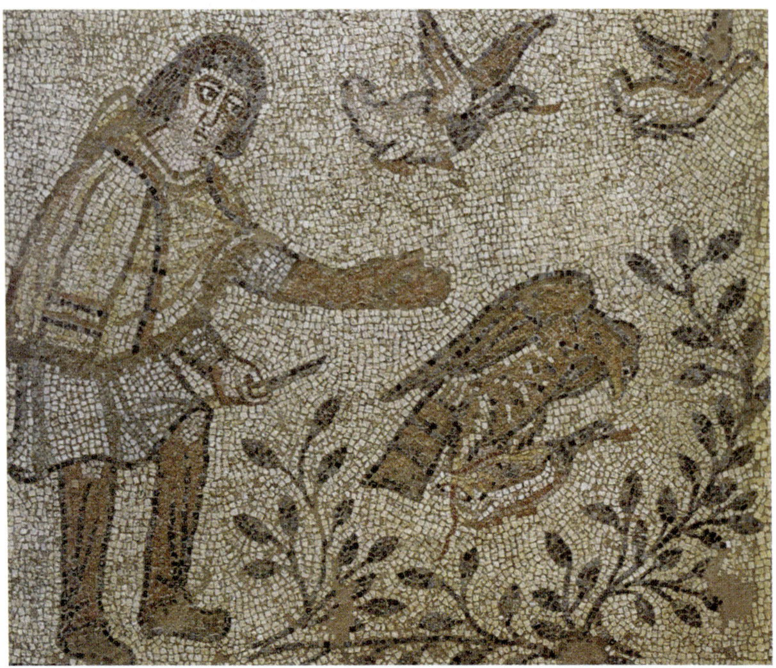

7 A hawk takes down a duck, mosaic from the Villa of the Falconer in Argos, Greece, late 5th–early 6th centuries.

the interaction of human and animal that was responsible for this victory. This image represents not a passive use of a hawk, in which it acts only implicitly as a tool for collecting quarry, but rather active hawking.[21] Moreover, the falconer is holding the leg of a fowl, making it clear that the hawk will soon receive her reward from the falconer's fist. The reason for using the female gender here (and throughout) is that the most highly prized hawks are, most frequently, female ones, being larger, faster and more powerful in general (even if sometimes hawkers use male birds as well as female ones).

Such motifs are quite widespread, and known also through Frederick II's *De arte venandi cum avibus* – see, for instance, an illustration in which a young man holding a falcon grasps a fowl's leg in his other hand (illus. 8). This miniature is not a hawking

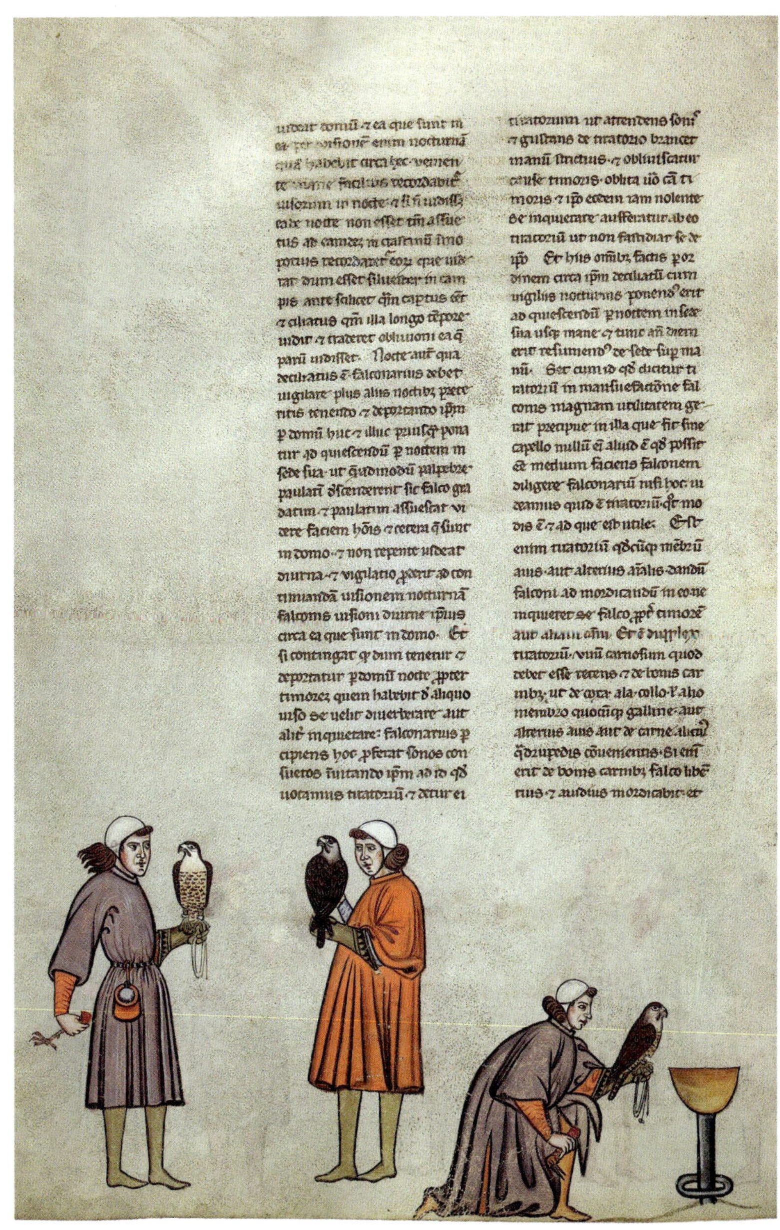

8 Frederick II, *De arte venandi cum avibus*, Manfred manuscript, southern Italy, c. 1258–66.

scene but rather depicts a subject that will be dealt with in the next chapter, namely the training and manning process that Frederick so eloquently describes. In addition to the hawk and her food that the man is holding, a *carneria* is clearly visible, in contrast to the Argos mosaic which does not show the *carneria*. The falconer from Argos looks like a mixture between the first and the third male figure from the Vatican manuscript. This underlines the existence of common characteristics in falconry imagery independent of cultural space and period of execution.

Many scholars have embraced the idea that the mosaics from Argos were made in connection with the conquests of the Vandals, which were taking place in the Roman Empire around the same time.[22] On the other hand, the mosaics themselves are rather characterized by their late antique Roman forms.[23] What is certain is that here we are dealing with a late antique type whose origin is not Graeco-Roman per se, but one that was adapted formally as well as culturally into this context. It is irrelevant whether the masters who crafted the visual programme of the Manfred manuscript knew Argos; they were almost certainly unaware of its existence. What counts are the common motifs that survive through the ages and become a visual repertoire of falconry.

The example of Argos is by no means the only one from that period. From Mértola (Portugal) to Tunisia, as well as in Madaba (Jordan), there are a number of surviving mosaics that reference the subject of falconry (even if only symbolically).[24] In other words, these cover the provinces of the Roman Empire across the breadth of the Mediterranean.

The mosaic in the Hall of Hippolytus in Madaba, dating from the sixth century AD, is of particular interest (illus. 9). It shows a man with a hawk on his outstretched fist, not hunting but with courtly women, including Phaedra next to him (identified in Greek letters above her head, a common way of helping to designate the *dramatis personae* in late antiquity). This scene is part of the story of Hippolytus and Phaedra, who had a burning desire for her stepson. The palace-like structure evokes Hippolytus' fabled passion for hunting within a courtly environment, even if it is only indicated here. It also prefaces, taking the story into account, the common medieval comparison of love to falconry, in which the luring between man and woman acts as an analogy for luring a hawk and the differences in perceived power relations between partners in both cases.[25]

It is, nevertheless, also quite clear from the mosaics how far this 'barbarian' practice had spread to Europe by the fifth century AD. Late antiquity or early Middle Ages? We will not enter this futile debate. Let us content ourselves with the facts. The Christian poet Paulinus of Pella in AD 458 expressed a wish for a dog and a hawk.[26] This implies that, even by this time, hawks and hounds were in vogue as important accessories for, or indeed symbols of, a respectable man.

In the third century AD, the author and astrologer Julius Firmicus Maternus wrote that 'those mortals who have Venus

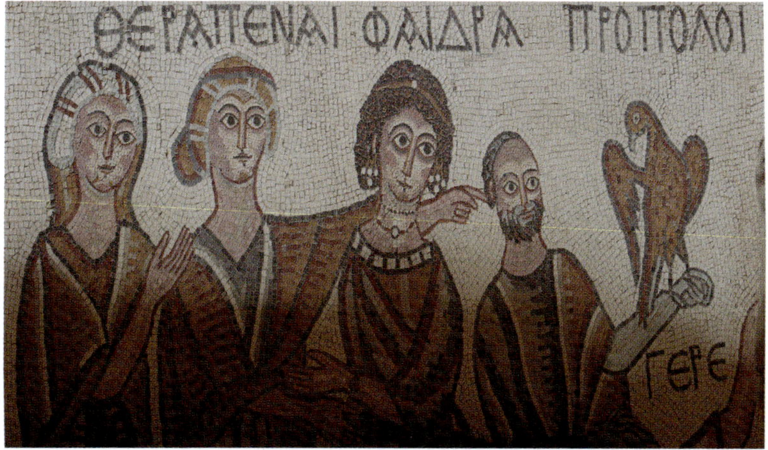

9 Phaedra and her handmaidens with a falconer, mosaic, Hall of Hippolytus, Madaba, Jordan, 6th century.

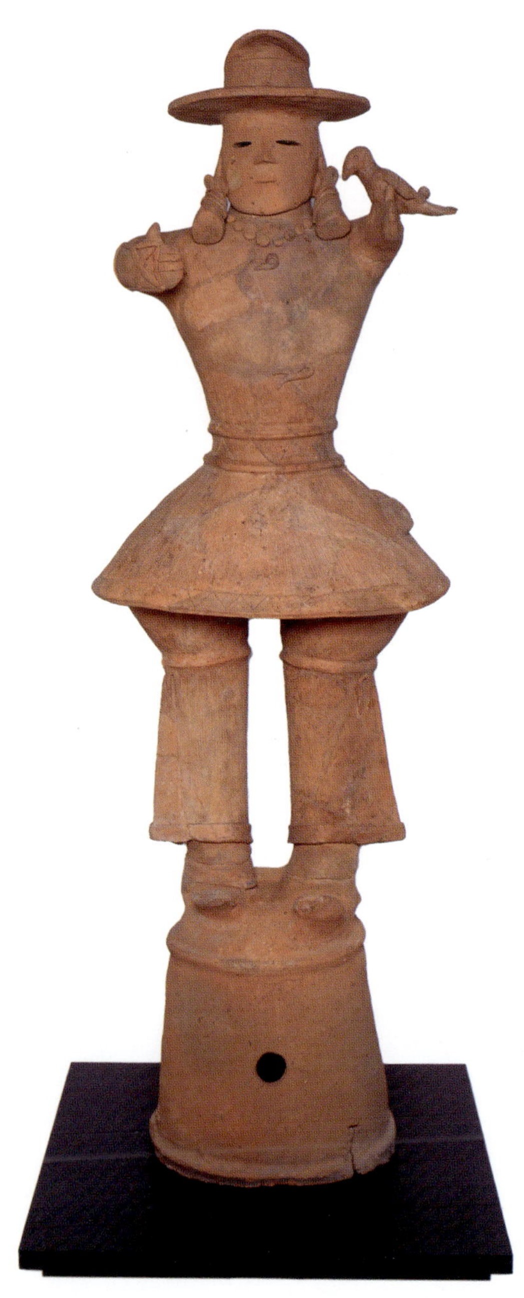

10 Falconer, clay, Japan, second half of the 5th century.

in Aquarius in their horoscopes are particularly fitted to use hawks, falcons, goshawks, eagles and other types of birds or those who have Mercury in Virgo.'[27] It is important to note here that falconry is placed between the goddess of love and the god of the travellers and protectors of commerce and communication: all human endeavours or attributes related to and necessary for falconry. Furthermore, it is also clear to what extent falconry was already a part of a Western astrological iconography.

To give another example from beyond the West, a famous sculpture from Japan, dated to around the second half of the fifth century, shows human–animal interaction and speaks again to falconry's worldwide dispersion, not only in practical but in visual terms (illus. 10). The quite abstract clay male figure wearing a hat as well as earrings, with its peculiar, almost geometric features, not only carries a hawk on his extremely short arm but has a glove on his right. The figurine probably represents the master of the ancient tomb (as a gatekeeper of sorts with his hawk as an apotropaic weapon) or even the ruler of the locality, underlining the fact that images related to falconry signified power, in turn connected to divine spheres.[28] From Egypt to Europe, from Central Asia to Korea and Japan, the same manifestation of power through falconry prevails.[29]

There are many different possible scenarios and actual routes as to how falconry came to Europe. It suffices to briefly outline some of them here without aiming for completeness, as these movements are highly complex. Nonetheless, some cases are important for our story – notable among them being the relations between Byzantium and Venice. One of many consequences of these links was a certain shared iconography of the sovereign connected to falconry that became visible later, for instance in the Pala d'Oro ('golden cloth', *c.* twelfth century AD) in St Mark's Basilica.[30] This golden retable of the high altar in Venice is a dazzling decorated piece with countless enamel plaques and

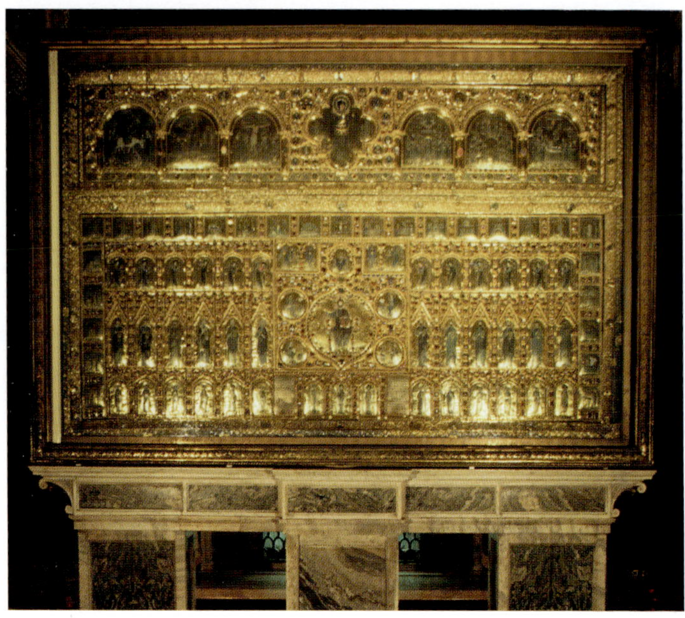

11 The Pala d'Oro, St Mark's Basilica, Venice, gold and enamel inlaid with precious stones.

gems (illus. 11). The central panel is dominated by Christ in Majesty, whereas on smaller plaquettes, among many other figures, riders appear carrying falcons that are clearly connected to a ceremonial act and therefore political legitimation (that of the Venetian Doge) of the object's religious function.[31] These enamel paintings, also depicting falconers, were probably sent as gifts by the Byzantine emperor Alexios I to the doge Ordelafo Faliero and were later incorporated into the Pala d'Oro (illus. 12).[32]

Another actual route of falconry is that the sport had already arrived in Europe with the Khazars and Visigoths.[33] The Frankish elites practised falconry in the early Merovingian period (from the mid-fifth century AD), and by the sixth century it was an aristocratic – even a royal – sport in Europe, no longer linked to mere survival, setting the trend for centuries to come.[34] In this sense falconry is connected to royal power. For instance, the Lombard king Rothari introduced legislation in the year 643 that punished anyone who stole hawks from the royal forests.[35] Long before Frederick II, Charlemagne (c. 747–814) underlined the importance of falconry for the court by keeping birds of prey and falconers.[36]

Around the late ninth to the tenth centuries, the falconer had a privileged status in the court of a Welsh king, according to the Laws of Hywel Dda (medieval Welsh law). This status demonstrates not only how important this profession was for an early medieval court but how much political power was connected to falconry, since in the manuscripts the falconer is named either above or directly after the court justice.[37]

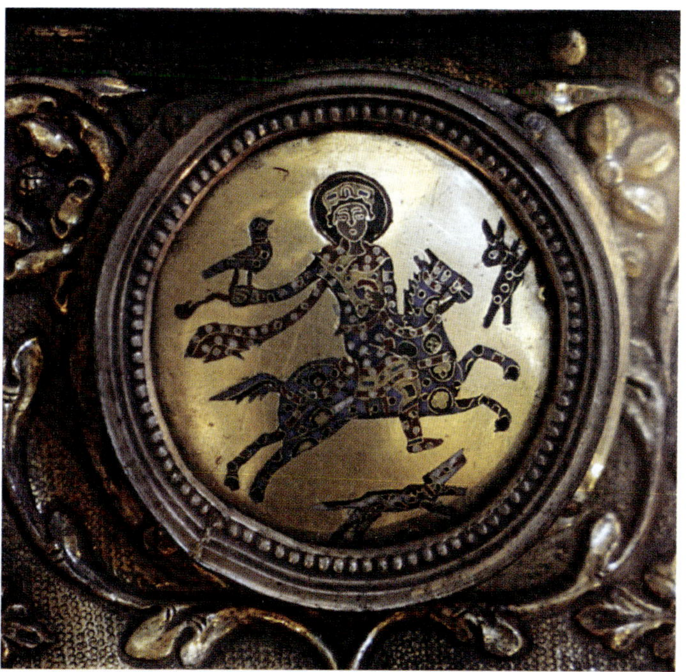

12 The emperor as a falconer on horseback, detail from the Pala d'Oro in St Mark's Basilica, Venice, commissioned in 976, expanded in 1105 and completed in 1345, gold and enamel inlaid with precious stones.

To sum up: attempting to place falconry's origins in a specific geographical area is a fruitless enterprise, since falconry can be traced to its very beginnings simultaneously around the world. The original purpose of hawking was survival, which meant not only a symbiosis with wild nature but, as a subsequent step, the training of a bird of prey in order to secure food. During the Middle Ages this process of culturalization turned hawking into a hobby among aristocratic men and women, going well beyond the mere purpose of hunting quarry. Elaborate objects, either those depicting falconry or those used for hawking (which may carry images themselves), were the last step in this process, reflecting not only the practice of falconry itself but, most of all, its power as a way of visually representing members of the elite.

The occidental images produced do not exemplify Western visual types, types only developed in that part of the world (unlike the theme of Venus and Adonis, to mention just one example connected to the paradigm of hunting). In addition, from quite an early stage, and most markedly by the Middle Ages, falconry became a unifying practice of sovereigns across regions, one promoted and practised through and in images. However, the parallel development of falconry in disparate regions does not necessarily mean that one tradition knew of the other, even if geographical interactions between those areas began very early in the form of gifts and diplomatic relations.

From the early Middle Ages, falconry was a common and unifying element in the Mediterranean, and so too were images of it.[38] Falconry does not have one origin; rather there were several origins from which it spread simultaneously around the world. In falconry, as in so many other fields of human activity, one can only speak of global beginnings, without awards for a first, second and third place in some imagined contest.

TWO

Human–Animal Interaction: Training and Tools

Quadrupeds 'are more easily brought under human subjection than [birds of prey], and they are readily caught by the use of force or are trapped by other means because they remain on the ground. Fully fledged birds, on the other hand, can be captured and trained only by finesse,' wrote Frederick II eloquently.[1] It is the interplay of human ingenuity and an animal's will that makes falconry exceptional and something that can certainly not be categorized merely as forceful subjection. What follows after the first, mostly abrupt encounter is a fascinating account of human–animal relations.

Human–animal interaction is the essential feature of falconry. The sophisticated procedure of handling hawks and hunting with them is probably its most important manifestation. This fundamental relationship between hawk and falconer has remained almost untouched throughout history, even if different techniques and technologies are situated within historical sociocultural contexts. Human–animal interactions in falconry not only concern securing food but also manning, training and even playing, as Helen Macdonald writes in *H is for Hawk* (2014) about her experiences with her goshawk Mabel.[2] Meaning 'loveable', the name implies a processual relation (in the suffix -able) that may even lead to affection (love-), an essential element of human–animal interaction, which is dominated by non-verbal communication.

One could even argue that hawking is the last step in a whole process of learning, even if the main outcome, hunting, is certainly the most representative; last but by no means least in visual terms. The relationship between hawk and human is one that moves between distance and empathy. The term 'distance' needs little further explanation, since there is a fundamental difference between the two species. Empathy relates rather to a common point of affective interaction, as in the case of Mabel. A good falconer should be able to feel the hawk's needs as if she were a family member.[3] This is a point that had already been raised in medieval times and was often linked to the ruler's ability to successfully interact with a hawk as he or she would interact with their respective human subjects, caring for them in the sense of a commonwealth.

Following this conviction, the sovereign should pass many hours with the hawk and, according to some sources (such as the fourteenth-century Castilian historian Pedro López de Ayala's treatise on falconry), should even, ideally, sleep in the same room as the bird to better reinforce the interaction and even substitution between the two living agents:

> It should sleep in your bedchamber, or that of its keeper, and there should be a lamp burning all night. In Spain falconers leave their birds untied, because if they flew off the perch at night, dreaming that they were hunting, it would be dangerous.[4]

In the anonymous fourteenth-century handbook *Le Ménagier de Paris* (The Good Wife's Guide), something similar is advised concerning the training of the hawk:

> At this stage of training your hawk, you must keep him on your fist more than ever before, taking him to law-courts

> and among folk assembled in church or elsewhere, and into the streets. Keep him thus as long as you can, by day or night; and sometimes perch him in the streets, that he may see and accustom himself to men, horses, carts, hounds, and all other things.[5]

That taking the hawk to church is advised, rather than criticized, is a subject to which we will return.

A miniature from a falconry treatise written at the end of the fifteenth century by the French hospitaller Jean de Francières seems to capture those ideas (illus. 13). A young man in a room with a prominently positioned bed has four hawks on a perch,

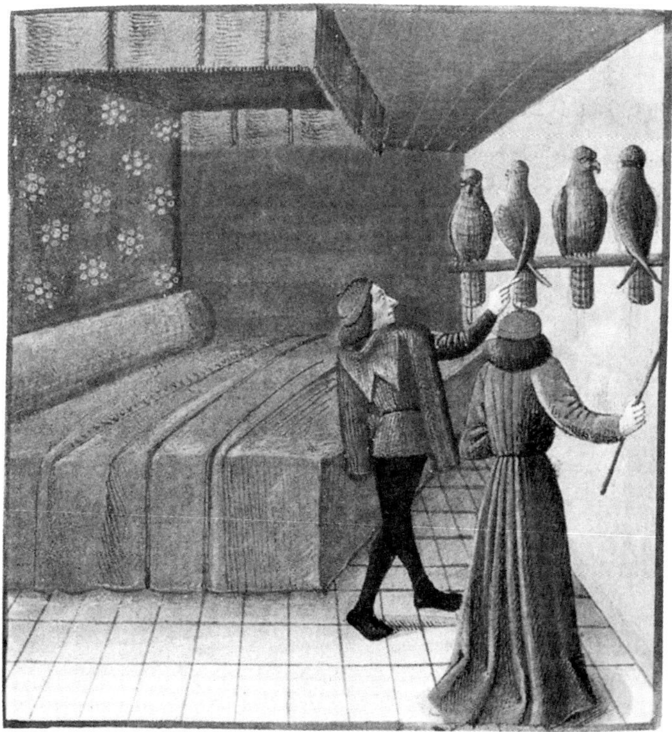

13 Instruction of a falconer, illumination from Jean de Francières, *Livre de fauconnerie*, late 15th century.

seen from different angles. He strokes the second hawk from the left with a wooden stick, a so-called *virgula*.[6] The man is accompanied by another male figure, who also holds a stick and seems to be an instructor, not only to him but to the treatise's potential readers and possible falconry practitioners. He presents only his back to the viewer and is therefore seen as a reference figure (a typical pictorial mode of identification).

In the miniature, there is a bodily, almost loving relationship with the hawk that connects man and animal through the *virgula*. To stroke the hawk's belly, as if it were one's child or even lover, is indeed a gesture of affection. The device plays a crucial role here to build a bridge between man and bird, connecting their bodies and so their 'natures' (beyond direct touch).

The treatment of falcons like humans was already documented at an early period. For instance, written records relate to a falcon's funeral in twelfth-century Syria; the body was treated as if it were that of a human, as was the grave. The falcon belonged to the Syrian poet and knight Usama ibn Munqidh, who treated it as his own child.[7] It is clear how certain virtues of the knight are transferred to the falcon and vice versa.

The Italian *condottiero* Francesco Sforza (1401–1466), founder of the Sforza dynasty in Lombardy, wept over his falcon's death as if it were a human companion.[8] The Mantuan courtier Mario Esquiola mentioned the tradition of such reactions: treating falcons as humans in fifteenth-century Mantua followed the path paved by Frederick II, who 'so loved the subject of his aerial pleasures, that he honoured some noble birds with marble tombs'.[9] It is clear that not every hawk had a grave, only noble and precious falcons. Some of them even had graves made of marble, a material usually reserved for nobles and sovereigns. It is not by chance that falcons had names such as 'Prince' and 'Emperor', as for instance in the Farsi name Shaheen, which refers to the peregrine and means emperor.[10] Tughril, founder of the Seljuk sultanate (1037–1194) in Persia and Iraq, also bore the name of a bird of prey.[11]

Omar Khayyam (1048–1131), a Persian mathematician, wrote in his book *Nowruz* (New Day) that the goshawk (*baz* in Persian) is the 'boon companion of the kings at the hunting grounds; they love it and rejoice it. The *baz* has some dispositions shared by the kings such as magnanimity . . . Therefore, it is more proper to kings than to other people.'[12] This is an almost naturalized legitimation of the elite's occupation with falconry, since the animal has a disposition similar to that of a king.

The interaction between nature and culture is clear in the relationship established between hawk and falconer, between tamed and untamed. The non-verbal communication between equals (hawk and human) discounting the sounds humans make imitating falcons and the noises falcons make themselves forms, together with the falconer's dog and horse, and even the quarry itself, an inseparable and interdependent chain.

The so-called 'waiting on' flight is an excellent example to underline this collaborative feature of falconry, as described by Frederick II:

> The falcon must be taught to circle about over the head of the falconer, that is, to wait on . . . instruction in waiting on is an intermediate stage between luring and active hawking, not only in the order in which it is taken up but in its very essence.[13]

But what exactly happens in waiting on? In more recent forms of the flight, the falconer's dogs – pointers or setters – first indicate the presence of concealed quarry. The falconer then releases the falcon (waiting on exclusively uses 'longwings' like the peregrine) to circle upwards until she is at an optimal height to stand a chance of success (her 'pitch'); sometimes so high the falconer may not even be able to see her. However, she learns the body language of the dogs and the falconer and relies on them to 'serve' her – to flush quarry.

This flight is utilized now for any quarry that is both very fast in flight (necessitating the falcon's height advantage) and will not move, once it knows a falcon is there, until deliberately flushed. In Frederick's day, waiting on was solely used for ducks: since there were no reliable pointing dogs, ducks were the only quarry that could be spotted by the falconer and be expected to remain *in situ* once the falcon was on the wing. Ducks stay on the water because they know that the falcon cannot attack them there. They will, however, leave it when compelled by the falconer – in Frederick's time, a drum was often beaten to flush them out. An image of King Edward III of England in 1328 – about eighty years after the iconic image of Frederick (illus. 2) – presents not only the throned king with a hawk on his fist under the blessing of an angel but a corresponding duck hawking scene in which he is accompanied by an entourage, with one figure even beating the drum (illus. 14).

Dogs were less frequently used at that time, since ducks need flushing promptly when the falcon is in the right position: they would often just keep swimming away from hounds. The same is true of more recently developed waiting-on flights at terrestrial game birds like partridge or red grouse, though they are more commonly flushed by dogs. In all events, the timing of the flush is critical since success depends on the falcon's position in relation to the quarry, the quarry's proximity to cover, wind direction and a host of other factors.

When the flush finally occurs, the falcon stoops – or swoops down – suddenly from her pitch and strikes the quarry with immense power. In some cases, when dogs fail – for whatever reason – to serve the falcon and flush, something extraordinary may happen: the falcon may punish the hounds for their lack

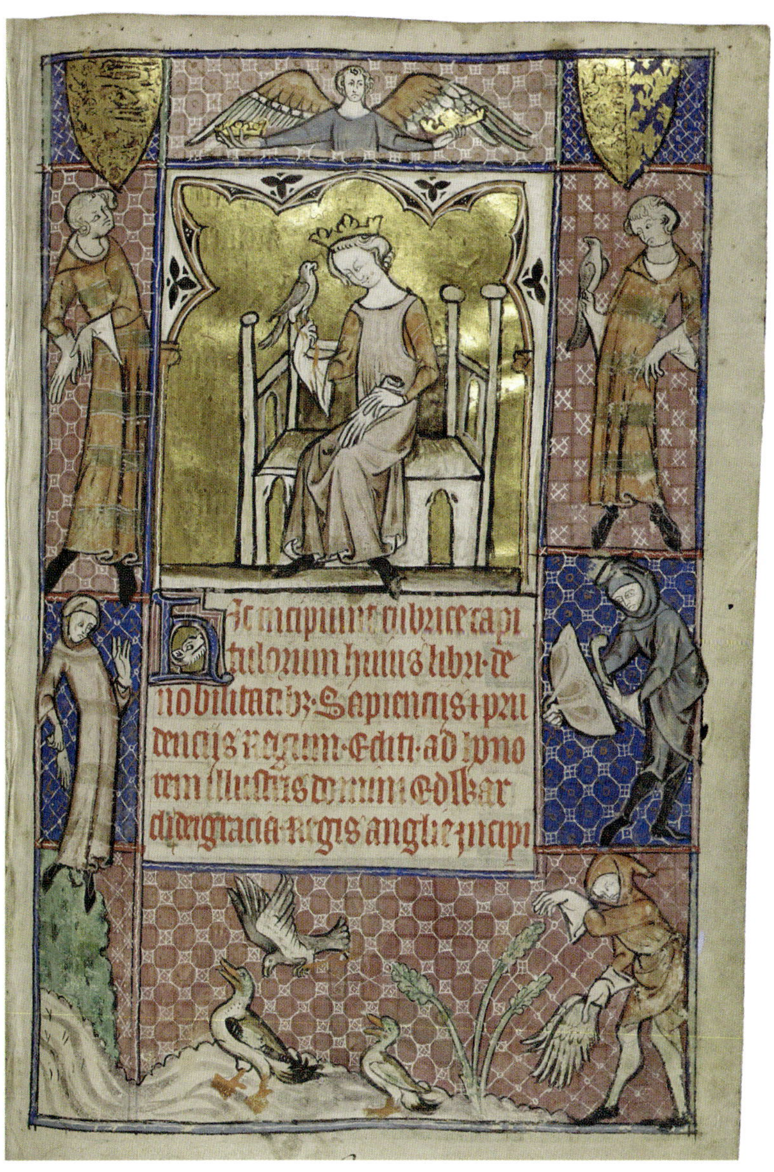

14 Edward III, king of England, enthroned with his falcon, illumination from Walter de Milemete, *De nobilitatibus, sapientiis, et prudentiis regum*, England, 1328.

of professionality by hitting them! This is done not with the intention to kill or harm, but most distinctly as punishment. In this sense one can speak of a falcon's mind. It was because of this that the famous German falconer Renz Waller (1895–1979) claimed that 'the falcon thinks'.[14]

The previously described waiting-on flight is, for several reasons, of central importance in this context: there is a team in which the falconer is only one of the agents, and certainly not the most important one, since the animals are the protagonists.[15] The quarry itself is of course part of the network, playing a critical role in the unfolding of the flight. While the falconer orchestrates the flight, deciding when to flush, the falcon also has to understand how best to act when the right moment comes. A certain spontaneity is central here since the dynamic interactions inherent in the flight, including those of all actors involved, as well as wild hawks or other animal or human interlopers and the weather, means plans might rapidly change. She may alter her approach to the quarry or abandon the flight altogether. This fact too allows us to speak of the falcon's mind, since the raptor must take certain decisions, usually in split seconds.[16]

It is remarkable, as contemporary practitioners also relate, that this communication occurs exclusively in the gestural-visual sphere: another indication of the visual power of falconry. According to Andy Bennett, a specialist in the visual capacities of birds, the visual acuity of a human being is comparable to a black-and-white television, while that of a falcon corresponds to a colour television.[17] In other words, the falcon monitors the field, like a superior kind of digital camera, until she is given a chance at quarry, for which she must learn to 'wait on'. The human falconer has to do the same, even if he or she does not have the same power of visual surveillance and in many cases may rely on dogs as his or her eyes (or indeed nose) – though the falconer seeks to give the falcon her opportunity. The quarry is aware of the falcon's presence and has a number of innate strategies and environmental resources to protect itself. However, its role is mandatory: without quarry, there would be no hawking. In many cases, the pointers' characteristic indication (that is, pointing) of the quarry's presence is an elementary gesture that is central for the visual perception of hawk and human alike.

The visual contact between hawk and falconer should, in theory at least, never be broken.[18] Part of the human's task – more specifically in waiting-on flights – is to train the falcon to pay attention to his or her movements; often the falcon can see the falconer, but not the other way around. A characteristic distich by the Irish poet William Butler Yeats describes this very situation, in the sense of the falcon's independence: 'Turning and turning in the widening gyre/ the falcon cannot hear the falconer.'[19] The hawk has her own will, and the falconer must take this fact into consideration. It is this constant oscillation of action and reaction that makes falconry such a complex and simultaneously appealing endeavour.

One could consider falconry a prime example of what the comparative psychologist Michael Tomasello has termed 'shared intentionality' (even if in this case we are looking at human–animal interactions): for instance, the mutual goal of taking quarry. Tomasello characterizes shared intentionality as 'joint action, attention and cooperative communication as social co-operation'.[20] This applies perfectly, for example, to the falcon paying attention to both the pointer's indication of where the quarry is and to the falconer's movements in the waiting-on flight. When Tomasello describes human thinking as being co-operative, one could apply this observation to falconry, where human–animal thinking is cooperative.[21]

Abd al-Rahman, who most likely lived in Baghdad around the late thirteenth to early fourteenth century, observed that hounds and hawks ought to get accustomed to one another, and learn not to fear each other, very early on, so that their cooperation can be successful:

> The hound should be present when they [the hawks] are called to the fist and when they are fed, so that they get on familiar terms with each other and like to be together and so that the hound becomes accustomed to them and keeps his eye on them when they are circling overhead.[22]

Frederick II also stated that one should train several falcons simultaneously in order for them to cooperate when flown together.[23]

In this sense one can speak of a collective body and mind. Collectivity is understood here in terms of a group, of different kinds of agents possessing various faculties and natures that solve shared problems or exercises on a non-verbal level, where training and repetition is mandatory. There is a union of those diverse elements that follow a similar goal or objective with different means and from various perspectives.

The interests of an agent, like those of the hawk, are not altered for the sake of collaborative union. Human and animal cohabit.[24] The falconer must cooperate with the hawk and understand her needs, even if humans certainly follow their own goals and interests. This goes similarly for the quarry, which develops a resistance to hunters. This interplay speaks to the union of dialectically opposed forces (nature and culture, human and animal). Intelligence and even beauty in the aesthetic sense can only be developed through social interaction, not through the animal's submission to the human, as Kurt Lindner, one of the pioneers of falconry research, claimed.[25] There is no hierarchy between hawk and human.

The goal is that the hawk operates as if in a wild state, yet one made possible by the falconer. An artificial wilderness is

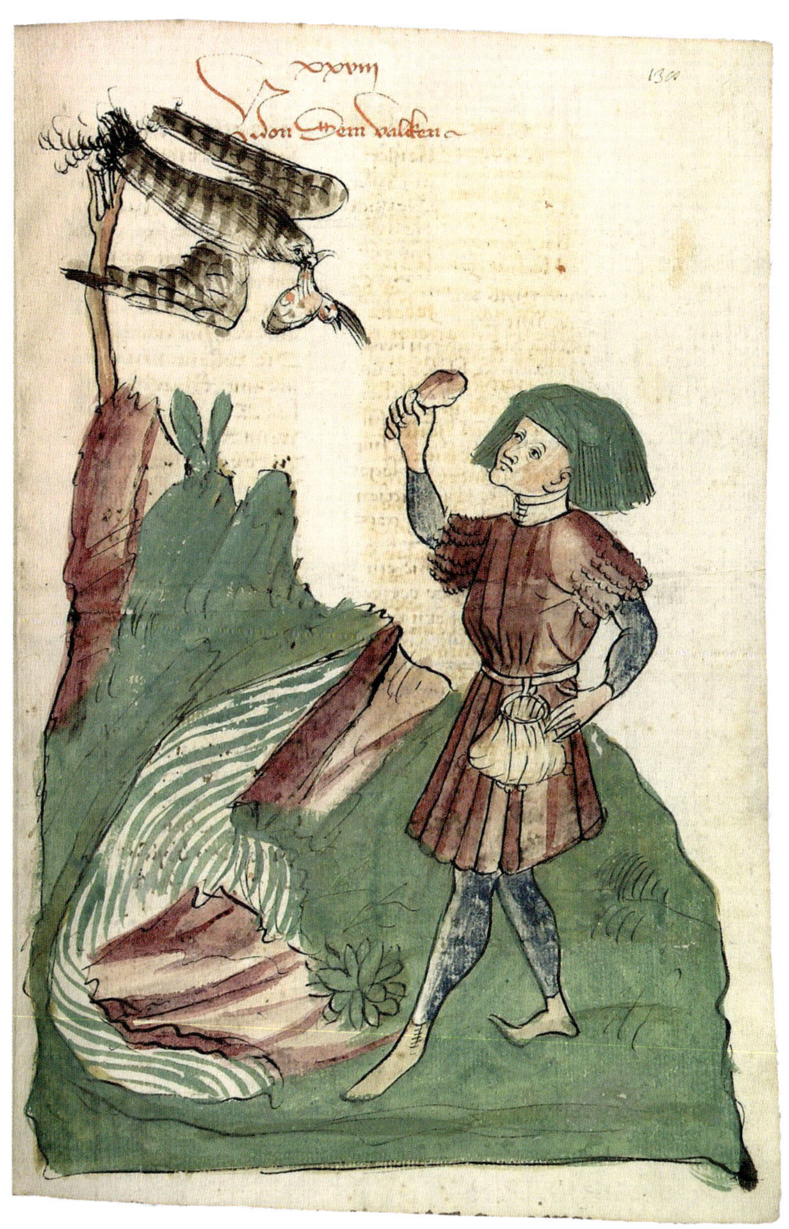

15 Folio from Konrad von Megenberg, *The Book of Nature*, Hagenau, *c.* 1442–8.

created by an experienced practitioner in which culture and nature merge with one another. In *De arte venandi cum avibus* we read the following:

> By the proper exercise of falconry raptorial birds are taught to tolerate the society of human individuals and their associates for hunting proposes, to fly after quarry, to behave without control just as they [the falcons] would in their wild state.[26]

The art is to artificially create a state that gives the hawk the feeling of being in its natural habitat. This fact presupposes a deep knowledge not only of the animal but of the quarry and the landscape in which one hunts.[27] At the same time, nature is culturalized, be it through falconry furniture, as we shall see, or even images that aestheticize the interactive processes of handling hawks and hawking itself.

In *The Book of Nature* by the German scholar Konrad von Megenberg (1309–1374) there is a telling image. The picture in the manuscript is connected to the workshop of Diebold Lauber (*c.* 1442–8) in Hagenau (illus. 15). A falconer, identified as such by his characteristic hawking bag, recalls a hawk in the air with a piece of meat taken out of his *carneria*, as if this would be sufficient to entice her back, given that she carries a songbird in her beak. What is striking here is the falconer and the way that he is coloured, since the image suggests the man has 'dived' into the processual forces of nature. The colours with which the green grass, the reddish stones and cliffs and the water are depicted can be found on the clothing of the barefooted falconer, who also adopts a rather elegant position, as if he were about to start dancing. The falconer is an integral part of nature here, even if his corporeal presence is deeply artificial.

We certainly cannot know what the hawk really sees or feels.[28] Although this impossibility brings in a gap that is never going to be fully bridged, we can, with our human faculties, put ourselves in certain positions and empathize with the animal, at least in an imaginative way. Images or certain falconry techniques enable this.

It is important to note here that the booming subject of animal studies mostly considers animals that are either tame or extremely wild. Is it enough to take the perspective of a frog or a shark to understand a problem? Indeed, does doing so make sense at all? In this context it is worth noting that falconry, because of its in-between nature, is barely considered by such publications. Falconry can be placed onto a specific shelf less easily because trained hawks are neither fully tame nor fully wild. It is exactly this in-between status that generates hawks' fascinating impact, and that of the connection of nature (their untamed status) with culture (the technique of falconry). This marginalization of hawking also occurs either because, most of the time, the animal's absolute autonomy should be placed in the foreground, or because only in extreme cases are the senses of exoticism or wildness considered.

If the hound is taken as the exemplar of the household's order, the hawk is the uncertain, even subversive factor. However, this model also has its limitations: inside the autonomous and autopoietic system of falconry, certain rules cannot be broken. Humans, even the sovereign, may not intervene. For example, Frederick II supposedly had to kill one of his beloved falcons:

> The Emperor Frederick was out hawking with a falcon, a sovereign bird that he loved more than many a city . . . The falcon saw a young eagle below it and followed it to earth and held on to it until it killed it . . . Furiously the emperor called a law enforcer and commanded him to cut

> the falcon's head off because he had killed his lord ['*avea morto lo suo signore*'].[29]

This imperial intervention shows that the hierarchy of nature cannot be supplanted, despite the fact that Frederick 'loved the falcon more than many a city'. It is an analogy of the hierarchy of courtly culture: Frederick, as a human emperor, defends the emperor of the air, the eagle. This could even be a metaphor of how the sovereign should act should any of his subjects question his authority. In this sense, the emperor must train his hawks to behave like his own subjects towards him.

Interaction with the hawk can be discerned in an image from a further copy of Frederick II's treatise, from the early fifteenth century (illus. 16). The emperor, wearing his insignia, is making a blessing-like gesture towards the hawk opposite him, which is shown in an imperial style of profile – one well known, as already mentioned, from coins and medals of emperors since antiquity. The human gesture is like an empathetic approach towards the animal. The hawk sits on a perch covered with cloth – almost like a throne – that does not resemble the common wooden ones. This suggests an anthropomorphic and symbolic approach on the artist's part. Here, practice and depiction again follow different paths.

Training, as a crucial point of interaction between the agents involved, as a process of enhancing specific faculties with the goal of catching quarry, is already established in words in the *Quran*:

> And those beasts and birds of prey which you have trained as hounds, training and teaching them to catch in the manner as directed to you by Allah; so eat of what they catch for you, but pronounce the name of Allah over it, and fear Allah. Verily, Allah is swift in reckoning (5:4).

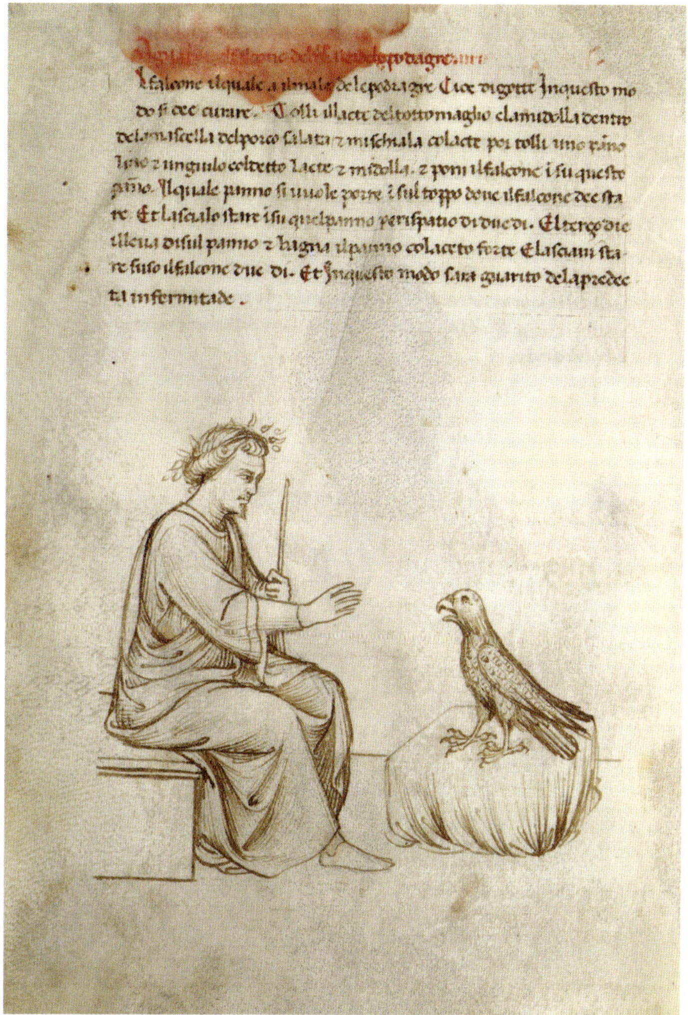

16 Folio from Frederick II, *De arte venandi cum avibus*, Treatise of Dottore Danchi, southern Italy, early 15th century.

Here we find a religious legitimation of falconry that also elevates humans as the absolute controlling element in relation to hawks and dogs. Their actions follow the will of a higher power, that of Allah. This underscores the significance of the practice in an Islamic context, something already observed.

It is once again Frederick II who gives further specific details about training and the interactions between human and animal: 'The falcon must learn to live with man and return to him promptly. Such virtues acquired by training, through patience and the passage of time, eventually become habitual, and, as it were, second nature.'[30] It is clear how this kind of collaborative togetherness of human and hawk is a process that can only be acquired through constant exercise. This is certainly no different, in essence, from other social practices. However, we observe here a higher complexity, since it involves divergent wills and goals that have to be somehow coordinated. The falconer is, as the trainer, the coordinator of the network, but nothing more.

Training engages and involves various senses, especially those of sight and touch. The emperor underlines, in the best Aristotelian tradition (for Aristotle, touch was the most important of the senses[31]), that touch can be found as sensation in the parts of a hawk's body that are the most fragile and precious, from the head to the feet (many diseases like *podagra*, or gout, attack this area).[32] However, scent and sound also play a crucial role in hawking: one thinks of hounds' extremely elaborate faculty of smell. Falconry involves different senses simultaneously and is therefore multisensorial. The Holy Roman Emperor does not remain silent concerning the role of the senses during training, writing:

> It is now clear how the falcon is manned by the sense of taste to take food against her normal instincts from the hand of man; and how, through the satisfaction of her desire for food, she will permit herself to be handled by man whose touch is normally abhorrent to her. By means of these two senses she is finally trained to tolerate unaccustomed sounds . . . All this should be taught to the falcon before she is allowed the use of her eyes.

> It is difficult to train at the same time all the falcon's senses, including that of eyesight, without prejudice to the status of the bird as a first-class hunter. What the blinded bird hears does not give her the same premonition of danger as what she sees or even what she feels. For all these reasons the falcon is to be trained by the three senses of taste, hearing, and touch before she is sighted.[33]

Not only sight, but also taste, hearing and touch should be trained. Food is the intermediary for this process. At the same time, a hierarchy of the senses is created, where sight is placed on the highest level, not only because it is so difficult to train but because it is the most powerful of the falcon's senses. On the one hand we think of the classic hierarchy of the senses, but, on the other, Frederick is quite pragmatic here: 'Since the disclosures of vision are much more hateful to the bird than the revelations of taste, sight must be disciplined.'[34] Through the metaphor of disclosure (of vision) and revealing (of taste), the central role of disciplining sight is underlined. It has to be, so to speak, eliminated (hence why the eyes were formerly sewn, or 'seeled') and then slowly restored as the hawk gradually becomes less afraid or nervous of humans. There is a parallel in this context to a work of art and a connoisseur, who acquires knowledge of how to see and hence gradually understand an image. In the work of the Arabic poet Abu Nuwas (756–814), one already clearly finds aesthetic, almost connoisseurly descriptions of a falcon:

> I would go out in the early morning with a glove for a trained falcon, a speedy catcher dressed in resonant bells. A noble bird trained delicately to capture its clumsy game. Its carnelian eyes clear of impure flecks, its eyelids healthy and unstitched. Its new feathers like a cloak woven by the most skilled weaver. Draped like a silk garment.[35]

Frederick II underlined the importance of the falconer's ability to imitate the sounds of hawks, so that, aside from using the lure, the falconer is able to call the falcon back with his or her own voice. In this sense the auditory dimension is also crucial.[36] One can therefore speak of communication through specific kinds of sounds, rather than language.[37]

Beyond this fact, Frederick also mentioned what in today's vocabulary we would call the multisensorial – one could even say synaesthetic – aspect of the practice, writing that 'an appeal to the sense of hearing, brings about a visual perception of the lure. These two senses together awaken the sense of taste through which she was first trained to come to the lure.'[38] The interplay of two senses activates the falcon's sense of taste. A good falconer should be able to feel and understand the needs of the animal.[39]

However, this multisensorial idea is also clearly manifested in the prologue of the celebrated ninth-century treatise on falconry by Moamin, an Arabic author and probable falconer:

> Kings enjoy very many pleasures . . . hunting seems to be most appropriate to kings . . . Because they live in the purer air, all the senses are delighted, all the parts of the body perform their actions more perfectly . . . Birds which also live off prey are the noblest and most remarkable instruments of hunting; for through them a man has happiness, joy and delight.[40]

For the English scholar Adelard of Bath (*c.* 1080–after 1152), falconry was the ideal pedagogical tool for royals because they could learn how to train, and, ideally, obtain wisdom, through hunting with birds of prey.[41]

We have already observed how the *virgula* was used as a bridge for enhancing the connection between human and animal, underlining the sense of touch through an artificial, wooden device. Such instruments, or items of falconry furniture, play a key role in demonstrating this engagement, which moves between embodied interaction and alienation. These techniques are also visual practices, so that there is an explicit connection between images or visuality and falconry. We will now pursue this idea through several specific examples, including hoods, vervels and lures.

A hood is a case, a container for a mobile, living being. It addresses the question of covering and uncovering, the presence and absence of the gaze, seeing and not seeing, focusing and targeting, and their opposites.[42] Falconry furniture in Vienna's rich collection of items relating to Emperor Maximilian I (r. 1459–1519) includes many hoods, one of which dates from around the turn of the sixteenth century (illus. 17). In the typical European (and Arabic) designs, thin straps or braces, most commonly made of leather, draw the hood closed, securing it on the hawk's head.

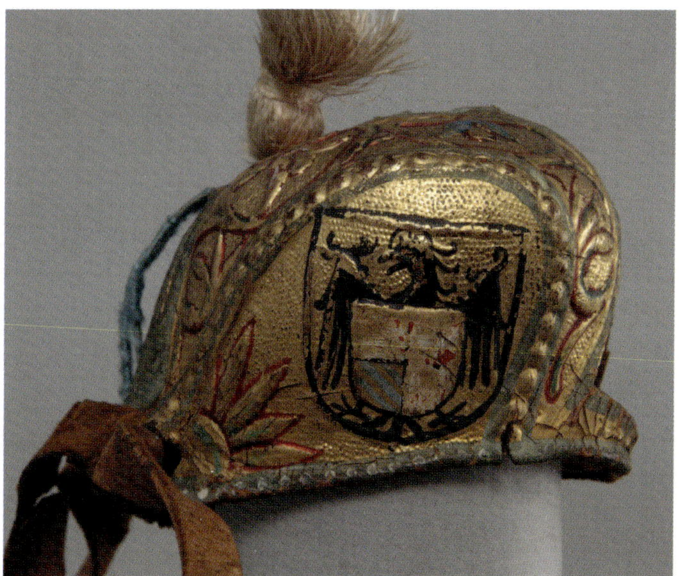

17 Hood of Maximilian I, northern Italy, 1494–1508, gilded and punched leather and paint.

Hooding has been a common transcultural practice since the Middle Ages, changing relatively little in terms of technique, and indeed basic designs, to the present day.

The hood was brought to Europe from the Middle East under the name of *burqa*. Again, in *De arte venandi cum avibus* we find more information about the device:

> The falcon's hood is a discovery of oriental peoples, the Arabs having, so far as we know, first introduced it into active practice. We ourselves, when we sailed across the seas, saw it used by them and made a study of their manner of manipulating this head covering. The Arabian chiefs not only presented us with many kinds of falcons but sent with them falconers expert in the use of the hood. In addition to these sources of knowledge from the time when we first decided to write a book, a complete treatise on falconry, we have imported partly from Arabia, partly from other countries, both birds and men skilled in the art, from whom we have acquired a knowledge of all their accomplishments.[43]

The hood should calm the hawk during the manning and training stages (manning, derived originally from the French word *main*, involves the hawk becoming familiar with sitting on the falconer's fist and getting accustomed to the ways of humans), and also before she hunts – preventing, for instance, her wasting energy attempting to fly at quarry that the falconer does not want to hunt, or in places she may not be safely or legitimately flown. It is not only a functional instrument but has an aesthetic autonomy that starts to be visible in Frederick's treatise. There, in the miniatures, it already speaks for itself by being visualized alone on the margin of a page, needing no reference to its actual function. We will return to this aspect with the example of the lure.

Every hood should be specifically tailored to fit an individual hawk and hence is unique.[44] Through falconry furniture in general, the never-to-be-achieved (and indeed seldom desired) tameness of the hawk and the immense gap between the bird and human is somehow diminished, or seemingly brought under moderate control. The inflexibility of the hood's leather must become the hawk's second skin: it needs to be comfortable, otherwise she will not remain calm. Hoods are often decorated with feathers, alluding to lightness and flying, properties of the hawk herself, bearing a dynamic relation to the leather's inflexible authority as a portable device.[45]

The hood additionally refers to a power that is connected to questions of sovereignty and is used as a metaphor for it, since it is the decision of the falconer-sovereign when (and what) the hawk should see and therefore hunt, or not see and hence remain calm. Hoods sometimes carried ornaments or even a coat of arms as a stamp of sorts, acting as visual devices marking the sovereign's power. The hood of Maximilian I highlights the symbolic quality of such items (illus. 17). The owner's emblem, here the double eagle of the Habsburgs, appears as an icon upon the hood's gilded leather. When carried, the hooded falcon becomes a symbol of imperial power, since it is in movement by virtue of being borne on the fist of a person, whether mounted or on foot, before its use in a royal hunt or during a diplomatic mission. When her sight is temporarily dimmed through the hood, the hawk becomes the iconic symbol of the institution (here the Habsburgs), under whose power she will subsequently act when the hood is removed, allowing her to target quarry. In other words, the hawk is under the auspices of the Habsburgs and should serve them, symbolically and in practice. Hoods frequently feature no figurative devices on their surface, though sometimes they do carry dazzling ornaments with powerful colours, as if the hawk's not-seeing condition is translated into abstract ornamentation.

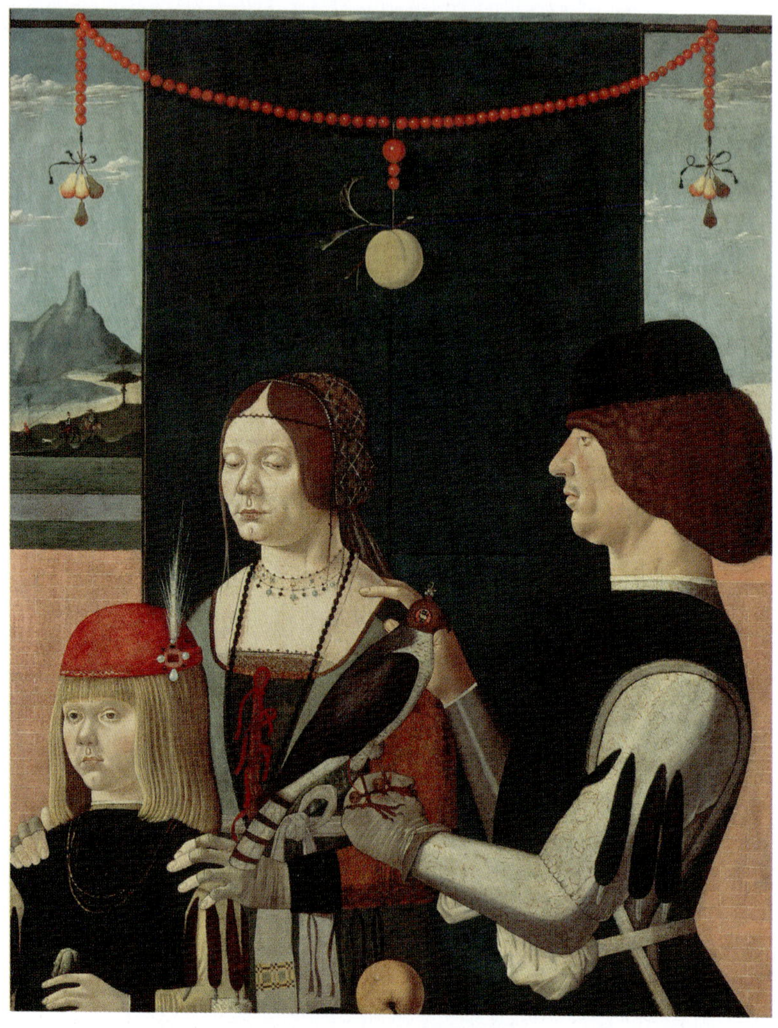

18 Painter from Ferrara (Antonio de Crevalcore?), *Family Portrait*, c. 1480, oil on canvas.

In a family portrait from Ferrara of about 1480, a man, appearing in profile, carries a hooded hawk in a reference to the outdoors: the painting also shows other male figures going to hunt (illus. 18). He is thus part of the outside, presented inside, whereas his wife has taken over the interior of the house with the child's education. The hood carries the family's coat of arms and appears in this domesticated interior as its material, mobile bearer.[46] It unfolds an abstract dimension in its haptic presence.

The red cords on the woman's clothing correspond to the hawk's jesses, with the (apparently) golden bells underlining the question of property. However, the man's gesture of carrying the hawk while putting his hand on his wife's shoulder also introduces an analogy by which both human and animal are, ostensibly, the man's 'property'. The hawk has its greatest power when it sees and hunts, as is the case for the wife, who is the head of the house, especially when the husband is absent and does not try to 'tame' her: things can change, at least for a moment, as the tale of Phyllis and Aristotle eloquently tells us.

One important but less commonly known item of falconry furniture was the vervel. Again, Frederick II describes it:

> Two rings or two stitches of cuirass, no matter whether they are of iron, bronze or horn . . . The unperforated end of the jesses, which must hang down at the back of the [hawk's] feet, will be inserted into the ring and the portion of the strip that will pass through this ring will be folded and sewn to the rest of the strap (so that it) will not have crossed the ring, or it will be knotted.[47]

Vervels could bear images of falcons with the coat of arms of the owner, and even be made of precious metals, like for instance those documented at the marriage of Lionel of Antwerp, Duke of Clarence, and Violante Visconti in 1368.[48] This speaks for the fact that falconry furniture was almost as important as the hawks: the clothes make the king.

However, even vervels made of precious materials such as gold may also simply bear inscriptions. A vervel from England from around 1399–1413, without an image, has a rather modest-looking inscription (illus. 19): 'I belong to the King of England,' reads the potential finder of the lost hawk.[49] This has a double symbolic aspect: it is as if the precious golden object, as well as the hawk that bore it, required no further explanation. The signature 'I belong to the King of England' is, in other words, connected to a specific dazzling golden object.[50] Both indications elevate the hawk's status, warning anyone who might dare to harm or steal her of terrible consequences. We know that people were heavily punished if they harmed a hawk. For instance, if a peasant hurt or injured a falcon, unless shown leniency by a sovereign, he or she would be blinded.[51] This is another kind of hierarchy that is constituted through hawking equipment.

Another example of falconry furniture with a striking visual dimension as a moving and even flying object par excellence is the lure. This recall device was used to attract the bird's attention: falcons, in particular, would be trained to respond to it from great distances in order to help avoid loss. Falcons that pursued quarry out of sight, or went to great altitudes and missed their

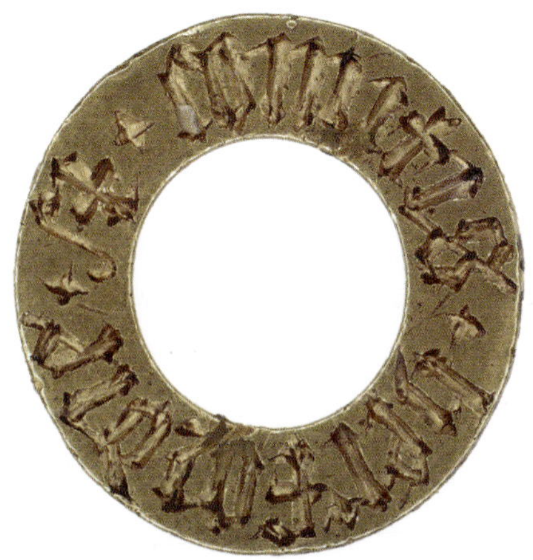

19 Hawk's vervel, England, c. 1399–1413, gold.

target, were likely to see something else in the distance and pursue that, in the past frequently resulting in permanent loss. The lure was a form of safeguard against this (though by no means foolproof), and the monetary and deeper personal value of the falcons made its effective use crucial. Today this problem has been partly solved through technological devices that help to track falcons, yet the ability to recall a falcon from afar rather than chasing her all over the countryside is still an important one for any falconer.

Frederick II commented upon the technique of luring:

> The lure is a symmetrical arrangement of wings by means of which the falcon is induced to fly back to the master. As the crane is the best-known quarry at which falcons are flown and as the gyrfalcon is the most noble of rapacious birds, the most skilled in catching cranes, and gives her finest performance in flights at them, we properly choose a lure made of a crane's wings; for it seems best to make the lure of the wings of the bird at which the gyrfalcon is usually trained to fly . . . When a wild falcon is called to the lure and is made familiar with that device, it is with the intention of making her forget her wild ways and return of her free will to the falconer.[52]

The lure, in that sense, helps the falcon to forget that she is wild – yet another aspect of her culturalization. Frederick also elaborated on the role of vision for the successful usage of the lure: 'keep the lure continuously in a falcon's vision . . . The falconer holding the falcon should watch her expression attentively and had [better] not permit her to fly until she has fixed her gaze intently upon the lure.'[53]

As other Habsburg examples from the collection of Maximilian I illustrate, the lure, which the falconer swings in the air,

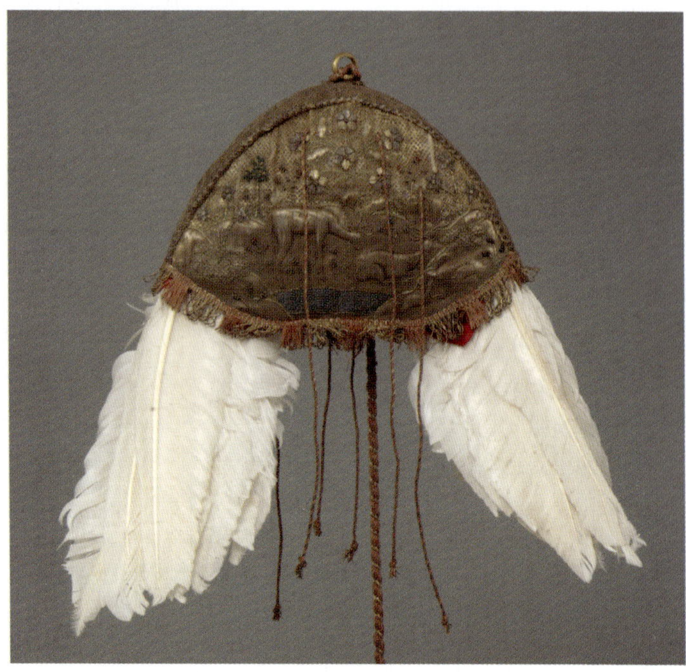

20 Lure, northern Italy, *c.* 1500, gold brocade, swing cord with tassel and modern feather filling.

was both a mobile decoy and mobile work of art (illus. 20). They may also be equipped with heron or crane feathers, and display images of quarry, even – somewhat surprisingly – of deer standing or sitting in a landscape. When the lure was not actually in use and in motion, the images depicting the deer could be admired by the assembled hunting party as a form of iconic trophy. Humans and falcons, then, were addressed in different ways. While the falcons perceived a lure in motion supposedly as prey, or at least as food, humans both handled and aesthetically admired the instrument when at rest. Lures provided a dual affordance for the dissimilar audiences that were simultaneously addressed.

Playing cards showing falconry furniture underline the process of abstraction of actual use into its mere visual depiction, something already indicated in the miniatures of Frederick's treatise with the hoods from the Manfred manuscript.[54] In the so-called *Ambraser Hofjagdspiel* (Ambraser Court Hunting Game, *c.* 1440–45), from the circle of the famous painter Konrad Witz, we can observe on one card two lures that appear asymmetrical on a red background, as if symbolizing red meat or even, at least to our modern eyes, the passion for falconry (illus. 21).[55] The card game also includes hounds, falconers, hawks and herons – in other words, the whole system of falconry, even if the agents appear individually on their respective cards. They are brought into interaction with one another during the game. In the case of the lures, these animate the other players to lure their antagonists.[56] They also underline the discrepancy between *kinesis* (movement) and *stasis* (stillness), because it is the medium of the card that may bring them into motion through the human

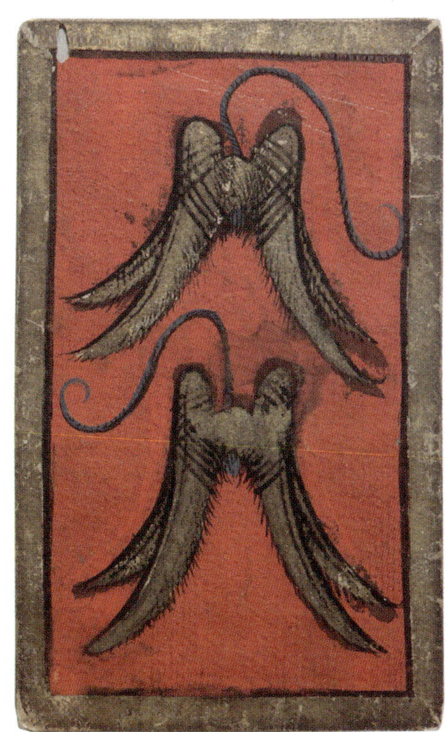

21 Playing card depicting lures, from the *Ambraser Hofjagdspiel* (Ambraser Court Hunting Game), workshop of Konrad Witz, Basel, *c.* 1440–45, pen and watercolour on cardboard.

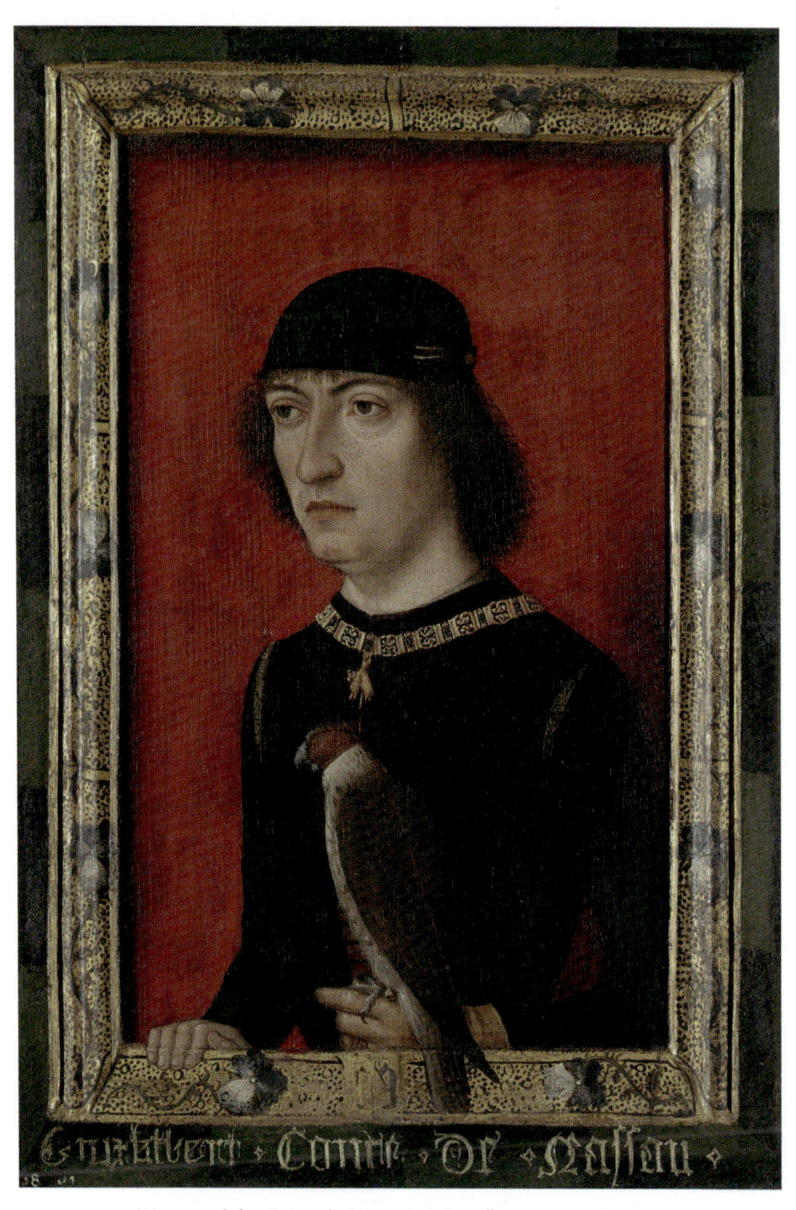

22 Master of the Princely Portraits, *Engelbert II*, *c.* 1480–90, oil on oak panel.

hand. Taking risks in the game is underlined by the contingent nature of falconry. What is at stake here, then, is the visual power of the instrument itself and its aesthetic appeal as such. This is also connected with the fetishization of falconry and its respective industry.

The handling of the lure becomes a powerful game with the seductive force of art, as seen in the Book of Hours of another passionate falconer, Engelbert II of Nassau (1451–1504). See the hint of *sprezzatura* (freely translated as 'effortlessness') displayed in Engelbert's portrait – the way he holds the hawk and the way he rests his hand on the picture's frame, painted in an illusionistic manner (illus. 22).[57] The concept of falconry being a technique of simulation connects to the painting's own illusionistic force.

The same holds for the body of a falconer, perhaps Engelbert himself, depicted in his sumptuous Book of Hours dating from about 1475–80 (illus. 23). Here, the *sprezzatura*, the *ars celare artem* (it is art to conceal art), shows in the body's S-line, enhancing the motions of both the falcon and the lure swinging in the air and, at the same time, the page's ornamental calligraphy.[58] In the same period, the last decades of the fifteenth century, the 'serpentine line' came to be seen as the essence of elegance and beauty – for example, the Parler school in Prague produced a series of statues around 1350 of the so-called 'beautiful Madonna'. The attempt to discipline one's own body correlates here with the game of disciplining the other (the falcon) through the *ars* of falconry.

The famous story of Zeuxis and his perfectly painted grapes that could fool even birds is transferred into the realm of falconry as a visual practice. The lure moves in all kinds of ways (physical and even emotional ones), and there is no hierarchy between the humans and animals involved.

Swinging the lure in the air and simulating flight is a spectacle of such sublime force that it becomes an epiphany in itself.[59]

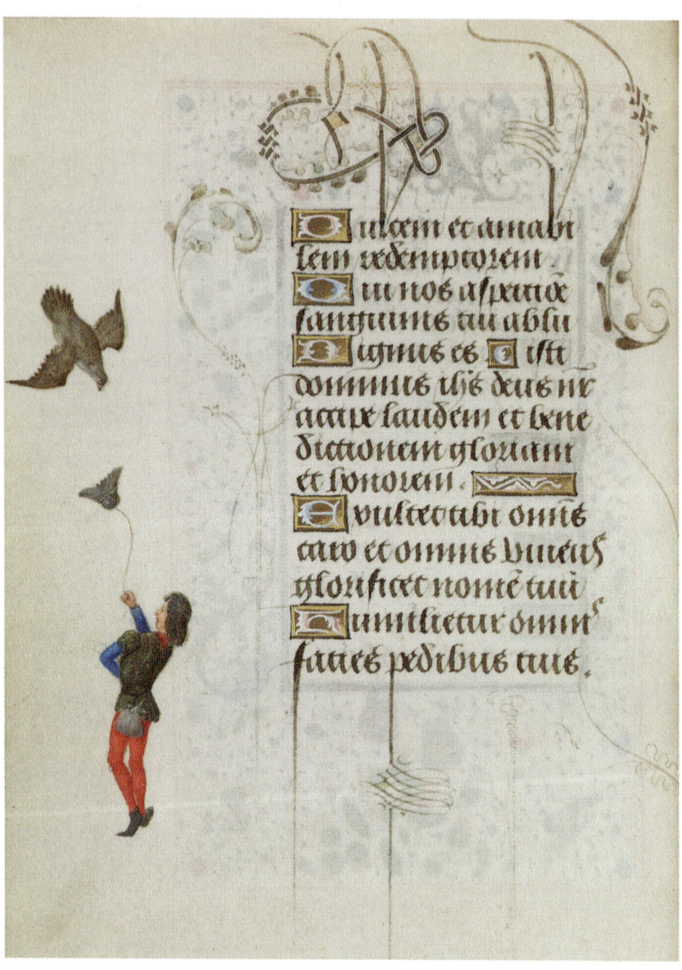

23 Return of the falcon with the lure, folio from the *Book of Hours of Engelbert of Nassau*, with illumination by the Master of Mary of Burgundy, Flanders, *c.* 1475–80.

Through this technique, the unity between instrument (lure) and symbol (simulation of flight and the supposed fooling of the falcon) is visualized. This means that the lure is at the same time a pragmatic technique and a symbolic, aesthetic object – on the one hand, the lure is perceived as another bird, yet on the other it is just a device that looks like a bird; the falcon recognizes this

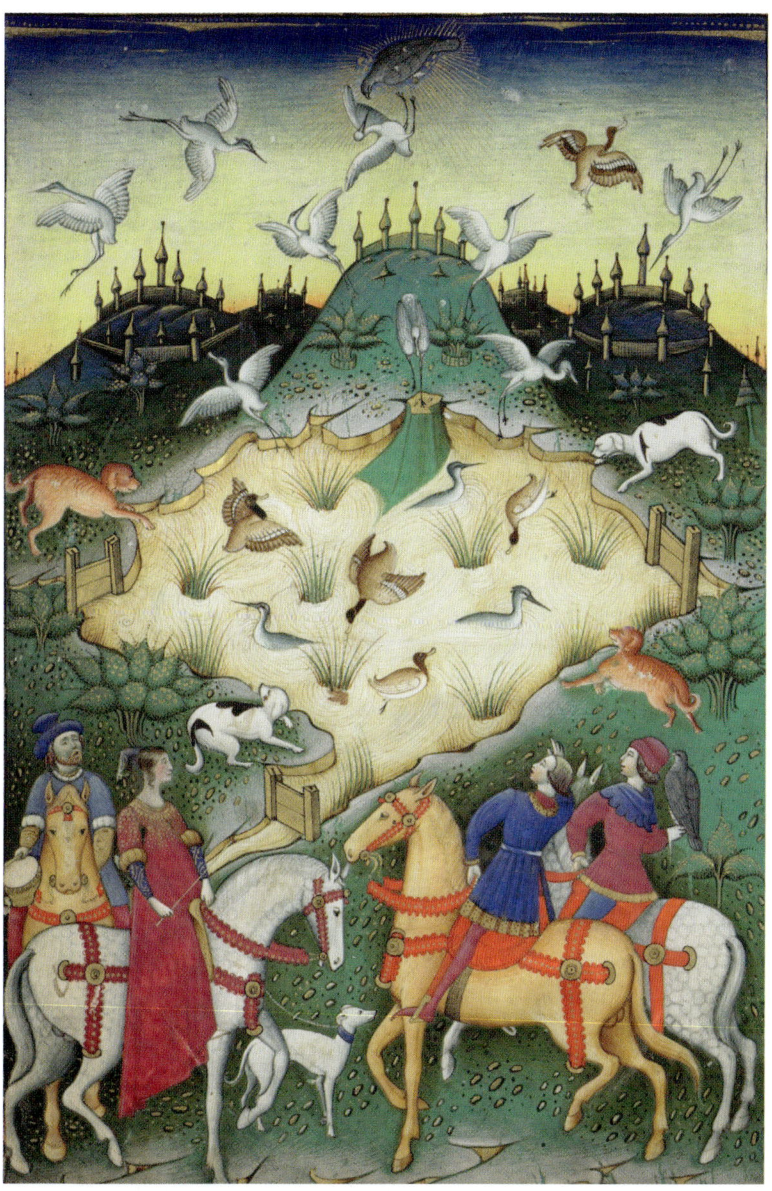

24 Hawking party, folio from *Traités de fauconnerie et de vénerie*, Antonio de Lampugnano, northern Italy, 1459.

and acknowledges both sides. In this amalgamation of sublime power, technique and functionality, falconry receives its elaborate status: somewhere between practical hunting, sport and art.

One image that represents falconry as the above-mentioned amalgam belonged to Milan's fifteenth-century ruling family, the Sforza; their copy of Moamin's falconry treatise contained an initial miniature masterfully copied by Antonio de Lampugnano (illus. 24). The pyramidal character of the image breaks away from any kind of conventional symmetry. The beholder watches the image as if through the eyes of a hawk, by looking at the main action above, where, like a thunderbolt, surrounded by radiant rays of gold, the falcon strikes one of the herons. The falconers who initiated this action become themselves mere spectators of the re-enactment.

As in the above-mentioned miniature, which is today in Chantilly, one can observe that falconry is a spectacle, a training not only of the hawk but of the viewers and their ability to see and understand this spectacle that sometimes moves extremely fast. This fact presupposes a habitual contact with hawks, here enabled through the medium of the image. So-called mirror neurons, bringing forth a certain bodily response and neuronal activity in viewing certain actions, especially if one is accustomed to performing those very actions oneself, seems to be a proper way to describe this process.[60] It is a sort of training of the beholder: the training of the falcon is a training of oneself.[61]

THREE

Power and Aristocracy

A detail from the famed fresco cycle in the Palazzo Schifanoia in Ferrara brings together opposing states of being that may be summarized as movement and stillness, tamed and untamed (illus. 25). In the bottom left of the *Allegory of March* fresco, a mounted hawking party is depicted with hooded, and hence calm, falcons; further to the left is a restless rider (note his garments, fluttering in motion) whose hawk appears set to leave his hand and launch itself towards the artwork's viewers. The hawking party in this allegory is led by Borso d'Este, Duke of Ferrara (who commissioned the frescoes, carried out by Ferrarese painters in his circle). Another part of the fresco cycle, the *Allegory of April* (illus. 26), depicts a falcon stooping upon a heron in an interior: while, admittedly, not an entirely suitable place for such an action, this only serves to underline its symbolic aspect. On the vertical axis underneath, a young boy gently strokes a falcon. It is important to stress here that falconry scenes are seen throughout almost the entire lower parts, and hence lower registers, of the frescoes. This is not a random pictorial decision but rather a symbolic one, visually accompanying Borso's acts of sovereignty.[1] Hawk and image are transformed here into a mirror of princes by shaping the actions and comportment of the courtiers.

Making visual contact with one's hawk was seen as a parallel to a woman looking in her mirror, as López de Ayala highlights in his *Libro de la caza de las aves* (Book of Bird Hunting, c. 1385–7): 'your eyes should be constantly on your hawk, as a woman's on her mirror.'[2] Beyond the gender convention of depicting vanity as a woman looking in her mirror, a deeply visual metaphor is being made here connecting eye, mirror and hawk. This was an important subject featured on the backs of hand mirrors, which commonly showed scenes of love and falconry as directly related to one another. The popularity of the subject was broadly contemporaneous with López de Ayala's treatise (illus. 27).[3] In none other than the thirteenth-century poem *Le Roman de la Rose* (The Romance of the Rose, c. 1230–c. 1275), probably the most famous work of medieval French literature, this analogy is eloquently drawn: 'For as the lure makes the noble sparrowhawk come to the hand at dawn and evening, so also with gifts can

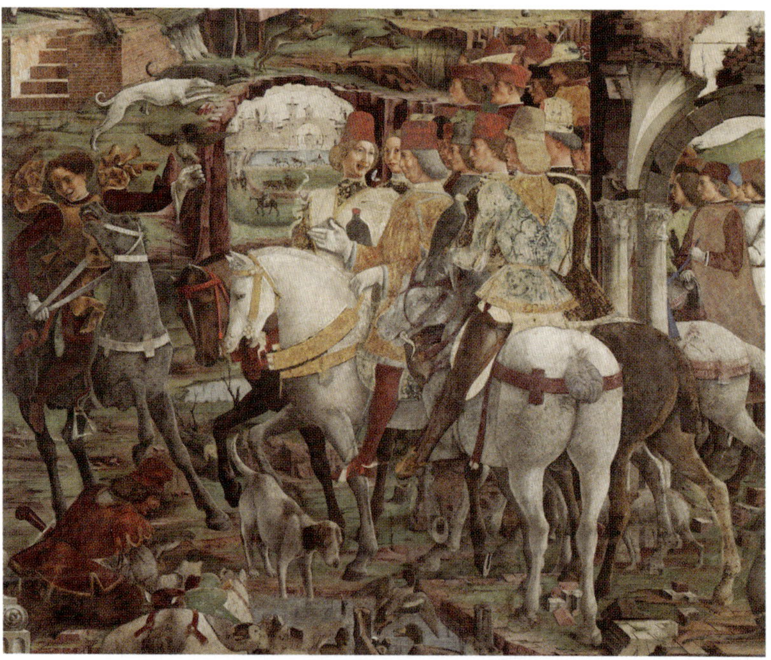

25 Detail of Francesco del Cossa, *Allegory of March*, c. 1468, fresco, Palazzo Schifanoia, Ferrara.

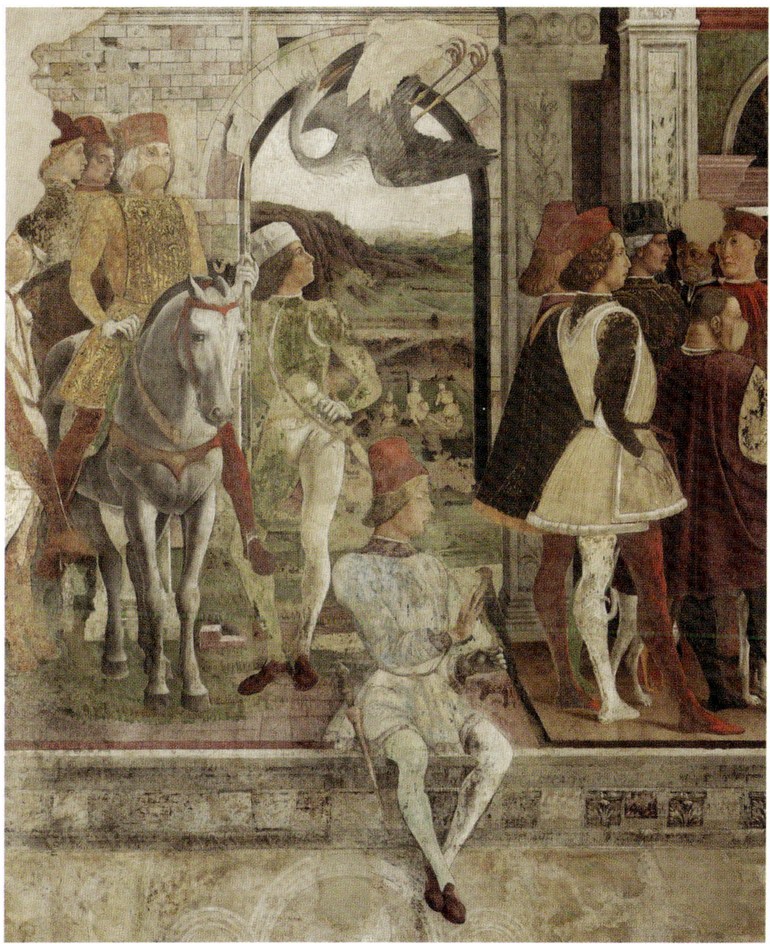

26 Detail of Francesco del Cossa, *Allegory of April*, c. 1468, fresco, Palazzo Schifanoia, Ferrara.

one make the proper prone to favour and to forgive courteous lovers.'[4]

Falconry has always been an 'exhibit', a spectacle, and this has changed little to date, if one considers the status of falconry today.[5] Particularly in the court, one could represent falconry as an artwork in motion, one that opens and closes its wings. This impetus was already found in Frederick II, and visualized in the

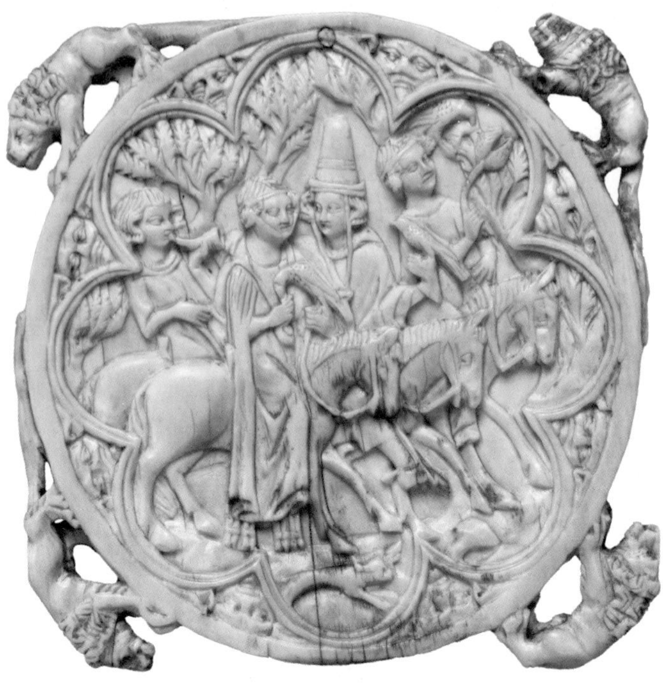

27 Mirror case, French, 1350–75, ivory.

miniature from the fifteenth-century French manuscript (illus. 3). Borrowing a concept from the anthropologist Clifford Geertz, we might construe the art of falconry as a performative practice, the flying and stooping falcon included; as a theatrical state in full motion.[6]

The falcon flying high above a territory fulfils the transformation of a natural landscape into a political one, substituting and extending the ruler's sovereignty over it.[7] The never-to-be-tamed hawk has to be manned and trained by the falconer, whose ability and power is demonstrated during this difficult task. A poem by Der von Kürenberg, one of the earliest *Minnesänger* (authors of *Minnesang*, a form of Middle High German lyric writing), known as the 'Falkenlied' (Falcon Song, *c.* 1160), underlines this idea:

> I brought up a falcon for more than a year.
> When I had him tamed as I wanted
> And when I had adorned his feathers with gold,
> He raised himself up high and flew to another land.[8]

Exactly at the moment when the falconer thinks that the hawk is tamed and he wants to dress her in gold, thus emphasizing the luxurious and aesthetic aspects of falconry, and therefore trying to fully culturalize her, she flies away from him, bringing to the fore the impossibility of taming. It is the proper interaction between human and animal that makes a sovereign a 'master' in ruling by acknowledging the falcon's autonomy and sovereignty. An important iconographic tradition, prevalent from approximately the tenth century onwards, shows how ruler and hawk were often directly associated with one another. This type of aristocracy on the move, and even of the sovereign (see

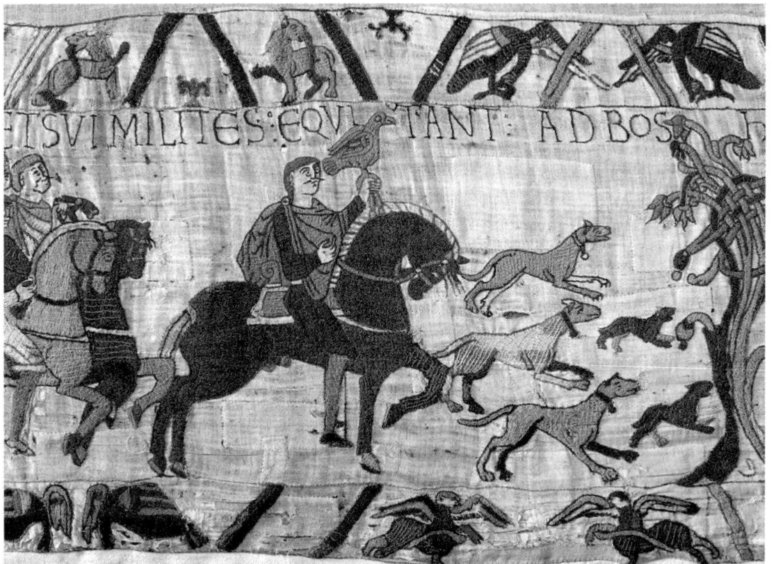

28 Mounted Harold with falcon, scene from the Bayeux Tapestry, c. 1070, embroidered cloth.

Harold Godwinson on the famous Bayeux Tapestry, c. 1070, illus. 28) is definitely not known from Western antiquity alone. It is rather a global motif with various kinds of visual representations.[9] During the medieval period, it is first and foremost members of the aristocracy (including women, such as Mary of Burgundy, who notably died while hawking in 1482[10]), the social group that commissioned most of the artworks of the time, that we find represented by visual testimonies of falconry. It is their symbolically laden narrative.

On a seal belonging to Sophie of Thuringia (1224–1284), we observe how the iconography of a mounted figure on a horse and carrying a falcon becomes an emblem of the countess. The motif has a visual power that mirrors the social and bureaucratic authority conferred by the seal (illus. 29).[11]

Knowing how to handle hawks was seen as an analogy for being able to rule the state. Culture, the ruler's handling of the falcon, was thus turned into nature, just as the quarry killed by the falcon could be turned into culture in the form of physical or pictorial hunting trophies. At the same time, the art of falconry had to be learned, to be literally incorporated. Europe's high-ranking nobles were trained in the art from childhood, as they were trained in dancing and horse-riding.[12]

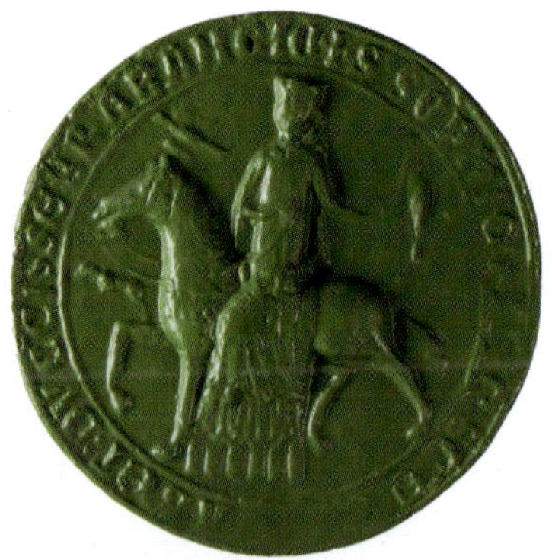

29 Seal of Sophie of Thuringia, 1248.

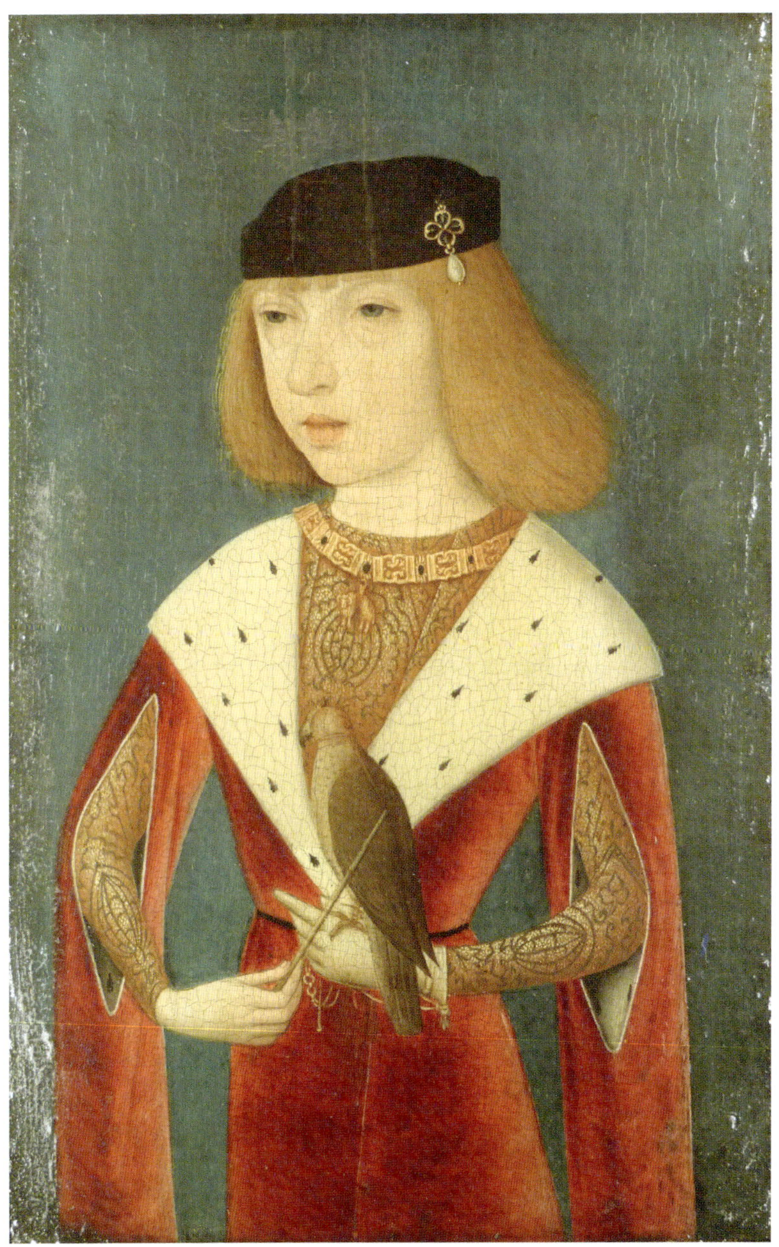

30 Master of the Legend of the Magdalen, *Philip the Handsome*, c. 1492, oil on wood.

Images of young rulers were an important subject of fifteenth-century portraiture. Falconry marked the threshold between childhood and adulthood in a prince's education, as we saw in Ferrara with the young courtier and his hawk (illus. 26). A telling example painted by the Master of the Legend of the Magdalen, today at the Musée de la Chasse et de la Nature in Paris, shows the father of Charles v, Philip the Handsome (illus. 30). Philip, like a kind of conductor, has a *virgula* in his hand stroking his hooded hawk, demonstrating how masterfully he can make use of the device. He also masters his subjects in an elegant fashion. A dynasty of power is crafted: a similarly composed image in Vienna shows Philip's son Charles v (indeed, it was often thought to depict his father because of their striking likeness).[13] The technique of falconry is manifested as a mobile legacy of power. López de Ayala refers to the essential role of falconry in a prince's education, claiming it trained patience and endurance, crucial skills for a future sovereign.[14]

In other words, mastering falconry encapsulated the essential features of a good prince. Frederick II writes that the ideal falconer is a young adult man who has already learned the art as a child, even if he gains real maturity only after adolescence: '[Children] ought to wait until they not only are skilled in the art but have reached manhood's age.'[15] Falconry was not simply a children's game. While games were always crucial for learning sociability and training various skills for real life, the necessity of dealing with the unexpected inherent in falconry made it a perfect school for young sovereigns.[16] Courtly hunting in general was a pedagogical instrument to train body and mind.[17]

Women used to fly lighter hawks like merlins and sparrowhawks, and young boys more than girls were seen with a falcon on their fist. Children started with smaller birds that were more easily handled or trained.[18] In the hunting treatise *Les Livres du roy Modus et de la royne Ratio* (The Books of King Modus and

Queen Ratio, c. 1376), the eponymous king mentions a number of good reasons for hunting with sparrowhawks:

> First of all because this hunt is good and entertaining and the sparrowhawks' stalking flights are very beautiful. Secondly, you are in good company, you line up across the fields, everyone has their sparrowhawk and you can see yours and the others' sparrowhawks. Thirdly, it is a hunt in which ladies can also participate. The fourth reason why one should be fond of hunting with the sparrowhawk is that the hunting season, although short, is beautiful, graceful and pleasant.[19]

There are, albeit quite rarely, medieval images of young women carrying hawks and accompanied by dogs, like the southern Italian figurine of the so-called *Falconiera*, from the first half of the thirteenth century (illus. 31).[20] The luxurious practice of falconry is encapsulated in the precious material in which the young lady is presented. For both reasons, the *raison d'être* of the object can only be fulfilled in a courtly context.

In a thirteenth-century Spanish translation of Moamin, mastering the art of falconry stood for mastering the art of governing, which was itself a major philosophical subject: 'knowing how to govern is an essential part of philosophy.'[21] According to the treatise, the essential features of falconry imitate life itself. Falconry is a model to learn how to conquer, to win but also to lose, as in real life.[22] Sovereigns must exercise and practise these techniques in order to rule successfully. Later, around 1513, Niccolò Machiavelli pointed out how the prince needed to know the nature of humans and that of animals. Using this knowledge, he wrote, properly enhances the sovereign's own authority upon his or her subjects.[23] As we have already observed, this was an idea prevalent in the Middle Ages.

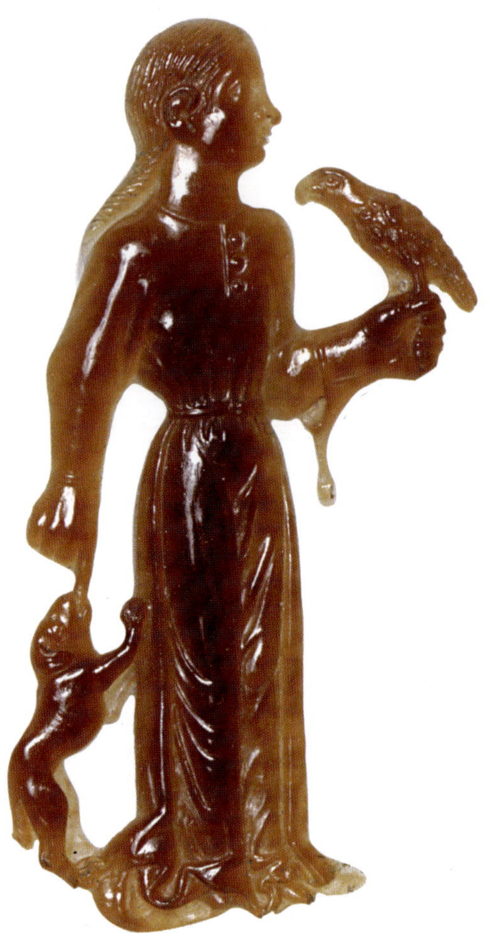

31 Young girl with falcon and little dog, known as *La Falconiera*, southern Italy, first half of 13th century, sardonyx agate.

The importation of hoods and hooding already testifies to a transcultural technique. It was shown in a previous chapter that Frederick II collected falconers from different continents, which indicates both the commonality and also the differences in falconry as practised across these environments. In this context should be mentioned the ninth-century treatise *Kitab al-Mutawakkil*, the falcon and hound book of the Abbasid caliph al-Mutawakkil, authored by Muhammad ibn 'Abd Allah ibn 'Umar al-Bazyar, who summed up older sources about the relationship between hunting, falconry and sovereignty. In this work it becomes clear once again how widely falconry was distributed worldwide, not only in practical but also in theoretical terms (in the form of treatises), and how widely it was seen as an exercise of government. The author explains:

> This is why kings of different people were so much occupied to ask their wise people to write books about how one should proceed and reign. And the one among the Greek philosophers who was best known for this was Eraclis, further Forforis, Plato and Hostar. And the most famous among the kings who commissioned them was Hifiridon. And also the sages of the Turks dealt with it. And the most famous king who commissioned works was Facan, the king of the Turks. And also the sages of the Persians dealt with it . . . Also many of the sages and kings of the Indians dealt with it . . . Likewise did the sages and kings of China . . . we [know of] no sage from among the Arab people who wrote a book that would be useful for hunting and the things that go with it, therefore I have written this book.[24]

Under the Umayyad Caliphate (661–750), not accidentally from approximately the time of the *Quran*, falconry had already advanced into a highly organized sport of the nobility, showing again the global dimension of the subject as a representational weapon for unfolding the elites' power.[25] Since a vast area of (today's) Spain was part of the caliphate, one may also consider the impact this had in Europe.

In the third quarter of the twelfth century, Constantine Manasses, a diplomat and humanist from Constantinople, described how Emperor Manuel I Komnenos (1118–1180) handled his Georgian falcon while heron hawking. Manasses believed that falconry, and hence the emperor's hunt itself, was not only entertainment but about victory and hence the conservation of hegemony in the Byzantine Empire.[26]

The aristocracy's occupation with falconry manifests in the way that hawks were referred to as princes or even emperors. The *Boke of Seynt Albans*, dating from 1486, includes a taxonomy of hawks corresponding to different positions in the court.[27] The king, for instance, is compared to the gyrfalcon, and the knight to the saker, to give just two examples. As one reads further, the treatise explains: 'For a prince: There is a falcon gentle, and a tiercel gentle and these are for a prince. For a duke: There is a falcon of the rock. And that is for a duke. For an earl: There is a falcon peregrine. And that is for an earl.'[28] This is not a unique case – the same list appears in an earlier British manuscript (*c.* 1340)[29] and Geoffrey Chaucer also linked the goshawk with royalty in his *Parlement of Foules* (*c.* 1382):

> There might men the royal eagle find,
> That with his sharp stare pierces the sun;
> And others [of which] scholars can fully tell.
> There was the tyrant with his feathers dun
> And grey, I mean the goshawk that longs
> For birds to sate his voracious hunger.
> The gentle falcon, that with his feet strains
> The king's hand . . .[30]

The hierarchy in the air is mirrored on the courtly ground, and vice versa, as in the episode between the eagle and the falcon of Frederick II.

Falconry could unify the community in a political, ritualized sense as a model of the state apparatus. Furthermore, the sovereign's political charisma corresponds to the size of his or her court, where falconry had a crucial role. Frederick combined his ability to run and rule the state and court with his ability as a falconer. In other words, this activity was used as a political field for experimenting with concepts of sovereignty.[31] Hawking was a kind of metaphorical management of a huge territory in miniature.[32] It was a worldly microcosm of the macrocosm, a living cabinet of wonders.

The most characteristic act of falconry in all its iconographical power through the centuries is of a human holding a hawk on her or his fist or arm.[33] One thinks here of the coin with Zeus and the eagle (illus. 5); the act can primarily be understood as a transmission of the power from a godly, mythical figure to a mortal sovereign. In that sense, carrying a hawk resembles, in gestural visual terms, a privilege that only gods and mythological figures seem to have, like Nike (victory), beyond Zeus. In the case of Hercules, who holds snakes in his hands, the similar gesture alludes to the elimination of the enemy, but in falconry it is about the union of participating factors or the controlling of the beast. In contrast to the case of Hercules, the submission of the other does not mean its destruction. It is rather about co-operation or even interactive shaping, as previously observed.

The historian Ernst Kantorowicz, in his book *The King's Two Bodies* (1957), elaborated on his thesis of the 'body natural' (the mortal body, for example the decaying body of a sovereign) and the 'body politic' (for instance his or her visual representation on a tomb). In our case, these notions apply not in the sense of an 'eternal' versus a 'worldly' body, but rather the symbolic substitution of the body through the falcon, as an avatar of the falconer, sometimes even supported through the medium of an 'eternal' image.[34] The extension of the sovereign in the air through the falcon brings in a dimension of contingency.[35] The sovereign is entirely at the mercy of his or her falcon. This fact may have subversive consequences, since control and power are transferred to a non-human actor with its own will.

The view from above is a divinely given privilege that used to be substituted through architecture, such as the clifftop medieval castles that we still find, even as ruins, around Europe. They enabled the sovereign surveillance over their territory.[36] What a ruler could not attain bodily seemed to be, at least symbolically speaking, possible for the falcon, which falls to earth, striking from above like a thunderbolt. Such a form of 'seeing' symbolized an all-seeing perspective and therefore power on the part of the sovereign, that is, a multi-perspectival viewpoint as an analogy to the hawk's borderless and uncontrollable movement. These all-seeing eyes are a divine kind of power similar to the eye of God, which surveys everything. In the so-called 'bird's-eye view', which is a human construction, there is an allusion to this fact.[37] In the substitution of sovereign and hawk we can speak of a vertical perspective of power. To see from above is a political act.[38]

As such, the act of carrying a hawk on the fist is a transcultural one that conveys a potency and power to act upon and rule others.[39] It is, in other words, in itself a disposition of sovereignty. In 'medieval' Persia there was an additional aspect related to this gesture involving foreseeing the future in terms of sovereignty and territory: it was said that 'if a falcon sits on the king's hand with ease and glances at him it is taken as a sign that new territories will be added to his kingdom.'[40]

The manner of carrying a hawk is connected to the iconography of the nobleman. As a product of late medieval imagery, the motif systematizes a long process of many centuries. One example originates from the circle of Andrea Mantegna, in the so-called Tarocchi Cards, a series of engravings from about 1465 (illus. 32). A male figure dressed in fine garments holds a hawk, towards which he looks gently. Underneath one finds the word

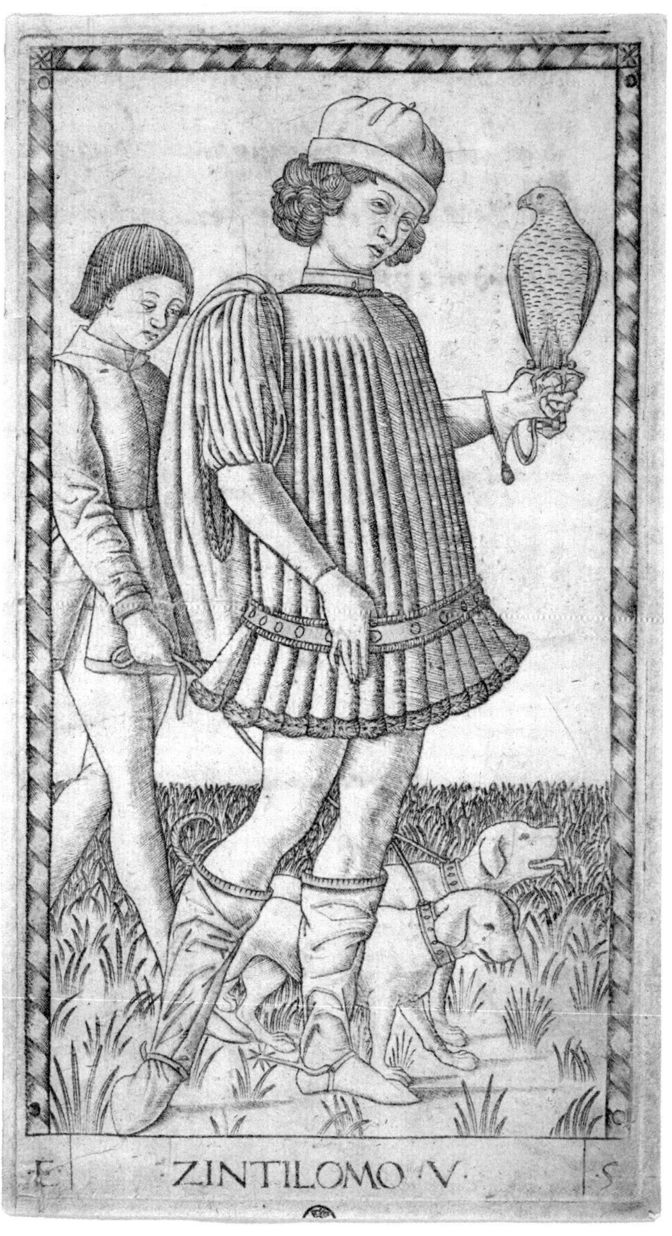

32 Master of the E-Series Tarocchi, *Zintilomo* (gentleman) from the Tarocchi Cards, *c.* 1465, engraving.

'Zintilomo' (*Gentiluomo* in today's Italian: gentleman).[41] Behind him is his servant, who holds hounds on the leash. Later, the author Baldassare Castiglione mentioned in his *Il Cortegiano* (The Courtier, 1528) how the prince usually has 'in times of peace falcons and dogs and all other things that pertain to the pleasure of great lords'.[42] In other words, Castiglione is verbalizing what was already visible in medieval examples: the idea of the falcon as an attribute of a nobleman.

In the iconography of the king or emperor, the example of the falcon is less represented, since the more common symbol of power was that of the eagle or lion, at least in a Western context.[43] Of course, the analogy of a lion or an eagle generally excludes the handling of those animals, while in the case of the falcon it is the very handling that manifests the technical virtues and skills of a sovereign. The prince or the count are more often depicted as falconers, but certainly not exclusively.

Falcons can, however, become symbols of an emperor's destructive power, as one can read in a letter by the Byzantine courtier Theodore Daphnopates, where a partridge given to him as a gift had been killed by the falcon of Emperor Romanos II (r. 959–63) and still carried wounds evidencing the struggle: 'I saw in that signs and symbols of your always victorious reign and its power against the barbarians.'[44] The affordance of the imperial and destructive power of the sovereign is substituted and carried out by his falcon. Additionally, Daphnopates alludes here to an imperial Byzantine gesture. This was part of a legend: the first emperor who interacted with hawks was supposedly Constantine, around 323. In the Bosporus, he saw a peregrine stooping at geese and immediately asked for its capture. The first Christian emperor was so fascinated by this spectacle that he decided to build the city of Constantinople on that very spot.[45] The foundations of an imperial city, today's Istanbul, were thus laid thanks to the lethal potential of a falcon. The story is also narrated in an Arabic manuscript from the eighth century by the falconer Al-Ghitrif:

> The first who hunted with birds of prey was the Byzantine king. He said: 'We found in the Book of Khaqan that a Byzantine king once watched a falcon hunting. He looked at him and was amazed by the clarity and smallness of his eyes and the beauty of his plumage.' The king said: 'The bird has a weapon, and kings have to adorn their courts with him.' So he ordered a number of them to be collected as an ornament for the court. Then a snake appeared to one of the falcons, and the falcon hopped on it and killed it. The king said: 'This is a king who becomes angry about what kings become angry about.' After a few days he sent a tamed fox to the falcon. The falcon jumped on it and let it escape with severe injuries. The king said: 'This is a giant king who does not endure injustice.' Then another bird passed the falcon, and the falcon jumped on it and ate it. The king said: 'This is a king who defends his territory and does not lose his food.' So Khaqan hunted with falcons as did the kings who came after him.[46]

The issue of the different techniques of falconry, culturally speaking, was initially addressed long before Frederick II. In the Persian *Qabus-nama* (Mirror of Princes) from the eleventh century, one can read:

> If you are fond of hunting, engage it with falcon, white hawk, royal falcon, leopard or hound, in order not merely to have your hunting without hazard but to ensure that what you take may be of service . . . If you should choose hawking, princes use two methods. Those of Khurasan never fly the hawk from their own hand, while the

> practice of those of Iraq is to do so. Both are permissible, and, if you are not a prince, you do as you please.[47]

Technique goes together with (princely) status, and hence diverse cultural habits according to the respective region: Khurasan in Central Asia, former Persia, and Iraq.

The falcon was part of an extended political body of rule. This underlines the performative unfolding of power at court as a unifying force. Falconry is a ritual that cannot be fully controlled because, as observed, the animal's subversive power can change the given situation at any time. Failure, however, is part of the ritual, even if, as the sociologist Pierre Bourdieu has argued, the primary goal of a ritual is to establish and conserve political stability and therefore not to question any authority.[48] Falconry is a productive element of disorder that helps to conserve order. How to behave in those unexpected eventualities that falconry frequently brings lies quite literally in the sovereign's hand.

The idea formulated in the *Oneirocriticon*, a dream interpretation treatise by the scholar Achmet of Basra (*c.* 653–*c.* 728), that 'the hawk and the falcon signify a position of power second to the king,' is still valid today and visible in mobile objects that enlarge or even defend the sovereign's territory, at least symbolically: jets or rockets carrying names such as *Falcon*.[49] The *Oneirocriticon* continues, remarkably: 'if the king dreams that he was hunting with a falcon . . . if he caught something . . . he will quickly strike down this nation and rule it through his lieutenant.'[50] This passage clearly raises the aforementioned idea of a substitution between sovereign and hawk. The ruling of the nation also occurs through the sovereign's hawk as his faithful lieutenant.

The connection between sovereignty and (physical) power is brilliantly described in the early thirteenth-century French romance *The Quest of the Holy Grail*, a 'medieval fantasy' par excellence.[51] One passage deals with the king of a barren country who, in battle, was mutilated between the legs and could therefore neither walk nor ride: in other words, he was incapable, in representational terms. For that reason, he stayed on a boat and fished and went by the name the Fisher King. During this period, his falconers used to hunt through his woods and took over governing, but not representational sovereignty.[52] This story highlights the importance of the image of the king who was practically impotent in a metaphorical as well as a literal way and therefore not in a position to govern.[53] Falconry is, in this case, an equivalent to running the business of, and governing, the state, while the impotent king is fixed, like a statue, in a representational position that enables him to officially remain 'ruler', at least ostensibly.

A striking and similar example with a more positive touch is a source from 893 that appears in the Welsh monk Asser's biography of Alfred the Great, king of Wessex (r. 871–99):

> Meanwhile, therefore, the king, between wars and the frequent hindrances of the present life, as well as the attacks of the pagans and the daily illness of his body, did not leave off from presiding over the government of the kingdom; engaging in every art of hunting; instructing all his goldsmiths and craftsmen, falconers, hawk-handlers and dog-handlers.[54]

Not only is representation of government (despite wars and illnesses of the sovereign's body) explicitly connected in this elegy with austringers (*accipitrarii*), who fly short-winged hawks, and falconers (*falconarii*), who fly true falcons, but craftsmen (*artifices*) and goldsmiths (*aurifices*) are also put into the same context, thus underlining the visual power of falconry and sovereignty.

But what about the falconers? Did they always originate from powerful elites? The common falconer by definition had nothing to do with aristocracy; he could, though, manage to climb within the hierarchy, acquire wealth and even become a member of the lower aristocracy.[55] There was nevertheless a huge discrepancy between an aristocrat or sovereign who was also a falconer and a professional falconer inside a court, who used to serve the ruler by facilitating his or her passion. In this sense one might ask: who is the actual falconer, or agent, here? The sovereign reminds one of politicians who open events by the symbolic act of cutting the ribbon. Following this, the falconers under the sovereign's protection are a further extension of power and have to manage the hawks, even if they remain secondary next to, or rather behind and certainly beneath, the sovereign. They are in this sense not so different from the falcon as a substitute and extension of power that serves, at least in representational terms, the sovereign.

When the twelfth-century Arabic knight Usama ibn Munqidh, briefly mentioned earlier, narrated the issue of training and handling falcons, he underlined, 'My lord we never train falcons ourselves, We have falconers and attendants who train them and go before us using them for the chase,' meaning that the actual job was done not by the ruler but by someone else.[56]

The falconers working in medieval courts were mostly male.[57] However, one example of a woman working in a hands-on professional role as a falconer, or at least carrying out routine management roles if not active in the field, is recorded as working in King James IV of Scotland's mews ('the birdhouse' of raptors). In 1496 a payment of five shillings and fourpence went to 'the wif that kepis the Kingis halkis'.[58] This was certainly not a noblewoman, though she could have been related to one of the male falconers at court.

The existence of a master or grand falconer in the court brought with it another kind of hierarchy, underlining the prestige of this form of hunting. Together with the master of hounds or chief huntsman and a forest ranger, the grand falconer had to oversee those courtiers or knights who were allowed to hunt – in other words, the privileged – on behalf of the sovereign.[59] That is, they were there to regulate falconry. Any violation of restrictions could bring heavy punishments. For instance, in 1251, Gilbert de Hauville, a falconer, was warned that 'the king will take severe measures if the royal gyrfalcons perish by Gilbert's default.'[60] Furthermore, in 1286, Edward I ordered the following:

> Although the king, by reason of his stay in parts beyond sea, does not believe that he will have his sport by the rivers within the realm this coming winter, he nevertheless orders the sheriff to put into defence all the preserved rivers within his bailiwick, and to cause in addition proclamation to be made that no one shall presume to hawk in the same with goshawks, falcons or other birds while the king is without the realm, and to so punish any persons found thus transgressing that their punishment shall cause to others terror of offending.[61]

Falconry and its exercise on the king's territory was solely a royal matter.

Falconry was a precious endeavour, last but not least, in financial terms, but most of all in terms of habit and social power that was visually highlighted. The courtly hierarchy also helped to develop the 'industry' of falconry.

When falconers act under the auspices of a specific court, they bodily and symbolically represent the power under which they may unfold their skills. They are not that different from the workshop of a painter, at which students and assistants operated under the name of the master. This occurs not only between falconer and ruler but within the wider hierarchy of falconry in the court. The court falconry establishment consisted of numerous people in different roles, under the grand falconer's direction, fulfilling the sovereign's wishes. There were falconers, trappers, under-falconers, cadge carriers and others who managed the mews.[62] In this sense one might even say that the one who caught quarry or trapped hawks was secondary, since everything occurred under the sovereign's auspices from the moment when the visual regime of the various actions was concentrated upon the ruler.

In contrast to the Fisher King, in physical terms the falconer was ideally a fit young man (less often a woman) in his prime, underlining the role of power and connecting body and mind. It was even said, almost in superstitious fashion, that falconry was responsible for hunting down illnesses, which is another kind of agency attributed to the practice.[63] A sovereign with an intact and fit body had to be as perfect and powerful as the animals with which he or she hunted. Transfer of power, and skills such as accurate sight, endurance and speed, are connected to the human–hawk relationship. López de Ayala commented in his falconry treatise precisely on this aspect:

> when a man is idle, without exercising his limbs and experiencing changes of air, his bodily humours grow stale and he is subject to sickness and diseases . . .
> To avoid these evils, those engaged in the education of the sons of kings and princes thought it good that they should go through the countryside for a few hours every day, taking fresh air and exercise.[64]

Frederick II crafted the image of the ideal falconer in words. It should be someone who is also a ruler of sorts, since hawking was a model of sovereignty, even if (and we will return to this) critical voices might be raised about that ruler's fixation on falconry, which resulted in the neglect of state affairs.[65]

Here, the Aristotelian concept of the *aurea mediocritas*, or golden mean – the desirable middle ground – is central, since the falconer had to be 'average', in this old sense of the word, embodying an equilibrium that was also necessary for a good ruler. The required equilibrium is a balance in mental as well as bodily terms. Frederick wrote:

> The falconer should be of medium size . . . He ought to be moderately fleshy . . . He must be diligent and persevering . . . He must possess marked sagacity . . . [as] he will still have to use all his natural ingenuity in devising means of meeting emergencies . . . He should also have good eyesight and see well in the distance, so that he can keep in view the birds at which he wishes to fly his hawk . . . He ought, in addition, to keep a sharp lookout on everything in the locality where he is hunting. It goes without saying that the falconer's hearing should be acute . . . A falconer should have a good carrying voice . . . He must be alert and agile in his movements.[66]

For Emperor Frederick, a falconer had to be multisensorial, agile and intelligent – similar to his hawk. Such virtues should be found in a sovereign. Frederick continues, recounting further features of the ideal falconer:

> He must be of a daring spirit and not fear to cross rough and broken ground when this is needful. He should be able to swim in order to cross unfordable water and follow his bird when she has flown over and requires assistance. He should not be too young, as his youth may tempt him to break the rules governing his art. Young people tend to

> become bored and to be attracted only by successful and pleasing flights.[67]

Such a description of the falconer was not simply alluding to a sovereign but was a direct reference to himself: Frederick II created here an alter ego almost, a self-portrait. The falconer should also be an all-around athlete, for instance a swimmer, as Charlemagne was.[68] However, Frederick did not stop here:

> The falconer must not be a sleepyhead, nor a heavy sleeper . . . He should not be the slave of his stomach . . . A drunkard is useless . . . A bad temper is a grave failing . . . Laziness and neglect in an art that requires so much work and attention are absolutely prohibited. The falconer must not be an absent-minded wanderer.[69]

Ancillary passions would detract from the actual goal. A codex of behaviour is created that parallels the proper mode of governance. The perfect falconer combines earth with sky and understands not just the language of the animals but that of the different elements.[70] In this way, because he can create and combine things, he is a second creator, after God. In an abstract and more implicit way, the falconer-sovereign embodies elements that can be compared to the originality and creativity of an artist. We have already referred to the relation between the two areas, and in the Coda we will take a further example into account, that of the artist as falconer.

We may also remark on the striking differentiation between falconry and common hunting in *De arte venandi cum avibus*, since the first is classified as an art:

> Here it may again be claimed that, since many nobles and but few of the lower rank learn and carefully pursue this

> art, one may properly conclude that it is intrinsically an aristocratic sport; and one may once more add that it is nobler, more worthy than, and superior to other kinds of venery.[71]

Frederick further underlines how 'we should pursue our studies of the falconer's science and art, not only to study the implements employed but to regard the artistic side of the sport.'[72] Science and art go hand in hand here. The falconer is not only an artist, he is someone possessing scientific knowledge, at least concerning the illnesses of the animal as well as its nature in physiological as well as behavioural terms. Another remark by Frederick demonstrates how beauty and technique can be viewed under a similar lens. Concerning the falcon's bells, attached to the bird in order that, in case of loss, the falcon's owner could trace it through the sound that it produced (not unlike shepherds' practice with their sheep even today), he wrote:

> Another method of attaching the bell to the body of the bird is to make a hole in the two medial tail feathers and so affix the bell. I am opposed to this plan, since the tail is thereby dragged down in an ugly fashion and the feathers themselves are likely to be injured.[73]

Falconry was pursued by commoners to secure food, like among the Bedouin. In the European Middle Ages, the aristocracy increasingly started to engage in falconry and became explicitly connected to this form of hunting. A particular visual narrative emerged with additional symbolic meanings in terms of self-representation and was also heavily enabled through luxurious artworks depicting aristocratic falconry scenes. This became so commonplace (through books, images and, later, films as well), that even today many connect falconry only with the upper classes. In the European tradition, however, there are some examples that show another kind of narrative, one that merits brief mention in order to gain at least a feeling for this visual ideology.

We see a falconer travelling out of town to go to the country in an *Allegory of Good Government in the Countryside* by the painter Ambrogio Lorenzetti (c. 1338; illus. 33). This fresco, on a wall in the town hall of Siena, shows wider social participation beyond that of the aristocracy alone. In another detail, one can identify a falconer already hunting in a cultivated landscape where other people are also pursuing their daily activities. Perhaps not coincidentally, the fresco offers a bird's-eye view.[74] It is

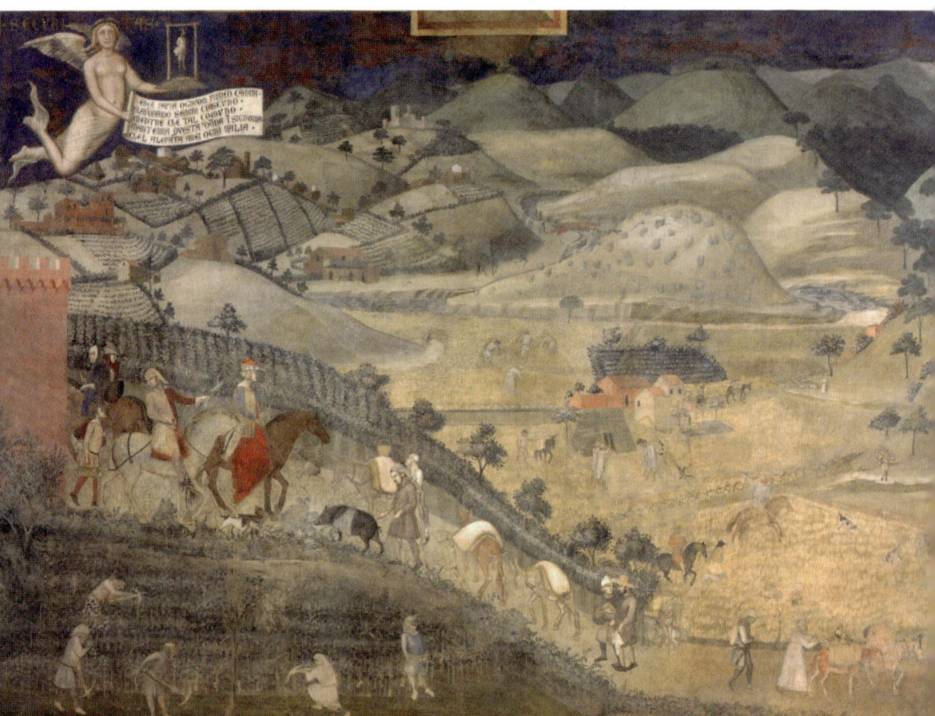

33 Detail of Ambrogio Lorenzetti, *Allegory of Good Government in the Countryside*, c. 1338, fresco, Palazzo Pubblico, Siena.

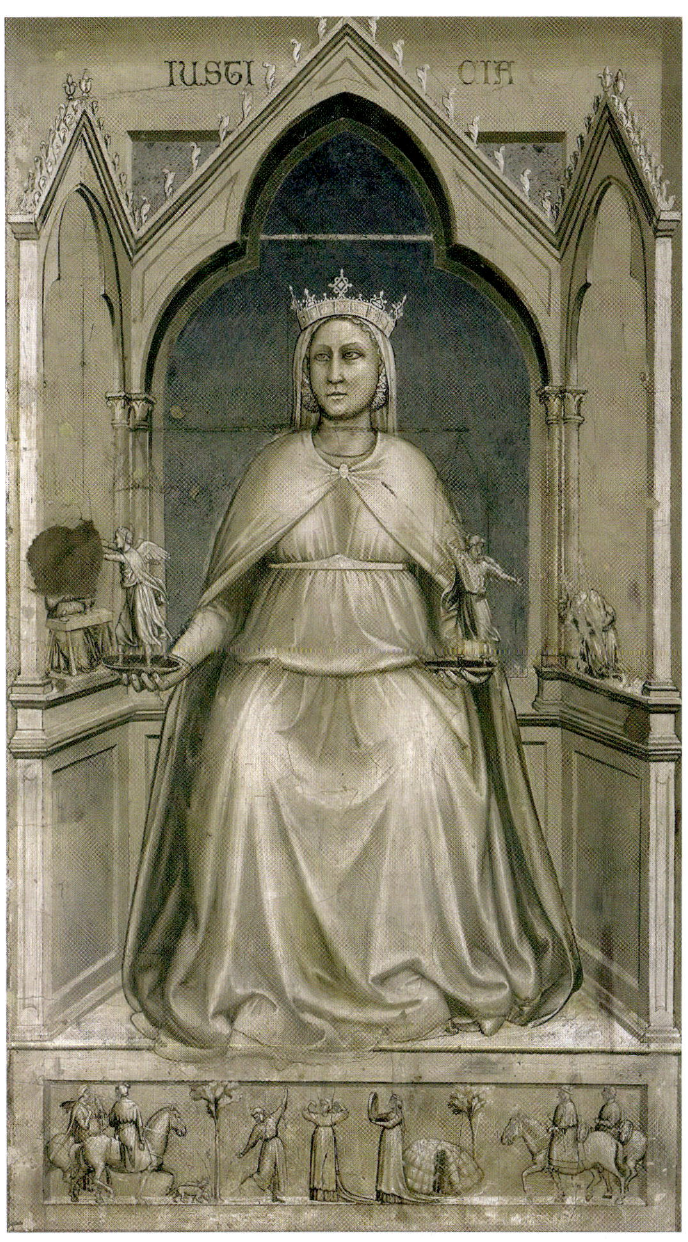

34 Giotto, *Justice*, c. 1304–6, fresco, Arena Chapel, Padua.

also telling that the scene, like so many falconry images, revolves around movement and mobility.[75]

Above the first falconer, Lorenzetti inserted the winged allegorical figure of Security, another indication of how the arts of falconry and good government tended to be associated with each other.[76] As has been argued, there is some affinity here with Giotto's depiction of justice in his Arena Chapel frescoes in Padua, with its inscription (freely translated) (illus. 34): 'as far as the arm of justice reaches, the brave soldier hunts, people sing and others trade.'[77] The falconers, mounted on their horses, seem to bring justice and security. These are clearly privileged individuals who may co-govern, but importantly it is a shared kind of power. In this sense, even if the class relations are not criticized, since the whole work is done for a representative part of the community, there is a republican echo here that goes beyond aristocracy. Such images reveal the different social worlds that resonated through falconry in medieval times. To a republican understanding, but certainly not exclusively, falconry was a commonwealth; one, also, in the sense of the stability that a good sovereign or a community brought in, as made manifest in images such as Lorenzetti's.

Another aspect not yet mentioned concerns the participation in falconry of women who do not belong to the aristocracy. There are, unfortunately, very few examples from the Middle Ages, and one has to come inevitably to the fifteenth century to find some cases. One compelling artwork is in Basel: a tapestry from 1468 showing wild men and women during deer hunting (illus. 35).[78] The often-treated subject of aristocrats hunting is represented, and the depiction operates with all the conventions of falconry's iconography. Is this a kind of world upside down, a way of depicting things that goes against order by way of visual criticism? The background, a 'tapestry in a tapestry' constellation, consists of ornaments; in this, there is no differentiation, formally speaking, from other examples of that period. However, the people who have hawks and hounds look different. All wear unique garments and head coverings that are neither aristocratic nor common. Their big beards and hairy appearance allude to a fashionable subject in fifteenth-century visual culture: that of the wild folk.

On the right-hand side of the tapestry, one discerns a woman with very long hair who, by contrast with the female figure linked to the man holding hounds on a leash, is not at home but outdoors, hunting. She is the only person holding a hawk, upon her glove, while the male figure puts his hand around her waist. The woman gestures tenderly towards him, a motif known from depictions of courtly love. Here the active element is the woman, not the man. Even the gestures have been interpreted as being courtly.[79] The whole field of the tapestry carries scrolls containing text, in which the relevant couple's dialogue reads: 'The hounds do hunt well, I would like to care for you,' whereas the woman with the hawk answers: 'Dear friend, let us be quiet, I hear the driving dogs.'[80] The erotic connotation is substituted through the concentration on the hunt, underlining again the woman's strong position in the tapestry.

But who commissioned such an object? It is no surprise that it derives again from the main socio-economic segment that could afford to commission such artworks and would have the appropriate space to exhibit such large tapestries. Hans von Flachsland, who owned the work, was a knight with strong connections to the city of Basel, being mayor there from 1454 to 1463.[81]

That this depiction is not an ironic one on the patron's part is proven by the way people in the image act. The wild folk behave similarly to fine people in terms of their manners. At the same time, the iconographic type of wild men and women has not changed its appearance, yet their behaviour has. It is as if, anthropologically speaking, love and hunting are existential

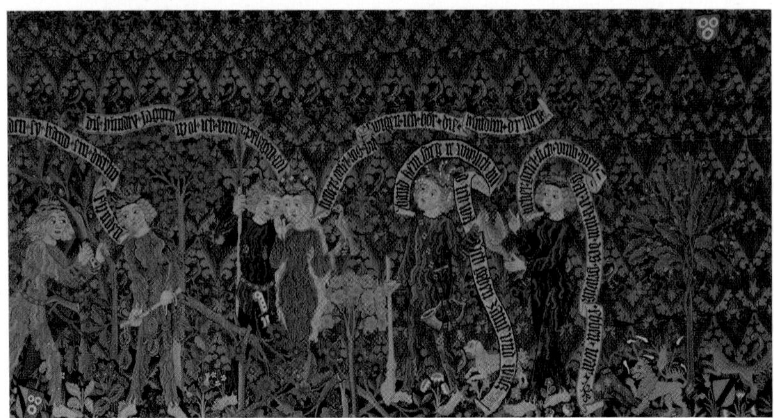

35 Wild men and women on a stag hunt, *c.* 1468, section of wool tapestry, Basel.

pastimes. Manning and taming refer, in this case, to the gender relations or to the different layers of nature (animals and wild folk). The human figures have language and instruments as well as codes of proper behaviour: in other words, they are not really wild. They are culturalized, like the hawks, showing their liminal position between nature and culture. The coat of arms on the tapestry underlines and legitimizes the deeds of the agents, as well as the power relations between them, creating a visual hierarchy. That the wild woman is carrying a wild hawk shows different levels of manning, the coat of arms marking the highest level. This indicates the untamed nature of both humans and animals on the specific tapestry, where wildness has, however, been 'tamed' through the persons who possess it. Wild men and women were often used as apotropaic elements helping to conserve order through disorder.

The common man, even less the common woman, is barely thematized in visual testimonies of falconry, especially in the Middle Ages. Their invisibility in visual terms is remarkable. This does not mean, however, that they did not pursue falconry.[82] In Brabant, even if this is rather an exception, from the fourteenth century onwards, anyone was allowed to take small quarry with the help of a hawk.[83]

There are a number of medieval depictions showing encounters between aristocrats and peasants in which falconry was used as a visualization of class distinction, since the latter could only hunt with certain weapons or animals and only with the sovereign's permission. In the famous Devonshire Hunting Tapestries (*c.* 1430–50), probably made in Arras, France, one can observe a lucid depiction of this socio-economic disparity (illus. 36).[84] Falconry has a double dimension here: a dialectic tension predominates over the people's social relations and transactions, which have variable modes of power within the social hierarchy, even within the hawking party itself, as one can distinguish professional falconers or other common people beyond the aristocrats. Different agents go about their daily businesses, as in the Lorenzetti painting (illus. 33), but in this case it becomes clear who the person in command is. This motif derives from the

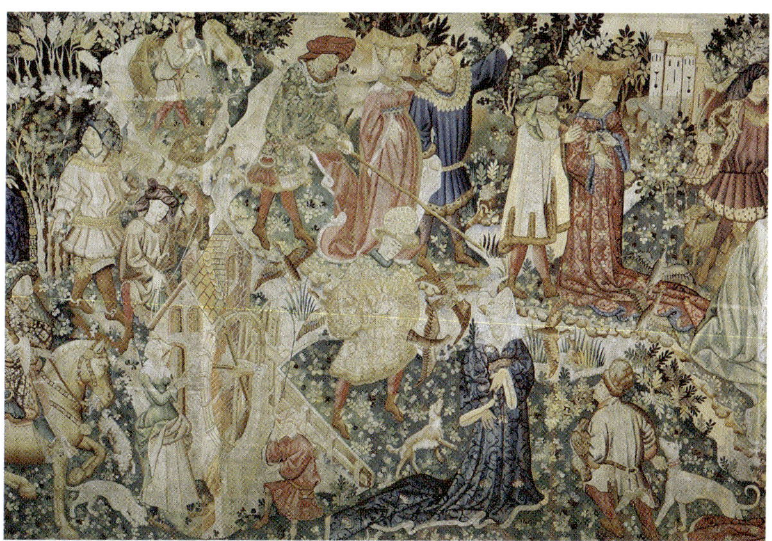

36 Detail of falconry from the Devonshire Hunting Tapestries, northern France, *c.* 1430–50.

tradition of calendar months in Books of Hours by the Limbourg brothers, where such tensions are also implied through visual juxtaposition. These medieval calendars often show labours and pastimes appropriate for each month, including ploughing, planting, harvesting and, of course, hunting with birds of prey.

Charles VI of France (r. 1380–1422) allowed falconry, by official decree, to be practised only by the upper classes.[85] But Frederick II eloquently summarizes the ideal of falconry as, at least seemingly, a classless quest:

> The pursuit of falconry enables nobles and rulers disturbed and worried by the cares of state to find relief in the pleasures of the chase. The poor, as well as the less noble, by following this avocation may earn some of the necessities of life; and both classes will find in bird life attractive manifestations of the processes of nature.[86]

FOUR

East and West Dimensions

Just like the ancient art of falconry, which originated in the East and spread throughout the European continent, its associated imagery has also traversed time and space, forging political alliances along the way. Falcons, much like images, roam and journey. Among the well-known falcons is the *Falco peregrinus*, commonly known as the peregrine falcon, or *Wanderfalke* in German. The name of a wanderer or peregrinator emphasizes the connection between images, falcons and motion as visual and tactile elements. In order to gain a comprehensive understanding, we will expand our perspective beyond Europe and explore the continuous exchange between East and West, a theme intertwined with the global origins of falconry. Falcons are inherently nomadic, just like images, while falconry itself similarly represents an itinerant, transcultural practice. This characteristic not only extends to the physical execution of falconry but also encompasses the visual and symbolic dimensions of the phenomenon.[1]

We will therefore deal here not with relations between East and West but rather with the simultaneously Eastern and Western dimensions of medieval falconry as an image in motion, and try to raise awareness about the complexity of such terms. By the Middle Ages, falcons and the images related to them already connected distant cultures, and they continue to do so today.

Falconry is directly connected to movement and mobility, not only from East to West or West to East. This also happens with images, which are in constant motion across the globe (something facilitated today via 'wings' in the form of invisible cables). This was already certainly the case by the Middle Ages, albeit on a scale different from today; the whole network of falconry (people, animals, falconry furniture, to mention only a few of the factors involved) presupposed mobility in time and space.[2]

It was the Holy Roman Emperor Frederick II who stressed questions of movement in conjunction with hunting: 'Hunting is nothing else but movement and exercise with the goal to catch wild animals,' he wrote.[3] Let us again not forget that Frederick brought together falconers from different parts of the world, sent by their respective kings, including those of the East (he refers explicitly to Arabia), in order, as he stressed, to better learn this art, since there were aspects of falconry that people from other parts of the world knew better or approached differently.[4] The case of the hood, mentioned earlier, which was directly imported from the East – specifically the Holy Land – can serve as a striking example. It demonstrates that there was an ambition to achieve an ideal kind of falconry by uniting several kinds of know-how. These were attributed to different cultures around the globe and their forces joined by being gathered in a single court, whose supreme authority also had the aim of bringing several cultures together under the tutelage of one empire. In this togetherness or unification one can recognize falconry as a transcultural practice. We will trace this idea by considering a famous iconographical subject related, surprisingly, to falconry, but also through textual and visual sources dealing with hawking, bringing East and West into productive interrelation.

Visual representations connected to falconry become increasingly important during the Middle Ages. One important example is the theme of the Adoration of the Kings, which explicitly involves movement from East to West since the kings travel from afar to be the first witnesses to Christ's new legacy: 'We have seen his [Christ's] star in the East, and have come to worship him' (Matthew 2:1). The subject as such is based primarily on the motion of objects – in this instance gifts – and people.

The theme of the kings' motion is underlined in a reliquary from Limoges that also demonstrates the mobile quality of the medium of the reliquary itself. It is dated around 1200 and shows again that falconry was visually characterized before Frederick II, at least implicitly, as if imported from the East (illus. 37), since the third king from the left carries a hawk on his hand. At the same time, the nature of the cult is manifested here, since beyond the image's programme, the reliquary with its internal space for bodily relics underlines the aspect of adoration in a double way: that of the kings' pilgrimage to Bethlehem as well as that of the beholders, making a pilgrimage to adore the reliquary.[5] In this way the latter are put in an analogous relationship to the former.

Above all, it was in fourteenth- and fifteenth-century Italy that the subject of the kings' adoration became increasingly related to falconry as if it were an essential part of its iconographic repertoire, since numerous depictions were produced during that period. The movement from East to West is brought together, in several cases, with political as well as courtly actualizations of the subject. Since kings from Eastern countries could (and did) carry hawks, they are often depicted with one on the fist at a time when hawking was in fashion. That this occurs in Italy possibly speaks to the role that Frederick II had in the process. Bethlehem lay in the West for the biblical kings, but not for the Italian artists who painted the subject. This underlines the relativity of such concepts.

Looking at Gentile da Fabriano's *Adoration of the Magi* (1423), in the Uffizi in Florence, it is not surprising to see that, above the youngest king, a man recalls a falcon to his lure in a manner

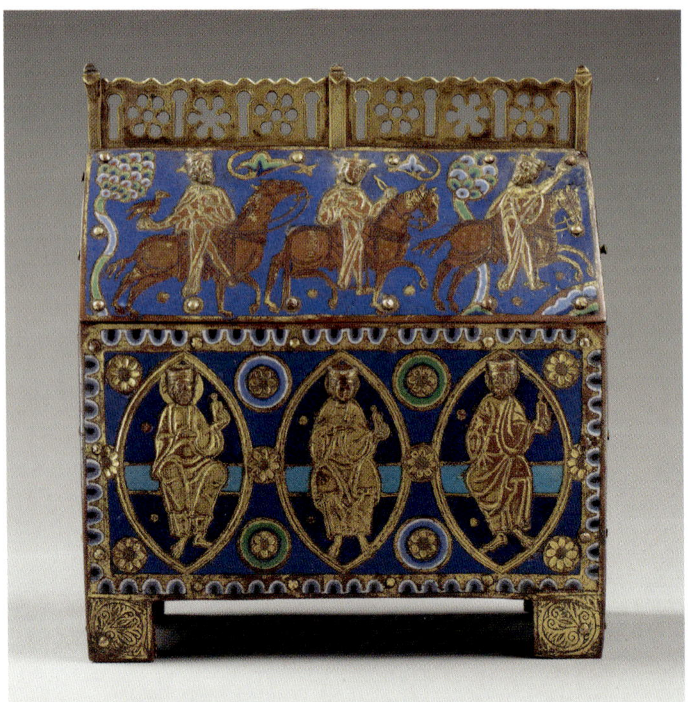

37 Reliquary casket with the Adoration of the Magi, Limoges, *c.* 1200, copper and champlevé enamel.

similar to the star paving the way for the Magi (illus. 38). The falcon wears bells, rendered in the artwork in the gilded, jewellery-like material applied over several parts of the painting's surface. This is the so-called *pastiglia* (pastework) technique, which creates a sculptural texture as it involves low-relief decorations in gesso built up upon the two-dimensional surface of a work.[6] Consequently, in addition to the visual dimension, there is also a haptic effect that dominates one's perception of the image, which is important since touch is an important sensorial feature of falconry. The golden appearance of the bells makes the image shine, also highlighting, at least on an implicit level, the luxurious quality of falconry as a pursuit. This golden shimmering accords with a tradition that, from the Italian perspective, was considered to be an Eastern one: it was often called, sometimes with negative undertones, the Greek manner, *maniera greca*, since it could be perceived in the golden background of Byzantine icons, thereby adding a formal connection between East and West to Gentile's impressive Late Gothic painting.

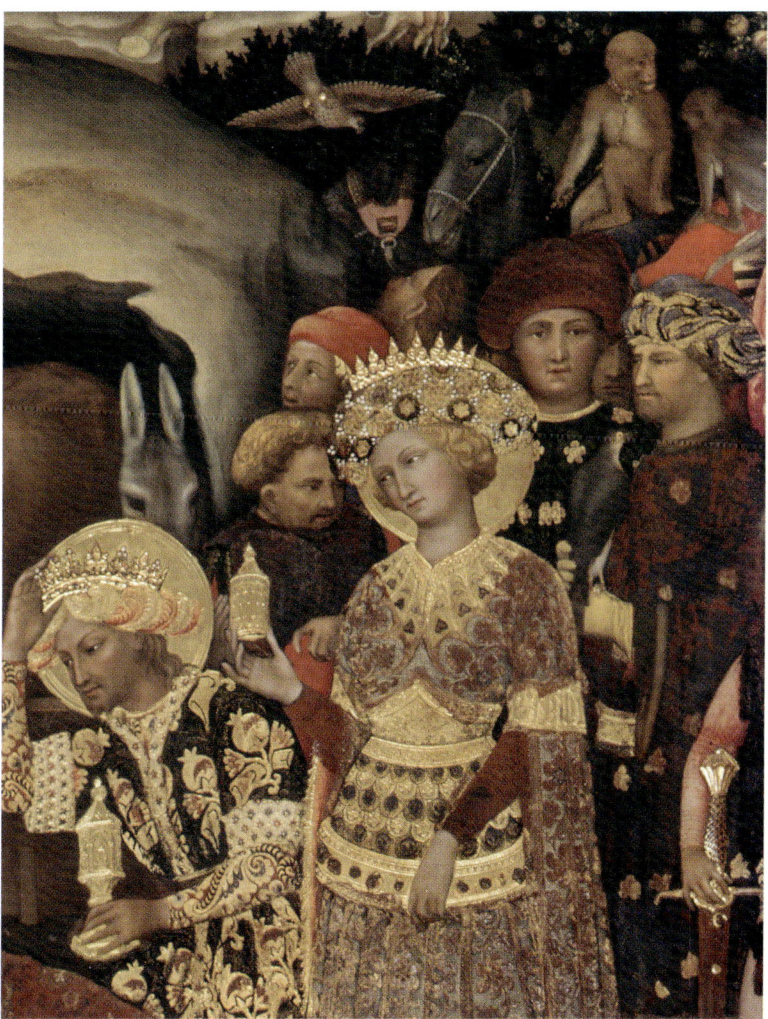

38 Detail of Gentile da Fabriano, *Adoration of the Magi*, 1423, tempera, gold and silver on panel.

It is certainly no coincidence that, between the luring figure and an additional male holding a goshawk, a person is looking outside the painting, in the direction of the beholder. We have here something analogous to the reliquary from Limoges: the beholder becomes a witness to the Adoration, but also to the falcon being lured. In this way, two independent practices are brought together. We are lured, like the falcon, to Gentile's image, almost blinded by its golden gleam. In the middle ground, slightly positioned to the right, another hawk is shown upon her quarry, having successfully achieved her objective, just as the kings have finally found their way to the Christ Child. In the background we may discern the depiction of the caravan, in which other hawks (one is bating, for instance) and also cheetahs are carried. We therefore become eyewitnesses not only to the arrival of the kings and their adoration of Christ, but also to their very nomadic pilgrimage, which is, physically speaking, a lengthy journey.

Attributes of the nobility of the Magi as well as concrete weapons for survival, the falcons in the caravan are a sign of their distant origin. The act of adoration was also suggested by, among other things, the mighty hawk, acting as an apotropaic weapon emphasizing the potency and power of the Magi.[7]

The most explicit connection between political-courtly environments and the subject of the three Magi concerning East–West interchanges is made in the frescoes by Benozzo Gozzoli, dating from about 1459–62, of the Magi Chapel in the Palazzo Medici in Florence (illus. 39). The kings' journey, rather than the act of adoration, is shown with breathtaking accuracy and dexterity across the tiny, narrow walls of the little chapel. Several hunting and hawking scenes are depicted in the different registers, where various species of birds of prey, in different positions, chase and capture quarry.

The facial features of the three kings are ostensibly those of actual rulers. In the case of Balthazar, it is possibly the Byzantine

Emperor John VIII Palaiologos (1392–1448), whose image was quite popular in Western Europe, as indicated, for instance, by Antonio Pisanello's medal made in Italy, whereas Melchior is shown as Joseph, Patriarch of Constantinople.[8] This is understood as another form of interaction between East and West, namely that of the approach between the two Churches, divided into Eastern and Western since the Schism of 1054.[9] Let us also not forget here the impact that falconry had in Byzantium.[10] This could be another reason for the presence of falconry in the frescoes and could explain the prominent position of the goshawk on the ground, just before the oldest king, looking away from the actual movement of the group. It has a portrait-like, even emblematic character because of its immobility and prominence (illus 40).[11] It is important to mention here that Piero di Cosimo de' Medici had a triumphant falcon as his emblem.[12] In this sense the hawk is a commonly shared technique, that enables the two different cultures to approach one another.

The image is a legitimization of the Medici and their sovereignty. In Medici Florence, processions through the city were spectacles often carried out by commoners, who were sometimes even disguised as the kings themselves or the caravan's entourage, as a kind of moving *tableau vivant*.[13] This participatory moment has a representative power that is connected to the community's social edifice through the subject of the Adoration. This is even more remarkable since the movement from the East to the West, as a legitimation of power, is also carried through the visual power of falconry, which combines once again the spatial dimension with the courtly and the political.

There is an additional element that deserves to be stressed here. It concerns the transcultural exchanges that are products of movement or, as we shall examine later, forms of diplomatic gestures. The term 'transculturality' seems here appropriate in order to grasp the phenomenon of East–West exchanges, because

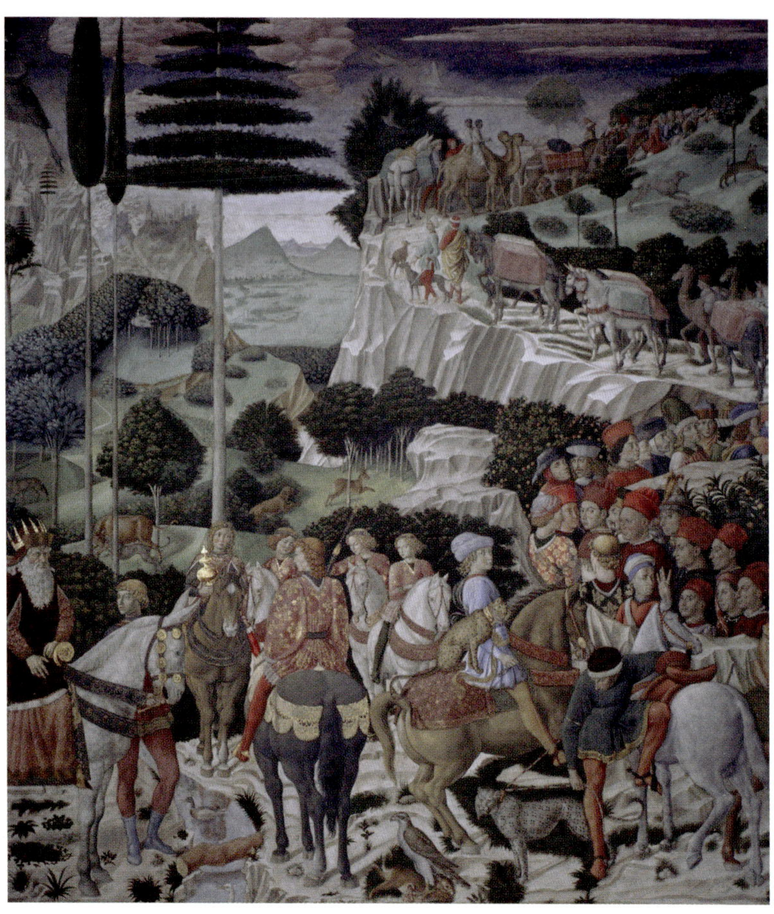

39 Benozzo Gozzoli, *Procession of the Old King*, c. 1459–62, fresco, Magi Chapel, Palazzo Medici-Riccardi, Florence.

it does not necessarily assume that such phenomena must take place globally or are to be found universally all over the world.

One of the main aspects of East–West interchange that concerns us here relates to the fact that those interactions, being also 'negotiations', were 'debated' through the medium of falconry and its images, bringing forward a critical encounter between diverse cultures.[14] Hawks and falconry acted as an interface for the relations between human agents as something commonly shared, enabling interactions between parties from different cultural and religious contexts. In other words, it is through the images and objects of falconry (from the animals themselves to falconry furniture) – not to mention, of course, actual hawking – that such diplomatic negotiations were able to take place. This commonly shared cultural technique, which manifested in different ways around the globe, enforces the mutual exchange of knowledge between the practising parties. This fact in turn obliges falconry to be perpetually in motion, because it is constantly enriched by these encounters.

Falconry is neither something hybrid nor eclectic.[15] It is certainly not exotic or foreign, nor is it about nationalistic dreams of 'purity' or about the Other.[16] Falconry is a wonderful example to demonstrate that there exists another way of interpreting such phenomena beyond the above-mentioned terms. They tend to bring in a rigid approach, a mechanical alternative of sorts, that does not do justice to falconry's playfulness and complexity. Hybridity, for example, is a mixture of different cultures

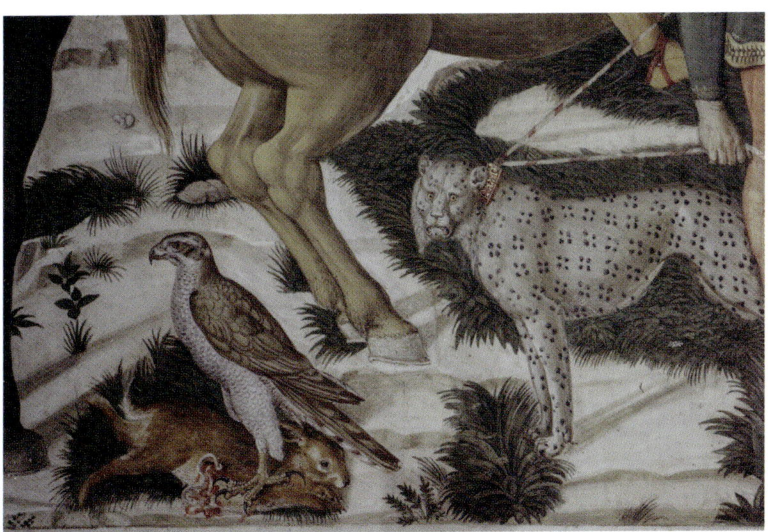

40 Detail of Benozzo Gozzoli, *Procession of the Old King* (illus. 39).

into one body, but falconry is a single body shared by different cultures.

Cultural mobility should be examined through specific case studies, as the literary historian Stephen Greenblatt argues, instead of attempting grand narratives.[17] Falconry, with its Eastern and Western dimensions, is an excellent example for this. Both East and West are approached here strictly in spatial terms, with the acknowledgement of the limitations of and existing discussions around these concepts. It is clear that the very position from which we talk about something influences our spatial perception and, hence, the concepts we use to describe a certain phenomenon. The very employment of such terms in respect to orientation is a deeply cultural one.

The art historian Hans Belting showed in his book *Florence and Baghdad* (2011) – and I do not want to question or validate the theory, but rather discuss it as an indication – that the Florentines did not conquer the world with the invention of perspective, but rather they took the developments of mathematics and geometry, and hence imported perspective, from the Arabic medieval world and particularly from Baghdad.[18] In this case we do have a rather static relation between A and B, or vice versa, even if – and this is the merit of the contribution – it questions a Western commonplace in the history of art by turning a common narrative upside down. The West is defined from the East and not the East from the West.[19] The example of the tulip later in the seventeenth century is similar, because it became something entirely Dutch, since it was sold as such, even though the tulip was initially imported into the Netherlands from Asia as a foreign flower.[20]

All kinds of static relationships are questioned through the model of hawking. Falconry was introduced to Europe as something barbaric – that is, linked to 'uncivilized' peoples – but very quickly this assumption vanished. Falconry was assimilated to such an extent that it became, as image and habit, something entirely European: it was even exported from the West later, at least in the form of images of falconry. Following that train of thought, falconry is not too far away from the example of the tulip, with the difference that it has not been nationalized. It is as European as it is Arabic, Chinese, Persian or Japanese.

The constant interactions between East and West are a kind of basic presupposition here in order to understand the mobility of the phenomenon, even if, or exactly because, the traces between import and export cannot be really distinguished. From at least since the early Middle Ages, falconry has been a unifying factor in the Mediterranean.[21] Furthermore, this spatial dynamic gained a new visual dimension through artefacts on the move, beyond real hawks and the falconers who moved from court to court in different spatial configurations. In this way, narratives of clear-cut movements or identities concerning the origins of the practice, which some try to pursue owing to national or even nationalistic convictions, become unimportant. The images in question are clearly transnational.

In his book *East–West Passage: The Travel of Ideas, Arts and Inventions between Asia and the Western World* (1971), the author Michael Edwardes discusses the character of the rocky landscape in the background of Leonardo's *Virgin of the Rocks* in the National Gallery, London (*c.* 1491–9 and 1506–8), as being an import from Chinese landscape painting.[22] He compares it with the characteristic hill formation of a painting by Guo Xi (*c.* 1020–*c.* 1090) and therefore with a (from a European perspective) 'medieval' Chinese image. Whether or not there is indeed a connection is of secondary importance here. The interesting point is that Leonardo's famous chiaroscuro, in Edwardes's argument, derived from Chinese prototypes executed almost four hundred years earlier. In this sense we have a visual transfer from Asia to Europe, an argument not so dissimilar to Belting's.

The aforementioned idea of falconry as a transcultural, shared endeavour connecting, rather than dividing, the East and the West is perfectly illustrated in a falconry episode in Boccaccio's *Decameron* (c. 1349–53), one that is much less widely known than his famous *Falcon* novella. In the ninth story we are introduced to Saladin, Sultan of Babylon, who at the time of the first European Crusade to the Holy Lands disguises himself as a merchant and travels to Italy to spy on his enemies and prepare himself more appropriately for the upcoming crusade.[23] In Italy, on his way from Milan to Pavia, he encounters the aristocrat Messer Torello d'Istria, who, together with his servant, is returning to his country estate with hawks and hounds, the typical accessories of an aristocrat, as already remarked. Torello considers Saladin and his entourage also to be aristocrats (ones even more highly ranked than himself) and persuades them to accept an invitation to his estate.[24] In other words, their first encounter occurs through the iconographic medium of hunting and, more specifically, falconry.

The next morning at Torello's estate, a further interaction, again related to falconry as a commonly shared social practice among aristocrats, takes place: 'Day came, and the gentlemen being risen, Messer Torello got him to horse with them, and having sent for his hawks, brought them to a ford, and showed them how the hawks flew.'[25] After Saladin leaves Torello's estate, the story continues in Egypt. Torello has, in the meantime, become a prisoner in a territory of which Saladin is the sovereign. The Italian continues to pursue falconry in the foreign land, as a result of which Saladin hears about Torello's dexterity in handling hawks, without knowing who the person in question is.[26] We have an inversion, a movement, or rather transfer, from the East to the West (Saladin) and vice versa (Torello), and the medium through which both men meet is again falconry. Falconry is the reason for an interactive gratitude, arising from mutually offered hospitality, while the prevailing hostility at the time between East and West becomes secondary. In other words, differences are eliminated because of common shared passions like falconry.

At the end, when Torello is safe and sound back in Pavia and joins his wife, it is now his turn to be disguised after Saladin's masquerade as a merchant: he appears to his wife as a Saracen, with Arab beard and garment. Both figures become, in other words, the Other, at least on a representational level.

Saladin and Torello's mutual acknowledgement brings to the fore their common passion, rather than their cultural differences. Falconry is in this case a universal language, a technique

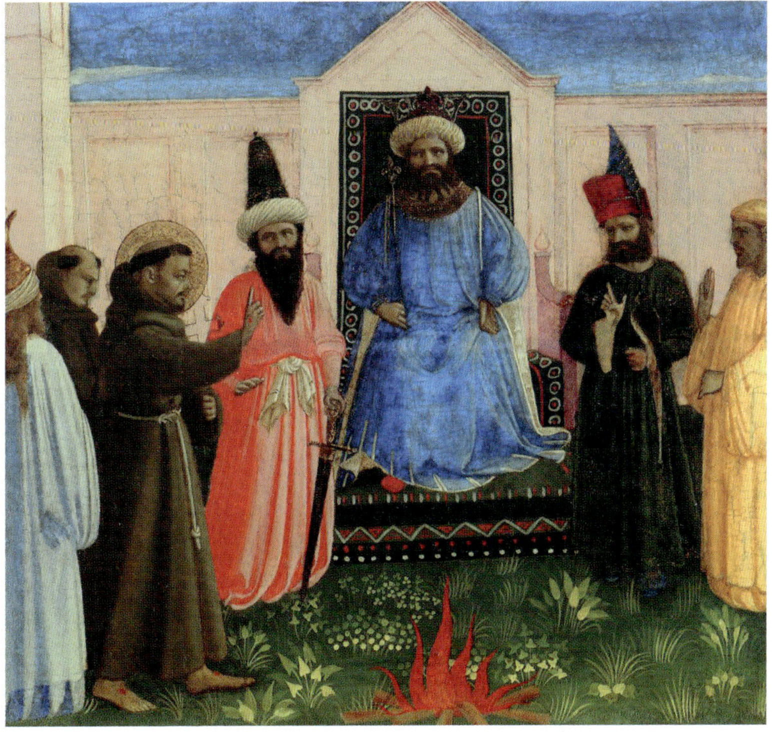

41 Fra Angelico, *The Trial by Fire of St Francis before the Sultan*, 1429, tempera on panel.

that enables negotiations even between opposing parties and eliminates differences in terms of religion and culture.

A situation that seems to be interpreted rather as a radical difference between East and West is shown in a painting dated around 1429 by Fra Angelico, showing St Francis in front of the sultan, who is engaged by the Christian saint to prepare a fire test for himself and the Muslim authorities (illus. 41). One of the men next to the sultan is holding a falcon, the other a sword. This underlines the practice's courtly dimension and connects falconry explicitly to a Muslim milieu. The gesture of St Francis, with his raised digit, that draws all the attention to himself and the fire test, is reciprocated by the gesture of the bearded falconer. The hawk has a clear-cut assignation, appearing in its culturalized 'natural habitat' as an essential part of Muslim courtly iconography and opposed to Francis's undisturbed faith. It is no coincidence that the episode takes place at a time (around 1219) when Frederick II not only undertook his trip to the Holy Land but also wrote his oft-quoted magnum opus. The audience of St Francis took place in the court of Sultan al-Malik al-Kamil at Damietta in today's Egypt, where the impact and knowledge of falconry was highly advanced. This is emphasized through artefacts like bowls, lamps and candlesticks: such objects often carry the transcultural motif of the rider with a hawk on his fist, appearing as an image on their 'bodies' (illus. 42).[27]

This certainly does not mean that, for Fra Angelico, falconry was only a practice cultivated in the East. As already observed, hawks have been depicted from the Trecento in representations of the Adoration of the Kings, as if they would connect, rather than separate, the East and the West. This observation can be strengthened through a comparable painting by Fra Angelico and Fra Filippo Lippi of the *Adoration of the Magi* (c. 1440–60), where, in a similar manner to Gozzoli's frescoes, the subject's political dimension is brought forward. One detail in particular, showing a goshawk taking a pheasant above the stable during the Adoration, hints at falconry since the hawk appears to be tail-belled, implying she is trained, and has perhaps been slipped (released directly to quarry) by someone in the caravan of camels depicted in the painting's background at the right (illus. 43).[28] What is surprising in the case of this painting is that it promotes the idea of the return of the Medici to power.[29]

We have already observed how the ninth-century treatise *Kitab al-Mutawakkili* makes it evident that falconry has an explicit political reference concerning governance. Kings in China, India, Persia, Turkey and the Byzantine Empire pursued this form of hunting, whereas the author writes that he did not know of similar cases in Arabia, hence, primarily, his writing the respective treatise.[30] Notably, however, it is in Byzantium (that is, the Byzantine Empire founded by Constantine the Great and the

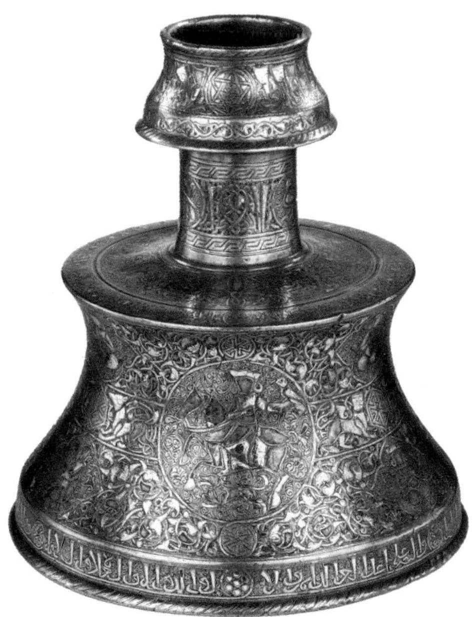

42 Candlestick with mounted falconer, southeastern Turkey, mid-13th century, cast bronze engraved and inlaid with silver.

establishment of Constantinople as the 'new Rome') that, according to the Arab author, the oldest traces of falconry existed, something that also reveals a historical interest in finding the origin of this art in as early as the ninth century.[31]

Such sources demonstrate not only that falconry was a known cultural practice before the transcultural exchanges between East and West, but that it was pursued in different areas for similar political reasons.[32] From that angle, the question of East and West brings to the fore again the problem of who is talking about what, and from which geographical region: the example of the *Kitab*, for instance, shows, as the author explained, that Arab falconry was strongly inspired by Byzantine (in this sense by

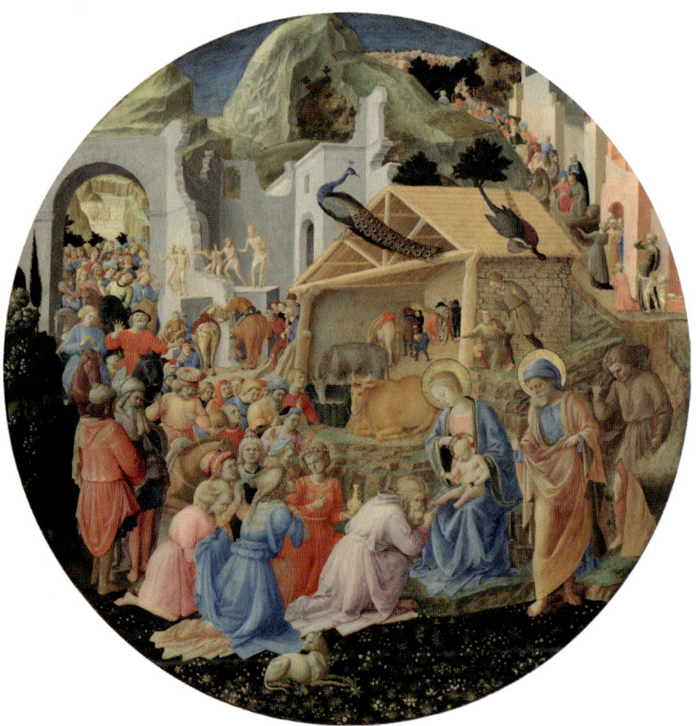

43 Fra Angelico and Fra Filippo Lippi, *Adoration of the Magi*, c. 1440–60, tempera on panel.

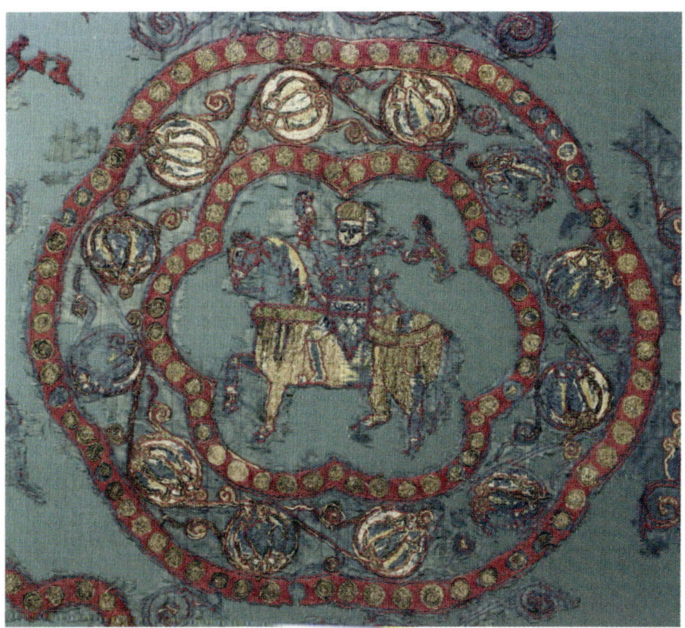

44 Detail with mounted falconer from the shroud of St Lazarus of Autun, southeastern Spain, 11th century, embroidered silk.

Western) and Persian (in this sense by Eastern) traditions.[33] From a Western perspective, though, the Byzantine Empire was connected to the East, as already observed in the case of the painting by Gozzoli.

Many examples exist that complicate our view concerning the relation between East and West, because they thematize through the subject, the place of origin or the artists involved exactly how unstable those entities actually were (and still are), or, better, how entangled their relationship was. We will look at three cases that should give us some insight into the issue.

A striking example from the early eleventh century, a detail from the shroud of St Lazarus of Autun, shows a mounted falconer. The medallion is related to images possibly produced in a Muslim workshop in Almería, Spain (illus. 44).[34] Here, many unequal elements of East and West are fused in one entity, because they

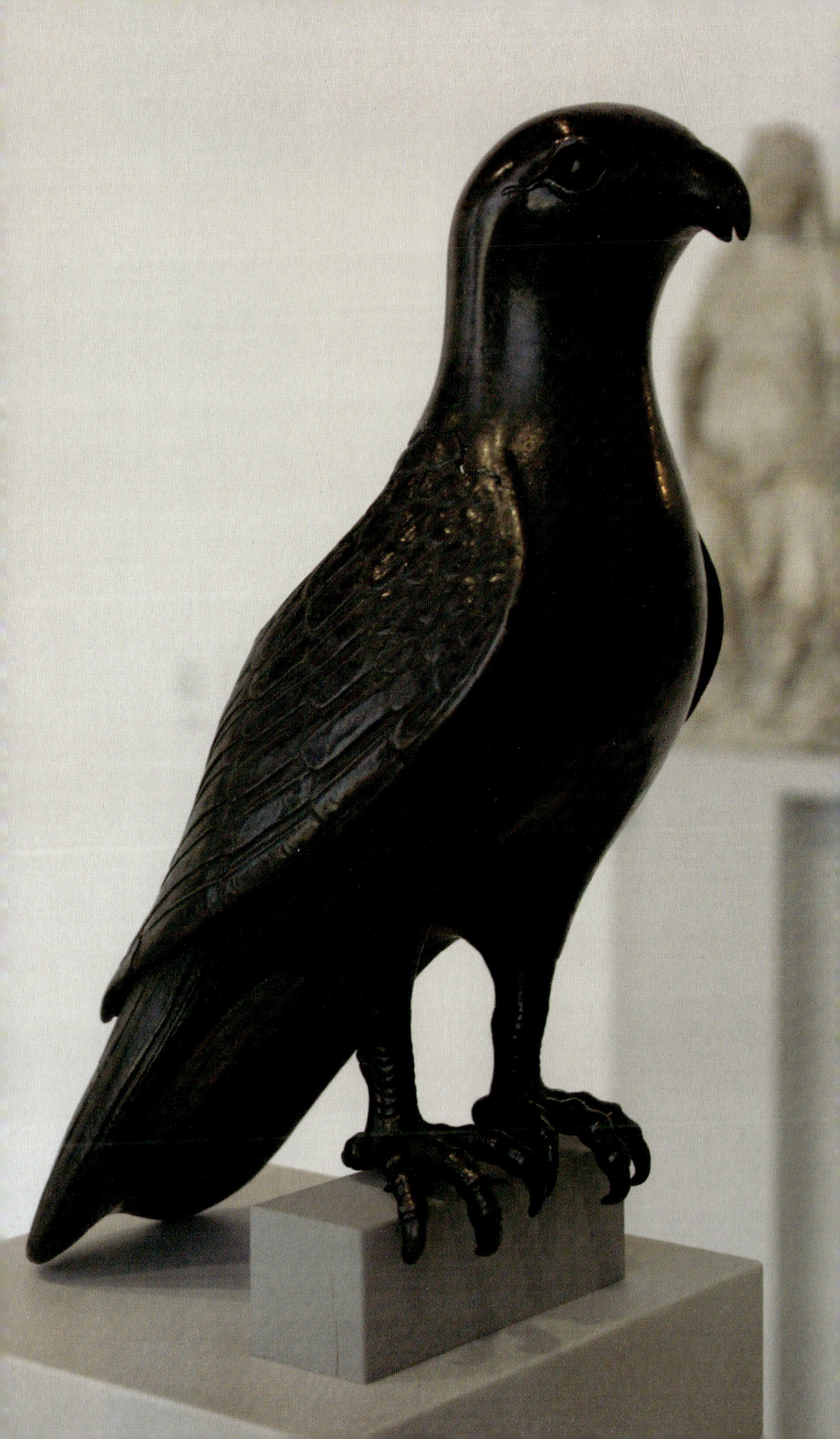

concern the production of the image as well as the subject and its place of origin: it is an object from Burgundy, produced in Al-Andalus by Muslim workshops, which suggests that falconry was an Eastern practice, since the rider depicted is clearly not European. Other riders are depicted on the shroud, carrying hawks on their fists and wearing turbans. Another rider has a beard and hairstyle which are perhaps Assyrian. This fact would connect him to the Mesopotamian area, where, as discussed earlier, falconry was pursued early on. In this sense the object is a transcultural image in motion that integrates supposedly opposing concepts in a single object.

The second case is a free-standing bronze statue of an upright bird of prey with closed wings, dating from around the thirteenth century (illus. 45). The rather rigid position with hints of detailed observation enforces the powerful appearance of the hawk and stresses its sovereignty. Only the area of the feet and the feathers are modelled, and, generally, the smoothness of the material dominates. The naturalistic movement of the claws implies that the hawk was possibly on a kind of pedestal functioning as a perch. There are no jesses visible, but the indication of a perch suggests falconry, even if only subtly.

The sculpture is thought to originate from southern Italy. Together with Sicily, this area was a melting pot between East and West.[35] However, no similar examples of statues exist from around this geographical area in that period: working with bronze was quite rare in southern Italy. The Mediterranean in general is, however, the most probable place of origin. This statement underlines to what extent this massive geographical space, traversing East to West and vice versa, has to be taken into account as a whole: through trade and the movement of objects, borders became relative.[36] Owing to such mobility, the transfers

45 Hawk, southern Italy (?), *c.* 13th century, bronze.

between the eastern and western Mediterranean, even in the Middle Ages, were almost invisible and therefore secondary.

For an Islamic impact on the bronze sculpture, either directly (as far as the artisan who produced it is concerned) or as a trigger for the assumed southern European workshop, one can look to similar bronze statuettes in the form of birds, among them falcons, known from Egypt, Syria and Al-Andalus. There are also falcons in the form of aquamaniles (water vessels), where their bodies often carry extracts from scripture and plant decorations, as a famous example from about 796–7 of a falcon eloquently shows (illus. 46).[37] The object has significant differences from the bronze from southern Italy. It bears Kufic scriptures that proclaim the name of Allah, as well as giving the name of the artist who made the object – a striking indication of the consideration of the artist as second creator in an Islamic context.

The courtly status of both objects is evident.[38] That the bronze from southern Italy (illus. 45) is not an aquamanile is on the one hand rather clear. On the other, it is quite certainly a courtly vessel, possibly an incense burner, since there is an opening on its back. These are again hints of an Islamic provenance or at least interaction; incense burners in the form of parrots and even falcons were widespread in the Islamic world. Such burners were also mobile, as our object is. An incense burner also creates a kind of meta-analogy between falcon and artificially made scent. Scent evaporates in the air, which the falcon dominates: here we are again in the multisensorial dimension of falconry imagery.

Our third example is a rather uncommon depiction of the biblical Pharaoh as a mounted falconer. In this sense it is as if the pharaohs were indeed thought to be the first falconers. The sheet is part of the so-called Hispano-Moresque Haggadah (a Jewish service book from 1275–1324 by an unknown creator, probably three members of the same workshop), originating from Castile (illus. 47).[39] Moses is shown at the side trying to warn the mighty

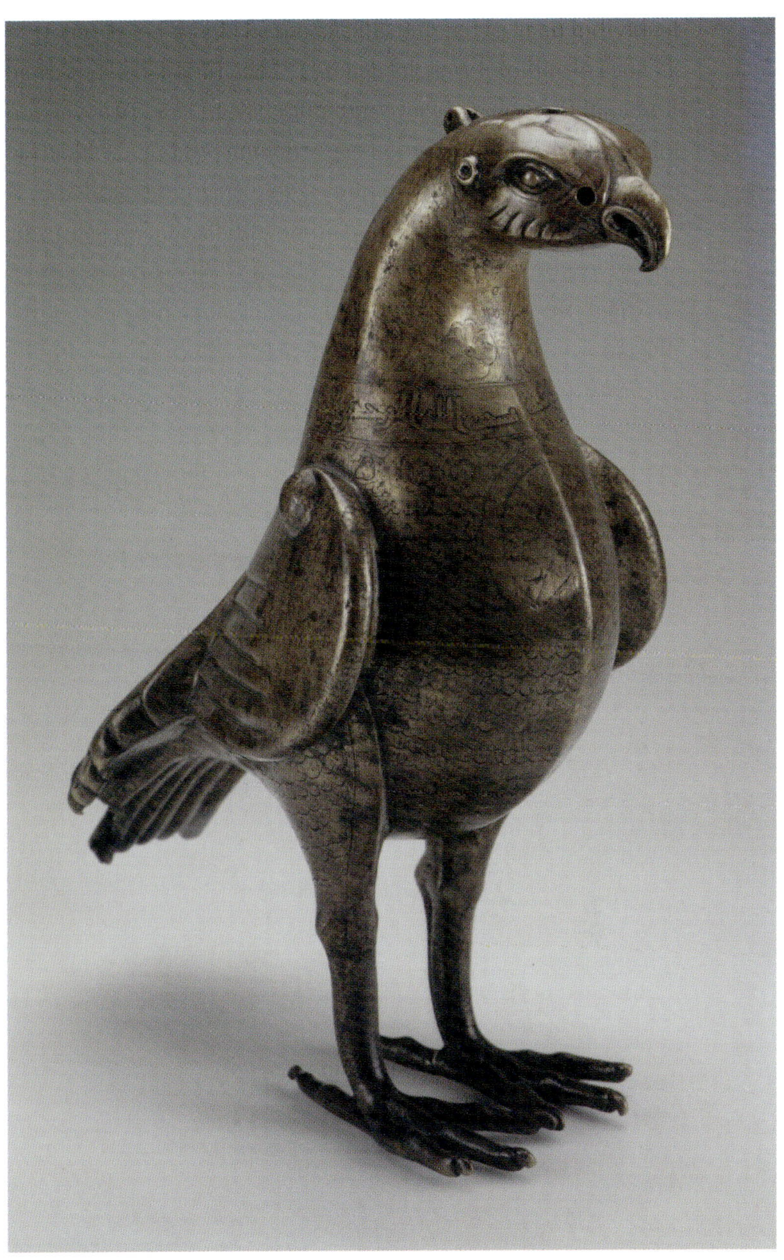

46 Aquamanile shaped like a falcon, Iraq (?), *c.* 796–7, bronze (brass), silver and copper.

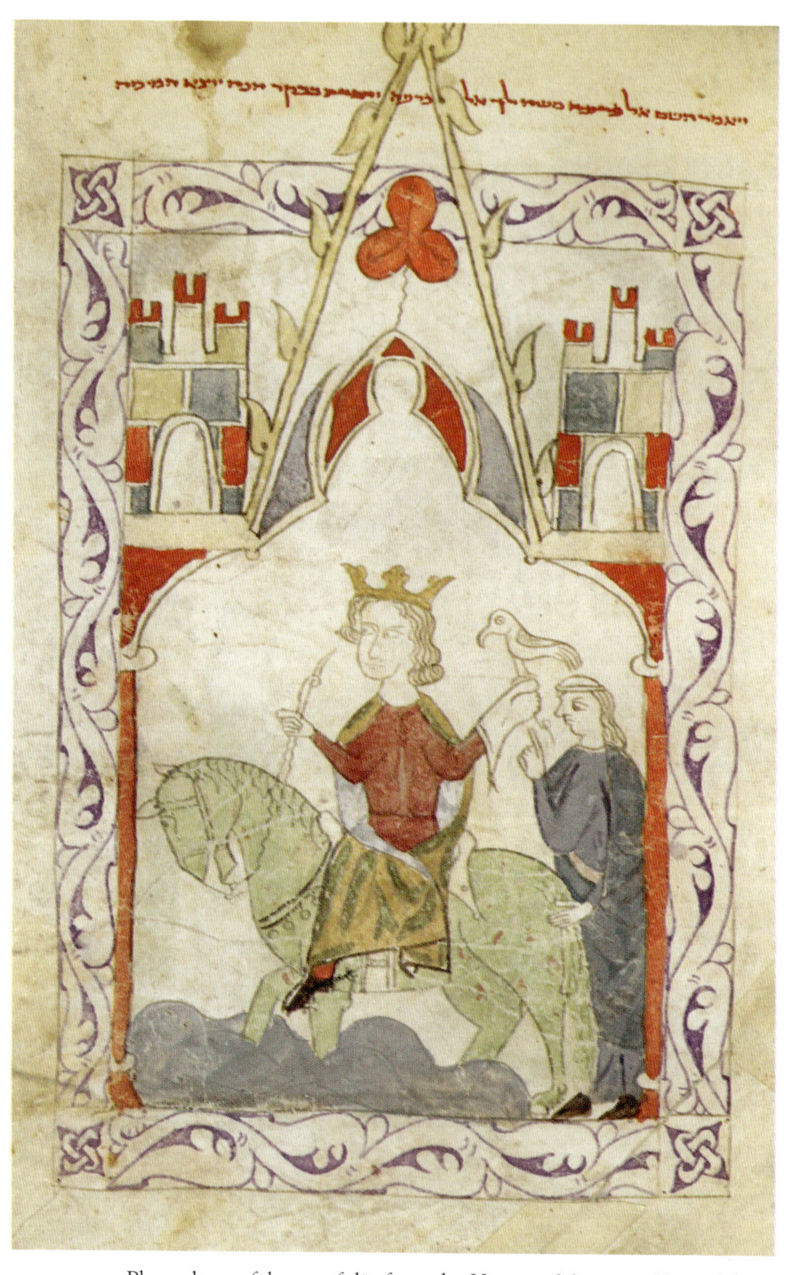

47 Pharaoh as a falconer, folio from the Hispano-Moresque Haggadah, 1275–1324, Castile.

ruler of the upcoming plagues (not unlike the weeping Ecclesia warning the pope, as we shall see). It is clear that the Pharaoh is neglecting his duties in order to go hawking, which was a common ecclesiastical criticism levelled at rulers, including Frederick II. In this sense the image becomes an object of critique, transculturally speaking, as we shall subsequently further observe.

What is revealing in our context is the case that the artefact literally embodies a symbolic unification of East and West: the Jewish illustrated manuscript of the Haggadah was produced in Europe. The medieval imaginative depiction of the East deriving from a Jewish context situated in the West gives the present inquiry a playful twist. Additionally, the image's creators could even have been Christians working in conjunction with their Jewish patrons.[40]

It is interesting to note that there is a tendency to search for a dominant presence in such examples of coexistence, as if this status of togetherness could not be enough. What counts, however, in terms of production, besides the actual subject of the image, is the eloquent manifestation of an intriguing interplay between East and West.

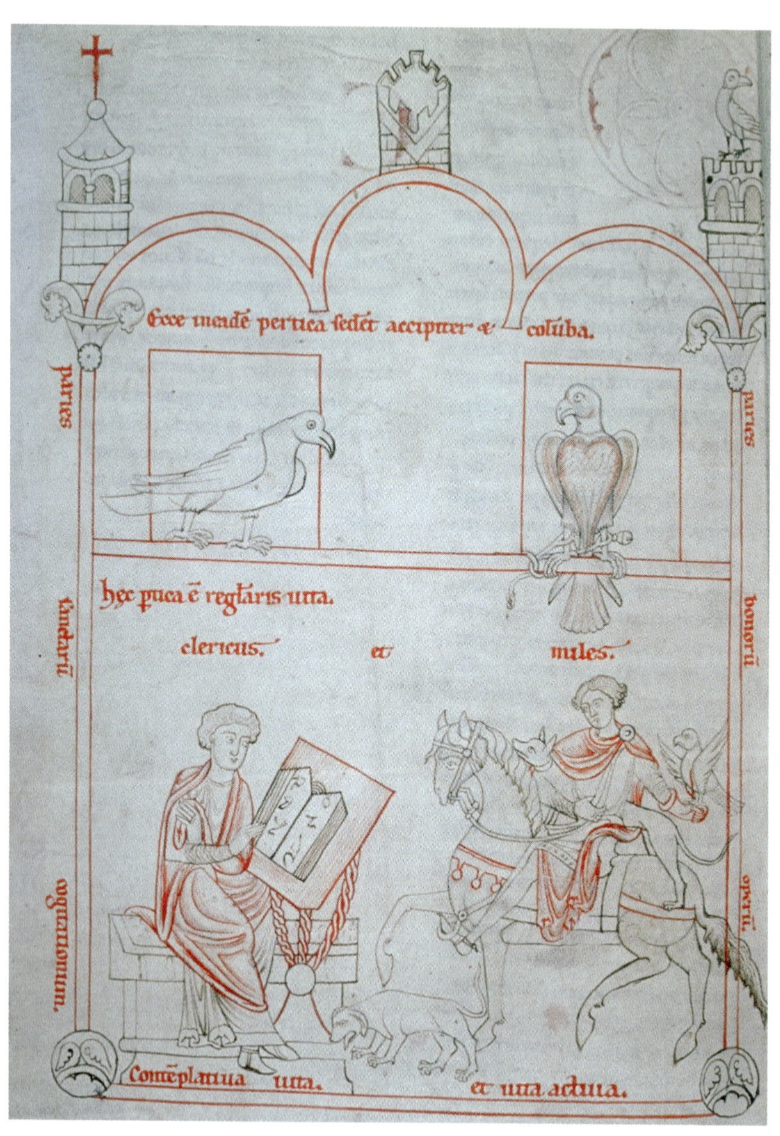

48 Falcon and dove, knight and cleric, folio from Hugh of Fouilloy, *De avibus*, 12th century.

FIVE

Chivalry, Warfare, Religion

Falconry was embedded in diverse, often contradictory visual and cultural spheres. Related subjects among them were chivalry, warfare and religion, which represented fundamental aspects of medieval life. It will be striking to follow the surprising connections in the usually opposing relations between chivalry and religion. Generally speaking, one can identify here an inconstancy of symbols and opposing concepts, including war and commonwealth, that were more often united than separated under the art of falconry.

Birds of prey were weapons, both literally and metaphorically speaking. This was the case with falconry's visual power as a commonwealth, already observed in Lorenzetti's fresco in Siena concerning good government (illus. 33). On the contrary, the focus of discussion should be shifted. Hunting, especially the practice of hawking, played a crucial role in aiding rulers to acquaint themselves with their territories, thereby enabling them to prepare for war effectively. This concept holds prominence across various cultures and is widely acknowledged.

Falconry, as a practice in political representation, simultaneously included the shepherd and the wolf theme, since the subject involves a dialectic tension that is similarly constitutive of the pursuit of falconry. How the one is part of the other but can suddenly switch to the opposite mode underlined the paradigm of falconry, which included security (the state of peace) and turbulence (a state of war).

A *cassone*, or marriage chest, dating from around 1445–55 can serve as an initial example. In Italy during the late Middle Ages, these highly decorated wooden chests would be given by the bride's parents upon her marriage and would transport her belongings to her husband's house (certainly one of a patrician or aristocratic milieu). On such a chest is a work by the Florentine painter Francesco Pesellino (1422–1457) which depicts the triumph of David and the story of David and Goliath (illus. 49, 50). In this case, there is a transformation from one mode into an entirely different one: from a peaceful activity to an aggressive pursuit that leads to the enemy's destruction. David enters the city of Jerusalem triumphantly, followed by soldiers and riders but also hounds and cheetahs, accompanied by music. The first part of this triumphal entry is, in effect, introduced by a rider with a falcon on his fist (illus. 49).

Directly beneath David, who stands upright with the head of Goliath, a young boy carrying a peregrine creates a connection

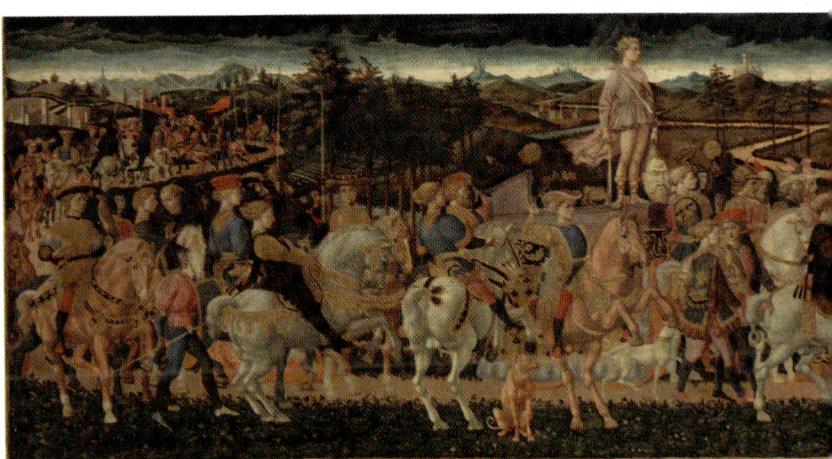

between the young shepherd and the beheaded Philistine giant. At the same time, on the young courtier's fine and rather contemporary (for the time) garment, one witnesses the falcon's striking power as an image within an image constellation that appears on the fabric and is juxtaposed with the real falcon he is actually carrying. Two different behavioural modes of the birds of prey are visually indicated. It is once again clear that the power of the image and that of the falcon have an analogous relation.[1]

In his *Lives of the Artists*, the artist and biographer Giorgio Vasari describes Pesellino's passion for depicting animals: he was employed by the house of the Medici for painting chests, including animal and tournament scenes, like the one observed.[2] In Pesellino's oeuvre, falconry appears repeatedly and moves within courtly worlds. On the other image of the *cassone*, the analogy between falcon and battle is quite explicit, since it shows David as a shepherd in a bucolic landscape with different animals around him (illus. 50). It is as if David's virtues as a future sovereign were already visible when he was a shepherd. These two

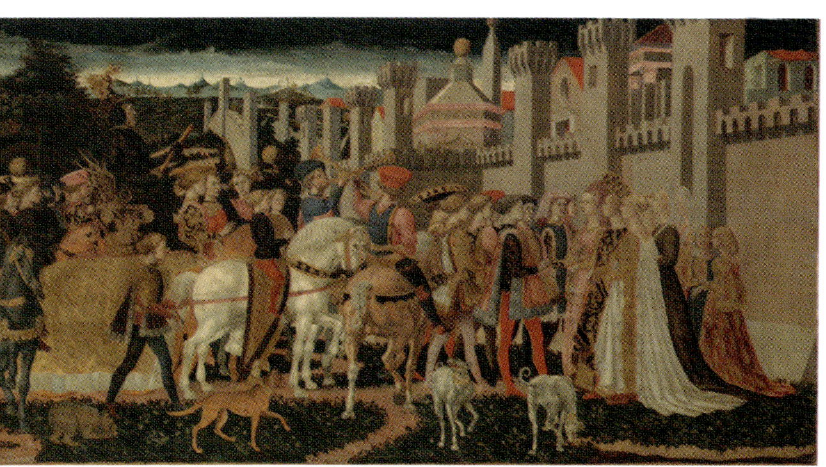

49 Francesco Pesellino, *The Triumph of David*, c. 1445–55, tempera on wood.

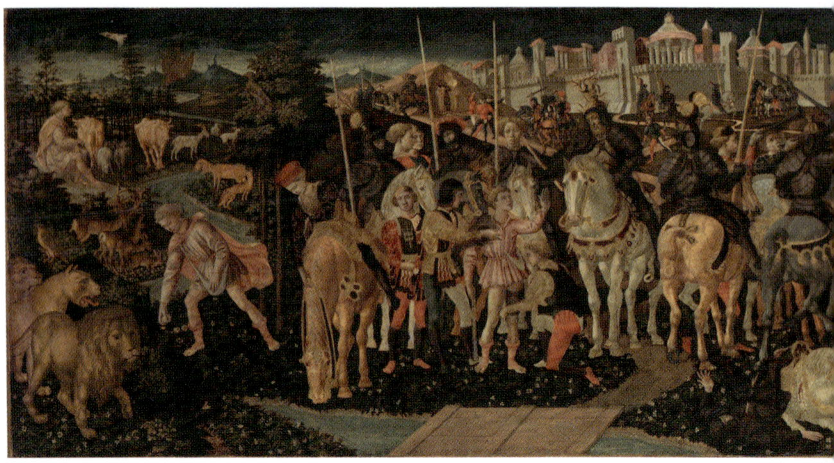

figures are a common component of political iconography: the sovereign often appears as a shepherd.

Exactly above David, who is in the process of choosing the stone with which he will spectacularly prevail over Goliath, a falcon is shown in her stoop, as if she might attack one of the deer, which in real life she cannot, at least not without the help of hounds. Thus we have here a symbolic element built into a realistic scene. This element introduces an aggressive character into the scene, which will soon become a battle. Rapidity, dexterity and even aggression, crucial features of a falcon, are transmitted to David, who, because of his 'Herculean deed', will become king.

It is known that David was a personification of the Republic of Florence, a symbolic figure embodying republican ideals.[3] One could argue that falcons as a sort of weapon in times of political unrest in a republic, are, symbolically speaking, figures of latent violence.[4] Added to this is the issue of movement, not only in the depiction but in the medium of the chest, which involves transporting and carrying, alluding to David's triumphant procession on the vehicle of victory.[5]

The falcon embodies the community's 'state' as an organic and simultaneously subversive symbol, so that the elements of

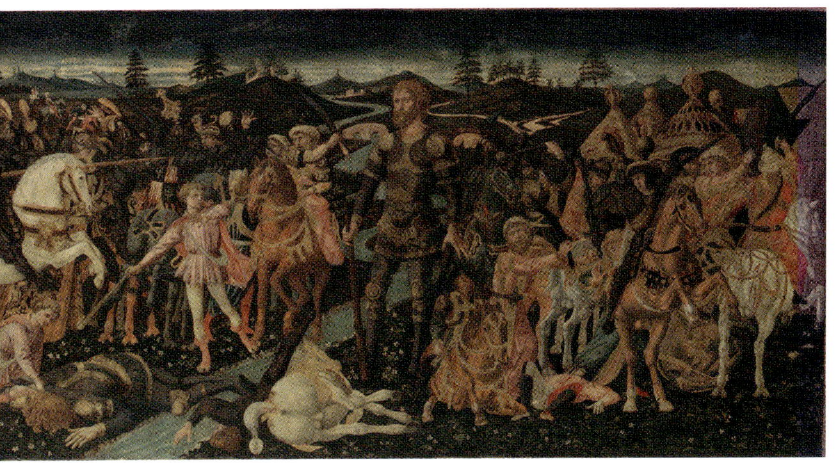

50 Francesco Pesellino, *The Story of David and Goliath*, c. 1445–55, tempera on wood.

both unity and discord are expressed through its singular wild and untamed nature. It is not only a weapon for sovereigns; it is also, intrinsically speaking, an autonomous weapon intervening as an independent power against humans. This is the reason the role of the agent is quite diffuse here, since the two parties, human and animal, shift constantly between activity and passivity, between who initiates the action and who receives it. The falcon's lethal power becomes, through falconry images, a form of lethal image. Her destructive power, which symbolizes the political power under which she acts (as in the case of Manasses in Byzantium), becomes, over time, commonplace in falconry in transcultural terms.

The natural physical power of the bird of prey is beautifully described by the scientist-philosopher and bishop Albertus Magnus (c. 1200–1280), who in his book on animals, *De animalibus*, underlined the following:

> The characteristic act of a falcon among raptorial birds is to fall with force on its prey . . . when it wishes to take

> game, it is in the nature of the falcon to ascend with a swift flight and with its talons held close to its breast, to fall with force on the bird with so powerful an effort that in descending it sounds like a raging wind, and it makes this attack not by descending directly or perpendicularly, but at an angle: because striking after such a descent it inflicts a long wound with its claws so that sometimes a bird falls split from head to tail, and sometimes it is found with its whole head torn off.[6]

From antiquity, hunting and war were thought to be two sides of the same coin. For instance, in the fourth century BC, the ancient Greek historian Xenophon understood hunting as a school for military service.[7] Both hunting and falconry were used as a model to exercise the art of war in times of peace.[8] In an antique saying, falconry is considered a sister of war.[9] Alfonso XI of Castile (1311–1350) brought the art of war under the same umbrella as chivalry as well as hunting: 'For a knight should always engage in anything to do with arms and chivalry, and if he cannot do so in war, he should do so in activities which resemble war. And the chase is most similar to war.'[10] The troubadour Adenes Le Roi (c. 1240–c. 1300), born in Brabant, wrote that the knight 'desires the battle more than the gyrfalcon desires the cranes, or the sparrowhawk the lark'.[11] Meanwhile, a Welsh poem from around the end of the fifteenth century by Huw Bulkeley of Beaumaris, written on behalf of Rhisiart Cyffin, Dean of Bangor, contains also an eloquent description of this very aspect:

> Was there ever a fine hawk on the crest of the tower with larger claws on a glove? The claw of the lad will make blood of wild birds to flow on to the grass in Anglesey: a bittern or a goose, he will not let them live, nor a heron nor a chick of a duck. His beak and

> hand are similar, wherever he comes, to a warrior's claw. We can compare two pointed objects, Huw's fist and that of this bird.[12]

This connection was not only a Western idea: the knight Usama ibn Munqidh wrote of hunting's similarity to a military expedition.[13] According to the political manual *Al-Fakhri* (1302) by Ibn al-Tiqtaqa, from Mosul, hunting helped the physical exercise of the troops in relation to learning different forms of warfare.[14] Indeed, falconers not only obtained important positions in court but also in the army, where they undertook leadership posts, enriching, with their knowledge and experience, a different sphere, albeit one highly related to their own specialization.[15]

Some medieval manuscripts make the falcon a personification of the knight.[16] The hawk helps the future knight to become one, if he is dexterous in this art, in a similar manner to the ruler who, as a child, matures through his or her exercise in hawking.[17] The falcon became as essential an attribute of the knight as the cross is for a dignitary of the Church. Knights were often associated with Mars, the Roman god of war. In later times, the famed early sixteenth-century frescoes by Raphael at the Villa Farnesina in Rome show falcons as attributes of Mars. Additionally, Albrecht Dürer depicted the emperor as a knight and warlord, with a stooping falcon above him in part of his *Triumphal Arch* (c. 1515–17) for Maximilian I.

In the *Canterbury Tales* (c. 1387–1400), Chaucer refers repeatedly to hawking – often in conjunction with love and chivalry. In Chaucer's tale of the student, 'The Clerk's Tale', for instance, the marquis neglects his duties to go hunting with hounds and hawks, enjoying, as the narrator underlines, all possible kinds of earthly delights. Since the narrator is a student, the discrepancy between the *vita contemplativa* and the *vita activa* becomes clear.

As early as the first half of the thirteenth century, the poet Jean Renart spoke of the ideal knight who 'whenever he wanted, he indulged in the pleasure of birds/ which I do not disdain'.[18] Chaucer also conceived an ironic portrait of the knight. The beginning of his story of 'Sir Thopas' contains a rather sarcastic account in which all the medieval clichés and attributes of the 'ideal' knight appear: he is beautiful and kind, brave in battle and a cavalier in love, a dexterous hunter and, last but not least, a skilful falconer.[19]

The radical difference between clergy and chivalry could not have been more clearly visualized than in a page from a twelfth-century manuscript of the cleric Hugh of Fouilloy's *De avibus* (Book of Birds) (illus. 48). Here, a cleric with a manuscript of sorts in his hands – and hence connected to spiritual activities – is juxtaposed with a mounted knight or soldier (*miles*), who is going hunting, carrying a hawk and accompanied by a dog. The two figures seem to be in the same interior, even if they are clearly depicted separately in distinct architectural worlds representing their own *raison d'être*: the cleric is under a cross and the knight in a fortress. Above them, two different, even antithetical types of bird appear: a dove and a falcon, as symbols of the *vita contemplativa* and the *vita activa*, the dove indicating the theologian and spirituality, thus passivity, and the falcon representing the knight and corporality, thus activity.[20] The falcon is even tethered, in contrast to the dove, which appears like another form of the Holy Ghost. This representation of the falcon underlines her non-domestication as a negative aspect of her behaviour. In this sense, her wild and aggressive nature is counteracted by the peaceful dove.

It is striking that the Greek word for falcon is *iérax*, deriving from the stem 'holy' (*ierós*), whereas there is a parallel theological connection in Christian thought of the falcon to greed and other sins.[21] In other words, the hawk carries antithetical attributes across places and times.

The deep-rooted connection between hawks and weapons shapes a bodily metaphor with an iconic and hence symbolic quality. The direction of the gaze as a connecting link between falcon and aircraft is visually captured in the film *A Canterbury Tale*, directed by Michael Powell and Emeric Pressburger (1944) and prefigures the analogy between falcon and drone. Through the gaze of a male falconer-soldier, a falcon's transformation into an aircraft becomes evident as a bond through successive images. The gaze makes the connection to what is pursued, and thus we understand that seeing is hunting.[22] The sequence begins with Chaucer's protagonists in his *Canterbury Tales*, where a medieval falconer is transformed into a soldier at the peak of the Second World War, when the film was made.[23] He is a living testimony to technological transformations. Falconry is, in this sense, an example par excellence of long duration that bridges the Middle Ages to modern times, a topic that will be dealt with in the Coda. These transformations occur right at the film's beginning as a frontispiece to the whole, in which characters and subjects from Chaucer's original *Tales* are modified to tell a wider tale of Britain's wartime experiences, just as the falcon is transformed, as if in a process of natural evolution, from bird of prey to automatic weapon.

The analogy between falcon, weapon and even war involves the aggressive nature of the falcon, as already mentioned, which manifests itself in nature and can become, through a specific motif, an emblematic feature for battle.[24] Fights between wild animals (for example, when a wild hawk drives off herons, which she instinctively sees as a potential threat), and indeed natural predation, only implicitly have common ground with falconry. Things are different when such contests are precipitated by humans or relate to them in any way, because then the term 'hawking' is appropriate.

Fights between wild animals already had a tremendous impact in antiquity as a theme. They would be raised to the highest aesthetic level in artworks, for example those based on the fight between the lion and the snake. These do not include any human interaction or intervention (unless staged at the Colosseum).

In Homer's *Iliad* (c. eighth century BC), one reads of combats between falcons and other birds as an analogy for the war between Greeks and Trojans, and that Achilles was acting like a falcon during his legendary battle against Hector:

> Thus did he stand and ponder, but Achilles came up to him as it were Mars himself, plumed lord of battle. From his right shoulder he brandished his terrible spear of Pelian ash, and the bronze gleamed around him like flashing fire or the rays of the rising sun. Fear fell upon Hector as he beheld him, and he dared not stay longer where he was but fled in dismay from before the gates, while Achilles darted after him at his utmost speed. As a mountain falcon, swiftest of all birds, swoops down upon some cowering dove – the dove flies before him but the falcon with a shrill scream follows close after, resolved to have her – even so did Achilles make straight for Hector with all his might, while Hector fled under the Trojan wall as fast as his limbs could take him.[25]

Later, in thirteenth-century China (Yuan dynasty, 1279–1368), we find depictions of combat between falcons and swans that appear to be without any human presence or intervention.[26] Not only paintings from the Yuan court but textiles and jades with this subject are known. These images precede fables and emblems with political associations, including those contests between herons and falcons that, later, became a popular motif in falconry scenes.

The story of Constantine's decision to found Constantinople in AD 330 after witnessing a peregrine's attempts to take a goose, spurring him to trap and train the falcon, has already been discussed. This is emblematic of the relation between political power and animal combat, where the latter has a feedback loop-effect on the person who takes the decision to intervene in nature. Even if humans are not directly part of these wild fights, as long as these are visible to them, they may be culturalized through human intervention, as in Constantine's case. In this sense the symbolic is embedded in the visual and aesthetic scene, since the latter gives stimulus to the former. The human (in the present case the emperor) is the wolf and no longer the shepherd, in contrast to Orpheus, who tames the animals through his music, or Christ, who unites all animals under his guidance as the almighty shepherd.[27] Dante even described Christ as a falconer, the faithful returning to him as hawks return to the human's fist.[28]

Even if the symbolic meaning of the contest between heron and falcon was not, emblematically speaking, established in the Middle Ages, its allusion to battle was already existent, as in the Manasses example earlier (Manasses handled his Georgian falcon while heron hawking).[29] In *Les voeux du héron* (The Vows of the Heron), a satirical poem from 1346, a heron taken by Robert III of Artois' falcon is presented during a royal banquet to Edward III of England with the following words:

> I believe I have caught the most cowardly bird . . . it is my intention to give the heron to the most cowardly one who lives or has ever lived: that is Edward Louis [Edward III], disinherited of the noble land of France of which he was rightful heir; but his heart failed him and because of his cowardice he will die without it. So he should vow on the heron and tell what he thinks.[30]

The seemingly weaker heron, because of its manoeuvrability and persistence, had certain advantages that made it a worthy adversary for the falcon. It is important to emphasize that some characteristics of the animal are bestowed upon the sovereign; ones that in this case are negative and somehow provoking, as if he were the heron himself. As an analogy this is connected to a demonstration of power as a possible challenge for battle. Indeed, the English were preparing to war against France.

From the Assyrian civilization, with its very early depictions of falconry, one finds the following written testimony: 'When . . . the falcon and the crow are fighting in front of the king and the falcon kills the crow the weapons of the king will rage against the weapons of the enemy.'[31] In other words, this omen sets the scene for a human battle that will have a positive outcome for the king. The motif of the wild animal fight (here falcon and crow, in other instances heron, crane and even swan) appears repeatedly in several semantic combinations, in different contexts and cultures. It is taken out of its supposedly natural environment and is culturalized and anthropomorphized. Through this, the concept of falconry as a model for training for upcoming warfare is established. The human agent is not only a passive beholder but also a trigger of sorts.

In the mid-fifteenth century, north of the Alps the motif of combat between falcon and heron appears more or less at the same time as the already discussed Sforza miniature at Chantilly (illus. 24). It is a work by Master E. S. (c. 1420–68), a German engraver of whom we know only the initials. He referred to the subject of falconry on many occasions in his prints (illus. 51).[32]

This rather small print, dated around 1450–67, refers to Venice, since her symbol, the lion of St Mark, is shown between land and sea. The animal as the embodiment, now, of a republic rather than an emperor is captured in the process of leaving the water in the direction of the land. A city (an allusion to the

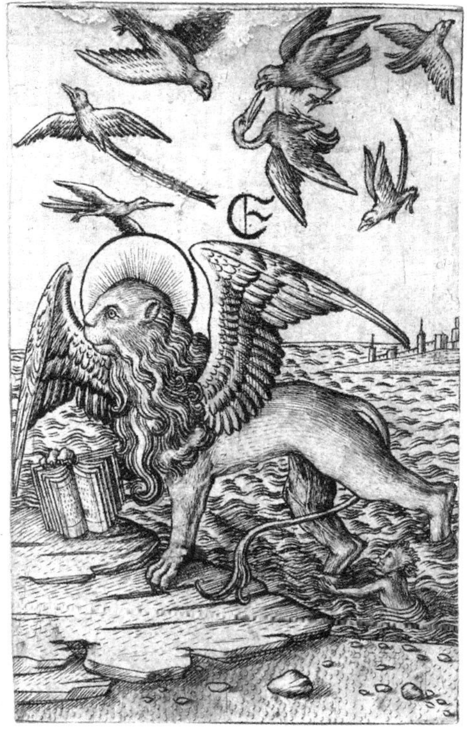

51 Master E. S., *St Mark's Lion*, 1450–67, engraving.

Serenissima?) is depicted in the background, while a man in the water seems to accompany the lion. In the air, different birds of prey and herons can be seen, among which we can clearly observe the battling falcon and heron.[33] This could be even interpreted as an analogy for the Republic of Venice, which, as an important sea power, could defend herself on the water but also protect the land of her territory, and potentially also strike back. The analogy between falcon, lion and Venice is thus made quite explicitly. The combat of the animals is a direct political representation with a republican touch, underlining again the falcon's dual aggressive and peaceful nature, visually captured in one entity. Defence and attack are two sides of the same coin.

However, beyond chivalry and warfare there is a striking, often antithetical representation of falconry within religion and the cult of images. In a dense passage from Erasmus' *In Praise of Folly* (1511), accompanied on the margins by drawings by Hans Holbein the Younger, the Netherlandish humanist brings image and animal (in this case hawks, visible in Holbein's image) into an explicit relation (illus. 52):

> I cannot pass by without bestowing some remarks upon another sort of fools . . . They hang up their ancestors' worm-eaten pictures and keep a long list of their predecessors, with an account of all their offices and titles, while they themselves are but transcripts of their forefathers' dumb statues, and degenerate even into those very beasts which they carry in their coat of arms as ensigns of their nobility . . . [they] cry up those brutes almost equal to the gods.[34]

It is important to note Erasmus' much discussed pre-Reformation critique of images: he saw images as luxurious things that might distract one from faith. Reinforced through Holbein's drawing of a nobleman carrying a hooded hawk, something that was already an emblem of falconry, Erasmus refers, not accidentally, to a coat of arms with beasts. In this sense it is also clear that his target is, among others, the aristocracy. Erasmus' book was published in 1511, but his critique, also involving falconry, could not have been conceived without the late medieval pursuit of hawking that was considered by many at the time to be a fashionable and highly luxurious activity – in other words, sensualist.

Erasmus' radical criticism pinpointed falcons and images, as well as their respective 'cult', as fetishism. There is, in other words, a pagan glorification of the hawk as a kind of god that reminds one of cults (of idols, images) similar to the Egyptian cult of Horus, which was associated with the luxurious pursuit of hawking. In this way, hawking is connected to the deadly sin of

STVLTICIAE LAVS.

illius æmulaberis. Hæc inquã atq; id genus alia, si sapiens ille obganniat, uide a quanta felicitate, repente mortaliũ animos, in quem tumultũ retraxerit? Ad hoc collegiũ ptinent, qui uiui qua funeris pompa uelint efferri, tam diligenter statuunt, ut nominatim etiã præscribãt, quot tedas, quot pullatos, quot cãtores, quot luctus histriones, uelint adesse, perinde quasi futurũ sit, ut aliquis huius spectaculi sensus ad ipsos sit rediturus, aut ut pudescant defuncti, nisi cadauer magnifice defodiatur, haud alio studio q̃ si ædiles creati, ludos aut epulum ædere studeant. Equidem tametsi propero, tamen haud possum istos silentio prætercurrere, qui cũ nihil ab infimo cerdone differant, tamẽ inani nobilitatis titulo, mirum, q̃ sibi blandiuntur. Alius ad Aeneam, alius ad Brutũ, alius ad Arctum, genus suũ refert. Ostendunt undiq; sculptas & pictas maiorũ imagines. Numerant proauos, atq; atauos, & antiqua cognomina cõmemorant, cum ipsi non multum absint a muta statua, pene q; ijsipsis, quæ ostentant signis, deteriores. Et tamẽ hac tam suaui philautia felicem prorsum uitã agunt. Neq; desunt æque stulti, qui hoc beluarũ genus, pinde ut deos suspiciũt. Sed quid ego de uno, aut

uitam illius.) Hic est uerissimus atq; ipsis acceptissimus, diuorũ cultus. Sed quoniã hoc lõge difficilius, negligit a uulgo, & ad faciles quasdam cerimonias confugiunt.

Cura sepulchri.

Quot luctus histriones. Durat hic mos adhuc apud complures Christianos, ex gẽtilitate relictus, ut conducti quidã plorent in funere, unde Flaccus. Vt qui cõducti plorant in funere dicunt, Et faciunt, prope plura dolentibus ex animo. Principes, equos etiã pullis obtectos stragulis, i hãc pompã inducũt, ceruice ad tibias alligata, quasi lugeãt, & dominũ requirãt. Huius spectaculi) Nam ista defuncti aut non sentiũt, aut suo malo sentiunt. Sed tolerantur in solatium infirmorum. Si modo tã moderate fiãt, ut ferri possint. Nunc aliquoties ambitio usq; ad insaniam exit.

Stulta nobilitas

Ediles creati.) Horum erat fabulas edere populo & uiscerationes exhibere. Nihil ab infimo cerdone.) Vide ut circũspecte taxat nobiles, nõ quosuis.

Sua cuiq; placent

52 Hans Holbein the Younger, 'A Nobleman and his Falcon', drawing in a 1515 copy of Erasmus of Rotterdam, *In Praise of Folly*.

luxuria (extravagance or lust). This discrepancy between criticism and cult as fetishism is reinforced through Holbein's critical drawing, although he paradoxically portrayed falconers (such as the English court falconer of Henry VIII Robert Cheseman) as well as noblemen with birds of prey.[35] In another drawing on the Erasmian text, the drawn margin by Holbein underlines the passage: hunting in general, and especially deer hunting, is criticized. People who behave like kings and hunt are actually the wild animals themselves.

In *The Seven Deadly Sins and the Four Last Things* (c. 1500) by Hieronymus Bosch, we see a falconer appearing under the sin of invidia (envy). This can be more or less related to Erasmus and Holbein, and reveals to what extent this kind of iconography has its roots in the late Middle Ages. In addition, the oppositions between classes are thematized in a detail from Bosch where a rich man posing with his hawk is juxtaposed with

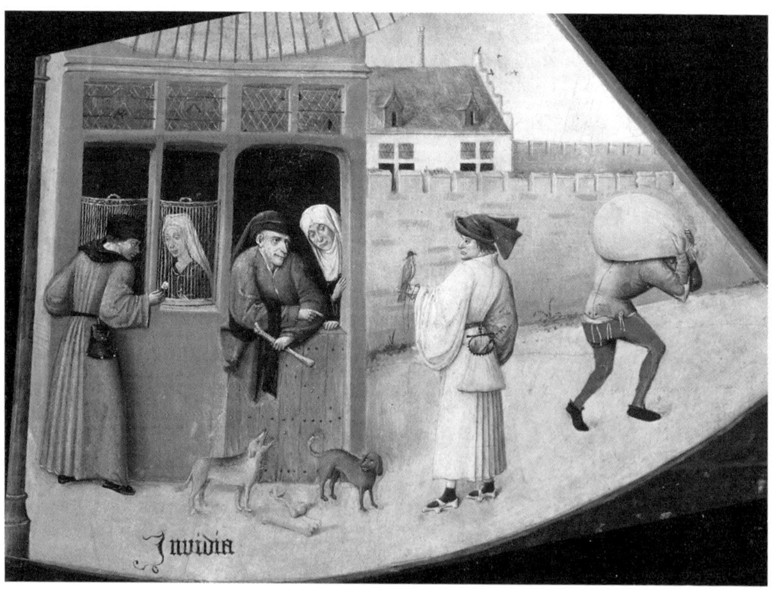

53 Detail of envy from Hieronymus Bosch, *The Seven Deadly Sins and the Four Last Things*, c. 1500, oil on wood.

someone who, practically unrecognizable (his individuality remains invisible), is carrying a huge weight (illus. 53).[36] Besides the hawk, a chicken's leg protrudes from the rich man's bag, implying the hawk's training. What is also striking is that the hawk is hooded, standing in relation to a man who looks towards it filled with blind envy while holding a piece of bone (directly beneath him, dogs are fighting over bones). Here we have a visual comparison between a moral concept and a social activity. The beholder's gaze is challenged through the picture's format: one must turn one's head and body in order to perceive the work in its entirety. This audacious image is not so dissimilar to Erasmus' use of the drawing above, which encapsulates his critique of the subject and its medium (the image). Image and hawk move between philia and phobia, love and aversion, addressing the very nature of cult and falconry.

We know from the sources that falconers went to church or made pilgrimages to shrines of the Virgin with *ex votos* in wax that depicted hawks, acting as idealized 'portraits' of their own hawks, and prayed for the return of their lost ones.[37] A thirteenth-century Spanish manuscript, the *Cantigas de Santa Maria* of Alfonso x (1221–1284), today in the library of the Escorial, elaborately illuminates this process. After losing his hawk somewhere in a rocky landscape, the falconer goes to a church to pray before a statue of Mary and the Christ Child, holding a sculpted hawk as an *ex voto*; in the next sequence, the lost bird appears miraculously, flying from above in the church's interior (illus. 54). The young falconer is ready to retrieve the hawk, whereas the bird's artificial substitute is already placed in front of the statue of Mary and the Christ Child. He is about to exit the church and gestures towards the statue: the image is responsible for the miraculous happening. The artefact has disappeared, as if the substitution of an artificial *ex voto* by a real hawk has been fulfilled. The miracle urges the beholders of the scene to pray

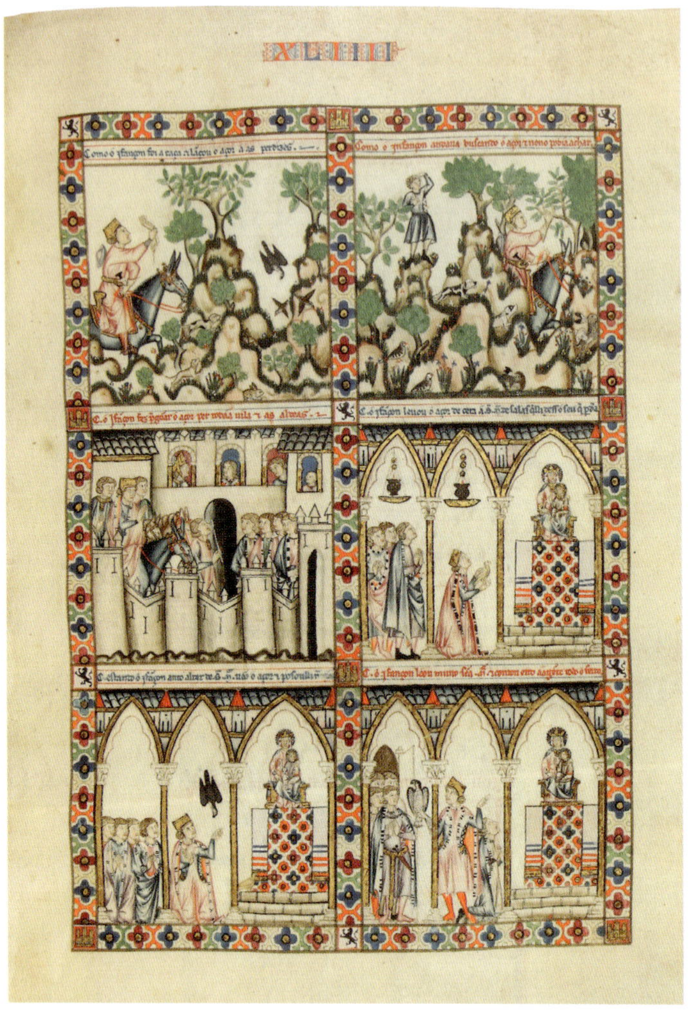

54 'Miracle of the Lost Hawk', folio from the *Cantigas de Santa Maria*, 13th century.

in front of the statue, as one can observe in the last scene. The adoration of miraculous images and the adoration of the hawk adds, at least metaphorically, another striking dimension to the Erasmian critique. We have already commented on the value of falconry at Alfonso x's court and the translation of the *Moamin* into Spanish, where hawking is related to political philosophy and hence sovereignty.

The illuminations of the *Cantigas de Santa Maria* accompany highly elaborate poems referring to falconry; some can be directly related to our image at hand. The poem is about a knight from Aragon whose goshawk was returned thanks to Santa Maria de Salas. The scene echoing the aforementioned illumination is described in the following way:

> He who trusts in Her with all his heart will experience what befell a nobleman in the kingdom of Aragón who lost a goshawk of his in the hunt. The bird was large and very handsome, and there was nothing in the way of prey of birds both small and large that it did not catch. The nobleman was very troubled that he could not find it and sent out a proclamation to all the surrounding country. When he did not find it in this way, he set out for Salas and took along a likeness of his bird made in wax. He spoke thus, 'Oh, My Lady, Holy Mary, I come to you with sorrow for my goshawk which I lost to ask you to return it to me. If you do so, you will have me always as your servant. Furthermore, I shall give you this wax in its image and shall always go about proclaiming your name and telling how of all the saints you are the best.' When he had said this, he went to hear solemn mass, but before he could depart from there, Holy Mary made the goshawk come to him, and he was very pleased. So that he would have even greater pleasure, She made the goshawk alight on his hand as though he were ready to go hunting with it.[38]

Different variants exist, and there are also other *cantigas* that refer to falconry, like that of the 'Moulting Goshawk'. This poem ends with a similar narrated episode involving an *ex voto* in front of a miraculous statue and the falconer praying for the precious goshawk to stay alive, addressing a central aspect of *ex votos*, which usually stand in for humans rather than animals. This episode again draws attention to the fact that hawks were treated almost as if they were human. This fact is enhanced through another aspect: *ex votos*, as already seen in the *Cantigas de Santa Maria*, historically included representations of hawks – for instance at the shrine of Thomas Becket at Canterbury Cathedral, from the early thirteenth century – with the hope that the owner's sick hawk would be cured; sick birds of prey were even taken to shrines, like the one to St Thomas Cantilupe at Hereford.[39] The hawk's image as well as the very animal itself were regarded as being as important as the other healing images of saints.

These poems were also accompanied by music and often sung. One can therefore speak of striking intermedial and intersensory relations between image, text and music. In general, this genre can be compared to the famous medieval German lyric form *Minnesang*, known particularly from the illuminated collection known as the *Codex Manesse* (c. 1300–1340). From approximately the thirteenth century, the lure has also served to bring an erotic connotation to falconry as a metaphor for conquering someone's heart.[40] In medieval literature and beyond, falconry is a favoured subject for forging erotic equivoques.[41] The phenomenon culminates in a very elaborate language, as in the use of falconry terms by Shakespeare (for instance in the *Taming of the Shrew*).

The *Minnesänger* known as Der von Kürenberg, introduced earlier, refers to women and falcons that one might easily tame, provided one lures them correctly.[42] In another saying, the man's gaze upon a hawk is equated to his gaze upon his own wife.[43] Let us not, however, forget here what happened with the hawk's assumed tameness in Der von Kürenberg. In this sense, the question of the hawk's resistive power is transmitted to the human agent. Seeing, hunting and taking into possession are all powerful actions that are metaphorically related to the hawk's strongest faculties.[44] Gazing or looking and being looked at are interactive moments that make the question of activity and passivity obsolete, because they concern rather a constant process of mutual exchange and interaction. There is, in other words, a visual analogy between power, gender and falconry relations.

Some poets of the love songs in the *Codex Manesse* were also rulers, bringing love and power into explicit playful interaction. Conquering as well as handling the untamed is crafted as a form of chivalric virtue, manifested in the dynamic scene of this book's cover. The texts and certainly the miniatures stress an almost utopian courtly ideal of love, embodying, among other things, the imaginative worlds of knights and courtly ladies. Some of them are shown in the active pursuit of falconry. The codex even includes a symbolic illumination of a knight, who literally has the head of a bird of prey. In this case, he becomes an emblematic figure connected to falconry, like many figures in coats of arms. For instance, in the late thirteenth-century romance of *Claris and Laris*, one of the Knights of the Round Table observes in his encounter another knight: 'He was well armed/ Nevertheless on his left hand/ He bore a good-looking bird/ For it was a moulted sparrowhawk/ It was not afraid/ For it was a marvellously manned hunting bird.'[45] The knight is once again constituted by his own bird of prey.

What interests us here is the fact that the poetic and the visual worlds are inspired by falconry as a peaceful endeavour, even if clearly combative moments involving hawking or the powerful tensions between the sexes also exist. We see, for instance, loving couples, identified through their coats of arms, such as that of Konrad von Altstetten (illus. 55). The sheet dates from around 1305–15. The couple touch each other and have dreamy expressions, while the man is feeding a hawk on his fist. It is a powerful metaphor for the relationship between the two figures, concerning manning, luring and attracting but also ruling.[46] The connection of falconry to proprioception and tactility obtains in the image from the codex an additional 'touch'. These are ideal depictions of love that became true icons of the Middle Ages, connected to chivalry and the court, where falconry appears as their essential and inseparable part. However,

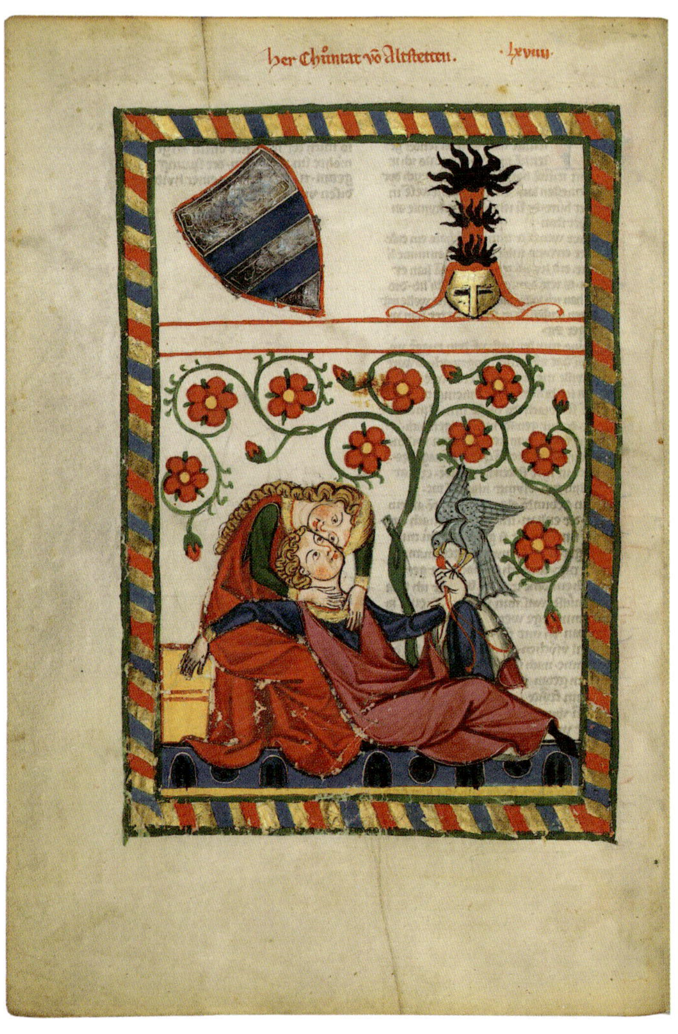

55 Konrad von Altstetten, folio from the *Codex Manesse*, c. 1305–15.

the man is not solely the active partner, luring the woman, since many examples to the contrary exist. For example, Baron Bertran de Born (*c.* 1140–1215), one of the major Occitan troubadours, not unlike the poets of the love songs in the *Codex Manesse*, wrote the following: 'I know a young moulted hawk, noble and graceful and swift, who has never taken a bird . . . She has taken me for a lover and given me more riches than if I were King of Palermo.'[47] In another poem, the protagonist's love and passion for hawking is actually substituted by his love for a woman:

> May I lose my sparrowhawk at first throw, or may lanners kill him on my wrist and drag him away, may I watch them plucking him, if I don't love thinking of you more than having my desire of any other who would give me her love and take me with her to bed.[48]

Let us go back, though, to the point of falconry's damnation: Erasmus' critique is comparable to a parody of falconry, a practice pursued also by Evangelista in his *Libro de cetrería* (Book on Falconry) from around 1470–74. It is important to note that this treatise was published during a time when the fascination and fashion for falconry was at a peak; a period also characterized by a moral critique connected to the luxurious practice of hawking and the habit of spending impressive amounts of money on the sport. In other words, it was a pastime of excessive vanity, according to the Spanish author.[49] Evangelista's book was even read by falconers, a remarkable paradox; the author was not uncritical towards religion, either.[50] Critique of and passion for falconry go hand in hand here, something that is perhaps not so surprising and which echoes the images' ontological status of moving between damnation and fascination.

During the Third Council of the Lateran in 1179, Pope Alexander III forbade members of the Church from carrying hawks during visitations. More or less at the same time, the Anglo-Norman satirist Nigel de Longchamp (1130–1200) underlined:

> The bishop runs from town to cast off his hawk.
> He spends more time in woods than sacred places,
> And values dogma less than [the] cry of hounds.
> He's troubled more when hounds are lost or when
> A hawk is hurt than when a cleric dies'[51]

Frederick II was praised by the pro-Hohenstaufen chroniclers for his falconry practices, because they understood hawking as a visual exercise for ruling. The court philosopher of the Germanic emperor, Theodore of Antioch, stated that kings could find no more pleasure than in hunting.[52] Other political voices, and most of all ecclesiastical accounts, attacked the Hohenstaufen emperor heavily because he neglected state affairs to go hawking.[53] That state affairs were, at least in representational and visual terms, dependent on hunting and in this case falconry in the aforementioned sense of commonwealth, was not in the purview of those voices.

Pope Gregory IX (1167–1241) also condemned Frederick II for his fascination with and passion for falconry. The pope underlined that the emperor degraded the prestige of majesty into a hunting office, and that instead of weapons and laws he was accompanied by hawks and hounds.[54] From an *imperator* (commander) Frederick II was transformed into a *venator* (hunter), and one of his most important attributes, the sceptre, became hunting equipment, something that also relates to the emperor's visual representation.[55]

It was, however, not only sovereigns who were criticized for neglecting their duties in favour of falconry: popes were also denounced for forgetting their papal duties. Denys, Bishop of

Senlis (1349–51), may have even written a treatise on falconry.[56] Popes of aristocratic descent like Clement VI (1291–1352), holding court in Avignon, were passionate falconers. In his private study room, the so-called Room of the Deer in the Papal Palace (Palais des Papes) at Avignon, which embodied the architectural entanglement of court and Church, one may still see today an impressive depiction of falconry, among other scenes of hunting and courtly life (illus. 56). The fresco is entirely freed from any religious connotations. It includes the most up-to-date courtly fashion of the times, alluding to the iconographical repertoire of the calendar months. In other words, we forget that we are in a papal palace.

In the early sixteenth century, Martin Luther accused Pope Leo X of neglecting his own duties because of his passion for hawking, pursuing earthly amusements such as falconry instead of taking the road of spirituality.[57] Knights and aristocracy in general had a direct connection to the papacy. Leo X was a Medici, the son of Lorenzo il Magnifico. Given this, it is no surprise that he remained a passionate falconer all his life. A contemporary source even remarked: 'Gentle and peaceable by nature, he was, nonetheless, so fiercely attached to this pastime that he spared not his wrath for anyone, were he stranger or known to him, when he acted against the duty of falconry.'[58] The pope's dedication to falconry clearly adds a further dimension: the head of the Catholic Church is stylized as a passionate falconer. This has a long history, as we shall see.

The pope as falconer is not part of his canonical iconography, probably because such a pursuit would even more explicitly connect earthly courtly deeds with spiritual ones, especially if one considers the ecclesiastical criticism of the practice.[59] Visual testimonies of this type exist, although they are not well known. One may find some surprising examples, however, in images of popes riding.[60] This particular motif, which survived in

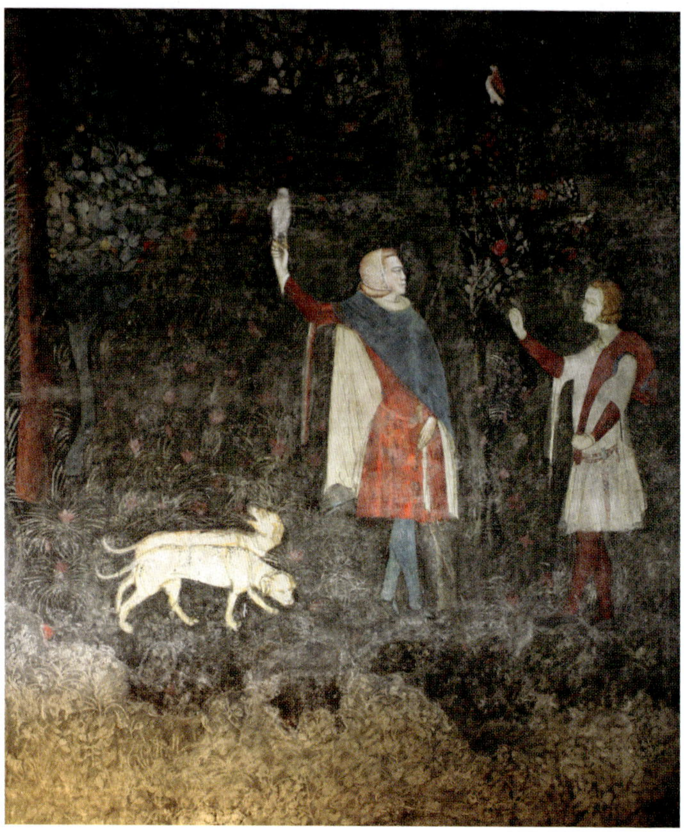

56 Robin de Romans, *Hunting Scene*, 14th century, fresco, Room of the Deer, Palais des Papes, Avignon.

various versions and media, involves Pope Clement v (1305–14) and exists from the fifteenth century: that is to say, images produced more or less one hundred years after the pope's activity in the highest position of the Western Church. Their existence speaks for the striking reception and visual legacy of a historical figure.

In all known visual examples, the pope is wearing his papal tiara and riding his horse in a pose more akin to that of a powerful sovereign, one that clearly derives from the political iconography of the emperor, since the one is the ruler of the earth and the other an intermediary between heaven and earth, as a successor of St Peter. The pope is carrying a hawk on his fist and rides in the direction of the countryside, obviously with the intention to hunt. He turns away from a female figure who appears under an archway with a sad expression (illus. 57). She is identified with the weeping Ecclesia, the Church, embodying Rome or, more accurately, the Vatican.[61] The scene is interpreted as representing the *profectio* (literally, 'departure'),[62] which alludes to the departure of the Roman emperor. On such occasions, special coins were issued.[63] We see here how a subject deriving from Graeco-Roman political iconography is attached to papal history and thoroughly transformed, since 'departure'

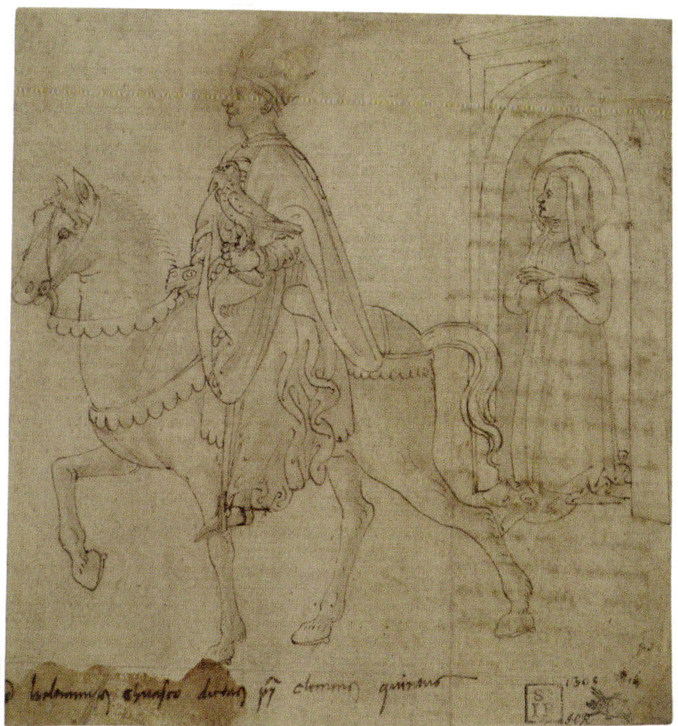

57 Circle of Fra Angelico, *Pope Clement V*, 1402–55, pen and brown ink with brown wash.

here does not necessarily mean a return. What is implied is the abandoned city, or, more precisely, the Church and hence Rome, as a worldly and spiritual power.

It was Clement v who brought the papal residence to Avignon in 1309 and ordered the construction of the Palais des Papes.[64] Thus, we are dealing with a visual critique of the pope. The pseudo-Joachistic writings (false writings of Joachim) with papal instructions are consciously falsely attributed to the apocalyptic thinker and theologian Joachim of Fiore (1135–1202), and were found in different illustrated editions (illus. 53 derives from this tradition), where various popes were connected to specific symbols.[65] These visual arguments have a clear negative dimension. The weeping Ecclesia, the spouse of the pope, is abandoned, and the pope goes to hunt with his other spouse, falconry, neglecting his duties, so the image argues. He takes the opposite road; this is why he is depicted riding from right to left, against the common Western convention. A visual position is taken alongside the verbal testimonies.[66]

It is striking that Pope Clement v was connected in pseudo-Joachistic writings to Joshua, the Old Testament leader of the Israelite tribes in the succession of Moses.[67] Thus, the pope is here directly compared to a warlord – literally speaking, a *miles Christianus* (Christian soldier) of the highest rank.

In scholarly literature, all images of riders with hawks are understood as representing Constantine if there is no other identification, especially if one considers that the specific motif was transcultural from its very beginnings.[68] The Constantine impact, as discussed earlier, could be related to the fact that Constantine, as the first Christian emperor, was also a falconer.

To sum up: the image of the mounted pope with hawk can be viewed as the legacy of an imperial gesture, transferred to a religious setting. This can be connected to the critique of falconry, which was also related to popes as messengers of the divine and sovereigns of the Western Church, and so of Christianity as a whole. In this way, a surprising mixture between seemingly opposed concepts, falconry and Church, is constructed visually, even though as a clearly negative exemplum.

However, it was not only popes and rulers who indulged in falconry. In the thirteenth century, the clergy were allowed to pursue hawking.[69] They hunted with smaller hawks according to their socio-economic status, thus forming another kind of hierarchy, similar to the one at court, though in both cases less formalized than some sources might lead us to believe.

The presence of the hawk within religious life on the one hand legitimized its usage, whereas on the other, as noted, it was attacked and criticized. Here one might ask: what place has a hawk in a church, or what does falconry have to do with religion beyond the example of the pope as falconer or the *Cantigas de Santa Maria*? An early example of a hawk in a church is found in the Gothic cathedral at Naumburg, Germany, dating from the thirteenth century. The kestrel appears almost as if hiding, as an accessory related to the different sculpted founder figures; figures who might have pursued falconry, since they belonged to the nobility (illus. 58). The hawk is found behind the iconic pair of Uta and Ekkehard in the western choir.[70] The animal appears as if entirely detached from humans. Yet a hint of human–animal interaction remains open; the bird is depicted as a natural element in a highly culturalized milieu. It could signify faith in general, which is embodied in the very church where the bird found sanctuary.

We saw in the theme of the Adoration of the Kings a goshawk in the act of taking a pheasant, an act that in the early frescoes of the Sistine Chapel, such as Ghirlandaio's *Calling of the Apostles* (1481–2), related to the issue of conversion, was interpreted as a symbol of faith.[71] This is opposed to the previously mentioned reading of the hawk as a symbol for greed, underlining not only

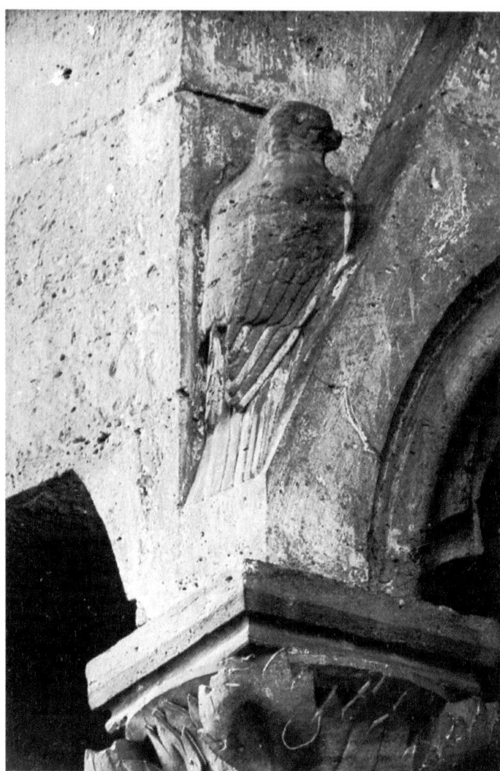

58 Hawk (kestrel), western choir of Naumburg Cathedral, 13th century (photograph early 20th century).

the instability of symbol but the dual and contradictory nature of the hawk itself.

An explicit critique concerning the carriage of hawks inside the church has also been formulated: the German humanist Sebastian Brandt, for instance, pinpointed in his *Ship of Fools*, his famed satire published in 1494, how men with their hawks made a lot of noise while in church, as if they merely wanted to show off their luxurious appurtenances.[72] In an English edition of 1509, the passage is eloquently translated by Alexander Barclay as 'They make of the churche for theyr hawkes a mewe [mews].'[73] In other words, sensual and immodest elements like hawks have no place in a church. They could draw attention only to themselves instead of the Holy Mass,

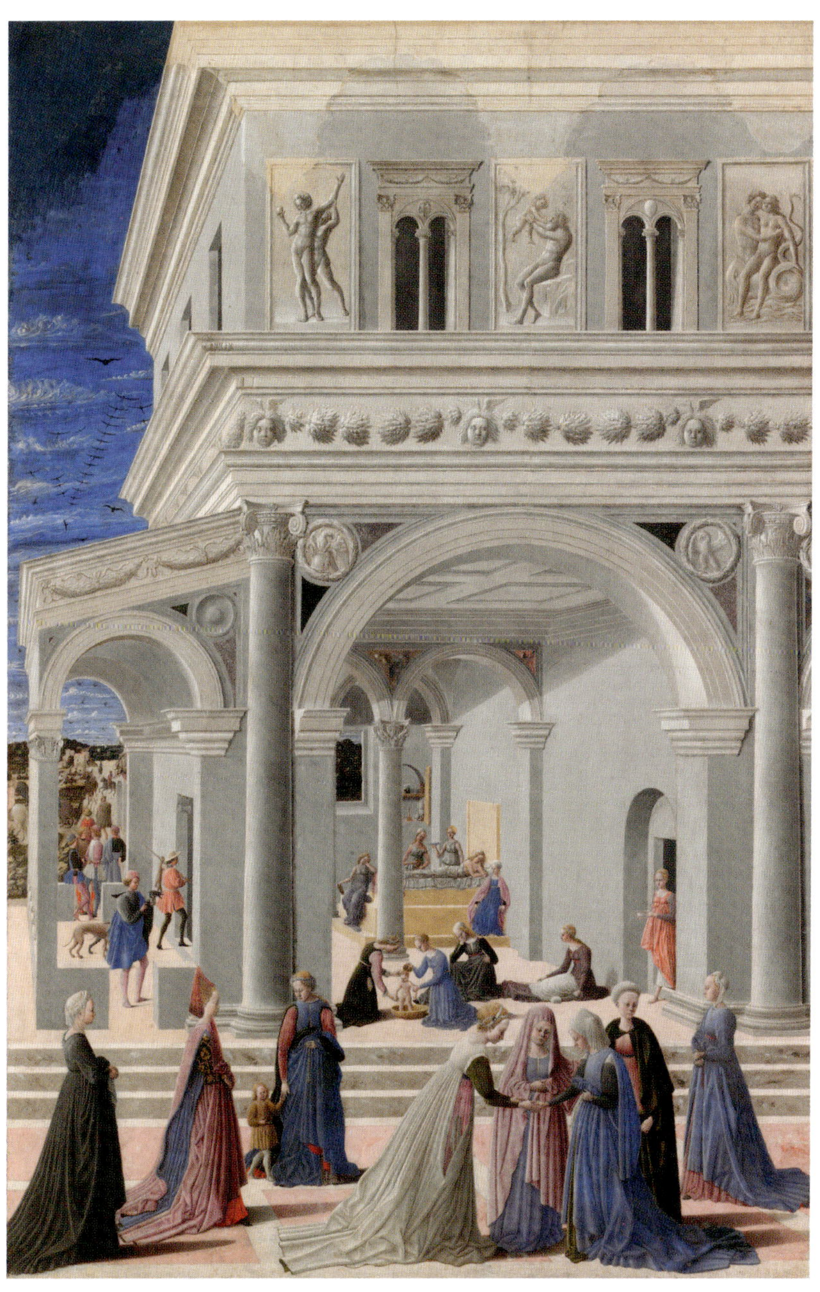

59 Fra Carnevale, *The Birth of the Virgin*, 1467, tempera and oil on wood.

having a structural relationship to the role of the images in theological disputes.

In a painting by Fra Carnevale representing the *Birth of the Virgin* (1467), the division between the specific event and everyday life in a certain milieu is impressively brought before our eyes (illus. 59).[74] It is clear that we are in a palace. There is a separation between inside (where the sacred birth of Mary takes place) and outside (the profane realm of falconers and hunters). Those elements, however, are not played against each other. They seem to be part of the same courtly sphere, since the ladies in the foreground unite both levels through their movement.

The abolition of the boundaries between sacred and profane concerning hawking becomes even clearer on the sarcophagus of the nobleman Raimondo del Balzo from 1375, which stands in the Neapolitan Basilica di Santa Chiara. On this, the pilgrim courtiers posing with generic hawks make it not only inside the church but even to the tomb (illus. 60). The centrally enthroned figure also carries a hawk on his fist. The profane and sacred worlds are not isolated from each other but rather are brought clearly together.[75] This is not an atypical conflation in papal tombs, and other tombs of minions of the Church as well as the state; similar examples can be found in Naples deriving from the early thirteenth century.[76]

At first sight, falconry and religion seem only to be opposed to each other, as already examined in the Hugh of Fouilloy manuscript (illus. 48). The merging of the opposition is representatively embodied in saints who were falconers and were depicted as such. This phenomenon is an ideal bridge to abrogate those dissentions and to bring them under one roof under the heading of cult, religion and falconry.

These saints descended, and this is crucial, from an aristocratic milieu and never really broke with their family tradition, even if they must have turned their backs on luxury in order to

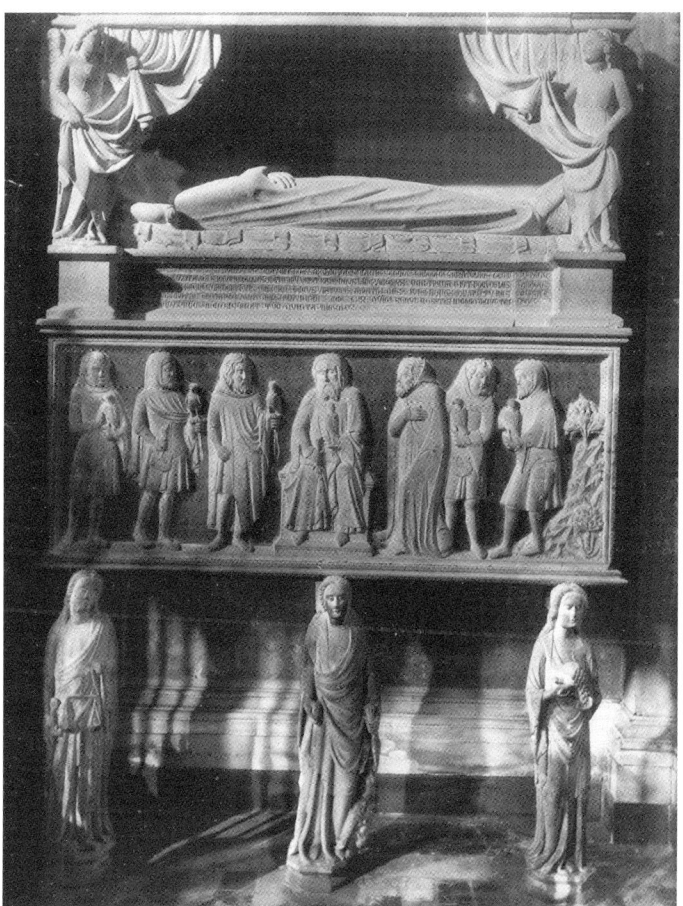

60 Sarcophagus of Raimondo del Balzo by Seguace dei Bertini, *c.* 1375, Basilica di Santa Chiara, Naples (photograph *c.* 1857–90).

become saints. In this sense they have a similarity to the pope, who in the Middle Ages and beyond descended from powerful and aristocratic, mostly Italian families. The hawk becomes here an *apotropaion* of her own being, a living memory of the saint's past life. This is the case in, for instance, a work by Simone Martini painted around 1320–25 and representing St Martin (a neat verbal allusion to the artist's name), who was a former knight and is shown with his entourage during the process of his

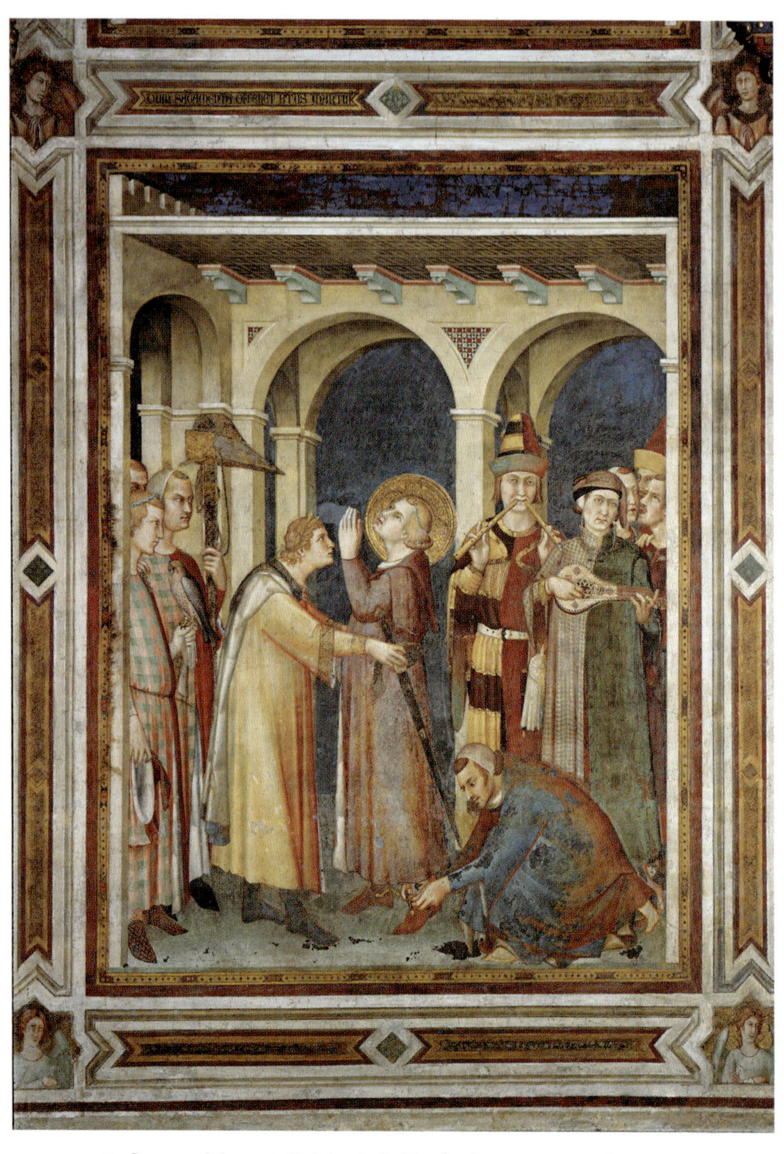

61 Simone Martini, *St Martin Is Knighted*, c. 1320–25, fresco, Lower Church of the Basilica of San Francesco, Assisi.

canonization – still carrying a sword. In this fresco in the Lower Church of the Basilica of San Francesco, Assisi, he looks upwards, that is, towards God. A halo hovers above his head (illus. 61). Martin is accompanied by two figures that bear his former life, as represented by a falcon and a harness. On the other side, courtly musicians with a singer shown at work may be discerned.

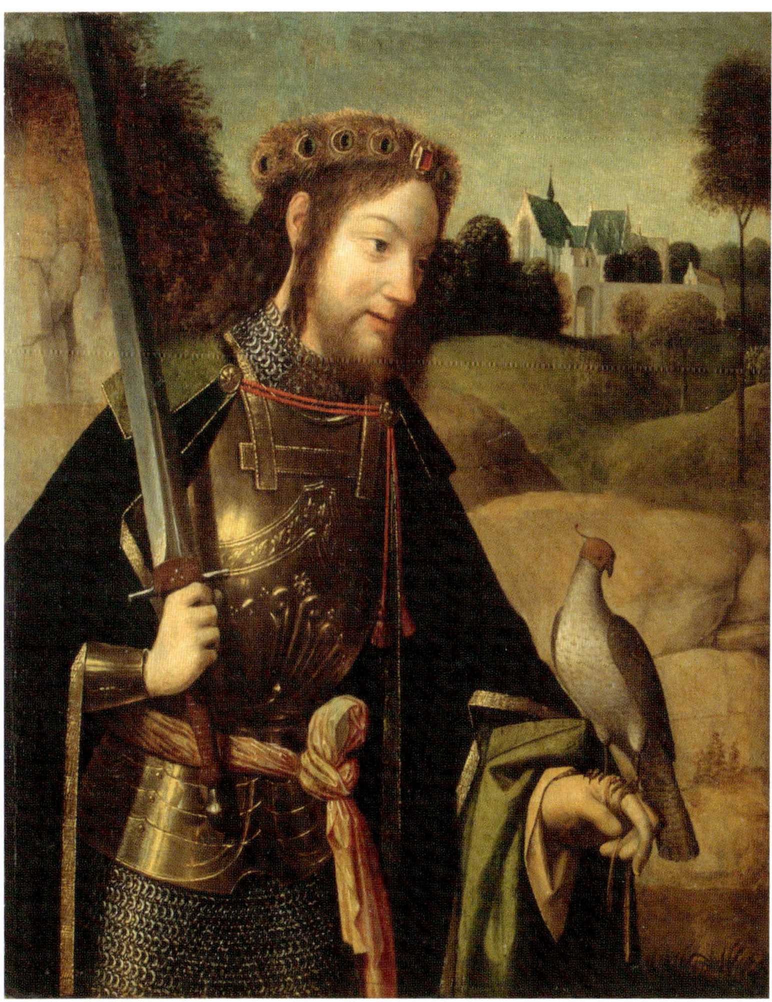

62 Geertgen tot Sint Jans, *St Bavo*, c. 1495, oil on panel.

Falcon and harness seem to represent the saint's past, although they are still visually present during his canonization.

This is not the case with figures such as St Bavo, the patron of falconers.[77] A former knight, Bavo married the daughter of a nobleman and dedicated himself to the art of war. Warfare, chivalry and religion are surprisingly close in St Bavo's case. An example from the late fifteenth century by Geertgen tot Sint Jans, who often painted this popular saint in the Low Countries, depicts Bavo as a knight carrying a sword as well as a hooded hawk on his fist. The hawk is placed exactly on the same level as the church on the background. The church seems to be the Cathedral of St Bavo in Haarlem, one of the centres of his adoration (illus. 62). Religious faith and knightly ideals often merged, as they do figuratively here.[78] The antagonisms between religion and falconry are united in the figure of a saint-cum-falconer.

SIX

Diplomacy and Gifts

Even to this day, sovereigns and prime ministers present falcons – either alive or in the form of artefacts such as sculptures or paintings – to other heads of state as gifts. Hawks are and were cherished in such circles for their unruly but ultimately tameable nature, as well as their symbolic political status. However, exchanging and trading falcons, a highly lucrative business, was already well established during the long Middle Ages.

Cultivating diplomacy through interactions with living creatures has proved to be a remarkably successful approach to forging mutual diplomatic ties. As living beings possess their own volition, it becomes essential to engage with their individuality to establish and display one's own sovereignty in their presence. The dynamics involved in building relationships with these untamed creatures are fascinatingly intricate, particularly when it comes to birds of prey, in stark contrast to the exchange of diamonds, which appears comparatively straightforward.

The transport and distribution of hawks occurred, from quite early on in falconry's history, on an international scale, like the sport's status as a widespread global phenomenon.[1] Apart from trade, one must also take into account gifts and their ritual exchange, spanning personal relations (in friendship or among family) to official encounters between sovereigns.

Beyond rulers in diplomatic missions, however, travelling merchants also tried to use hawks to obtain access to a powerful sovereign and gain financial benefits.[2] This fact sheds light beyond political power relations onto the financial interactions between different parties. Hawks and falcons, similar to artworks and other luxuries, presented a challenge that enabled adventurers to try their luck and enrich themselves.

Falcons incarnated claims of power and sovereignty, connections and alliances, but they could also be the cause of disputes or even war. This notion is embodied in the hawk's peculiar nature, which unites aggressive and peaceful aspects. This double symbolic connotation has always been an integral part of the nature and culture of falconry. Falcons and falconry were not simply passive elements of mere political representation, but their exchange and, even more importantly, their role within political iconology triggered or even constituted spheres of interaction and diplomacy. Hawks, falconry furniture and indeed falconry images were and are material-symbolic entities. Gifts of hawks were agents of political as well as transcultural encounters and established, at least symbolically speaking, those very relations.[3]

Animal gifts had functional and representational purposes within the same court, as well as between the sovereigns of different courts. There was a particular interest in falcons, which were special in terms of rarity and origin and therefore had considerable value, not exclusively measured in financial terms, since value was often translated in other forms of reciprocity, for instance alliances.[4] In addition to this, the aesthetic dimensions of both falcons and falconry were of paramount importance, being a further indication of the sport's political materiality.

The gift not only brings forth dependencies but also obligations, and conserves or reinforces power relations between different parties. This obligation remains as long as the debt is not returned; in some cases, the non-returnable nature of the debt can prove to be more powerful than its cancellation.[5]

The sociologist Marcel Mauss, in his classic study *The Gift: Form and Reason of Exchange in Archaic Societies* (1925), defined the obligation to give, to conserve and to react or reply as fundamental aspects of gift-offering.[6] This forms the basis for any kind of debt constellation, since every gift is connected to the burden of a rejoinder, especially when a debt is intrinsically bound to a political order.[7] According to Mauss, the gift constitutes the reciprocal counter-gift, whether it is of a material or other nature.[8] Moreover, gift exchanges also offer opportunities for transcultural exchanges. These do not move in a simple linear way from A to B and back but rather demand a continuous interaction in which the goal of appropriation is not always given or visible.

The sovereign's political wisdom is measured in the acknowledgement of the other, non-human party without trying to subjugate the animal, but rather to cooperate in a non-verbal way in order to achieve their respective goals. A successful interaction with the hawk would prove that the sovereign was also capable of cooperating with humans. There is also, however, another dimension: to give a hawk as a gift means simultaneously to acknowledge the sovereignty of the other party.[9] To successfully practise sovereignty in conjunction with handling hawks denotes a ruler's central virtue, as discussed. Through the symbolic substitution of sovereign and falcon, acting as his or her avatar, the issue of paying tribute or even obedience, and simultaneously signalling warning, are incarnated in the bird. In this way, the animal becomes a vehicle of a visual and non-verbal diplomacy.[10]

A hawk's life was as precious as that of a human. If one stole a hunting bird, one's own life might be forfeit; indeed, in some areas in Central Asia, no distinction was made in terms of punishment for killing a human being or killing a hawk.[11] This merging of human and animal can be directly connected to territorial claims; to 'possess' a falcon meant to exercise power over land and air and, at least on a representational level, parts of the world.

The maintenance of the 'reason of state' is, symbolically speaking, secured through the diplomatic deployment of hawks. The emperor, or sovereign in general, tried to influence other courts through the giving of falcons. This strategy was equally applied and was even of greater importance when employed towards enemies.[12] Hawks were talismanic *apotropaia* of diplomatic relations, protecting the inside against the outside.

Through the trade routes, and from the perspective of the falcon as a vehicle of exchange, the transculturality of the phenomenon becomes clear. The sea routes in medieval times, along which the trading of falcons took place, could extend, for instance, from the Baltic Sea to North Africa. John, king of England (1166–1216), received gyrfalcons as a present from the king of Norway.[13] Gyrfalcons were the most precious of the royal falcon gifts. Originally from Greenland or Iceland, they belonged to the most sought-after category of hawks – and not just in Northern Europe. There was a connection between the exclusiveness of this species and the king of Norway: the gyrfalcon was tangibly presented before the eyes of his subjects as well as to sovereigns from distant lands.[14] Since falcons could not be bred in captivity, one needed to acquire them through trade.

The resulting problems of sickness and maladaptation of the birds to their new warm climates represented a huge challenge for anyone wanting to possess a gyrfalcon in southern regions, occasionally even leading to the death of those beautiful white birds. Today, with hybrid gyrfalcons, which are in this sense entirely adapted and possess the genetics to handle warmer climes, the whole issue has gained another dimension.

Falcon gifts were also employed to secure certain conditions for territorial claims or favours, such as in the case of Charles V, who bequeathed the island of Malta to the Knights Hospitaller on the condition that they would send him as a remembrance a white falcon (meaning a gyrfalcon) every year.[15] The Habsburg emperor also helped the king of Tunisia to regain his throne, in exchange for which the ruler had to send him six falcons every year.[16]

Turkish soldiers captured Jean de Nevers, the future Duke of Burgundy, during the Battle of Nicopolis in 1396 and asked for a ransom of twelve white gyrfalcons, which was one of the most costly conditions they could set, owing to the sheer expense of sending ships and crews to obtain them.[17] This shows the substitutional relation between territory, animal and human as a principle of exchange. The demand shows that the Ottomans were perfectly well informed about Burgundy's important infrastructure concerning falconry, which had flourished since the thirteenth century. Highly in-demand professional falconers and trappers from the Low Countries, including Burgundian territory, stood out.[18] López de Ayala refers explicitly in his treatise to professional trappers from Brabant, because not only did they trap hawks, they were also involved in the trade of falcons (especially gyrfalcons) from Norway, which were brought by ship to Germany and then carried to Flanders.[19] These professionals were in constant motion, going to Paris, England or Cologne to sell their catch, while simultaneously importing sakers originating from the Balkans, the Black Sea and even the Middle East through Levantine trade.[20] The North and the West exported falcons to the East and to the South, and also imported them through the latter, highlighting once again, from yet another angle, the global mobility of the phenomenon during the Middle Ages.

Gyrfalcons also had a special importance in Eurasia, in monetary terms as well as in those of prestige, since their export was a monopoly of the state; these precious birds of prey were used for encounters between sovereigns throughout Eurasia.[21] In other words, the phenomenon knew no borders, thus emphasizing once again not only the boundless nature of the falcon but also the transculturality of the practice itself.

Important political events were reason enough for gift-giving.[22] Falcons were sent also to bishops and Church dignitaries, beyond others like counts and countesses, dukes and duchesses, landgraves, city officials and, not least, in the case of the Burgundian court, the Grand Master of the Teutonic Order.[23]

The search for falcons and a thirst for collecting more broadly reinforced the trophy-like character of falconry. Falcons were in that sense natural, self-mobile artworks, having literally their own agency. From the point of view of collecting, hawks and images have a further relation. Some human agents involved in the practice of falconry also wanted to possess a transcultural and, insofar as it was possible, complete collection of hawks that would permit them to show off as collectors by uniting all kinds of different animal features and skills, in an almost encyclopaedic manner.

This passion for collecting went so far that kings were even held for ransom, as in the case of Jean de Nevers. Sometimes, alliances were made with the sole goal of the sovereign acquiring a hawk that did not originate from his or her own country and was not part of the collection.[24] This trend is clearly mentioned in a source dating from 1270:

> It is to Boston fair that the King's falconer goes to buy the birds that come, probably, from Norway or from Iceland. For under Lincolnshire [in the Pipe rolls, medieval English Treasury records] we meet not only with Norway hawks, but with an Iceland gerfalcon, and in that country the birds appear to have been treated almost as currency.[25]

From this passage, a hierarchy of gyrfalcons in terms of value becomes evident, with a distinction between the grey gyrfalcons (commonly termed 'Norway hawks', as above) and their white Icelandic counterparts. In the case of the latter especially, these highly prized birds of prey were understood as a form of currency. However, this was not only the case with the most precious hawks: for instance, some court officers in Brabant were able to pay the sovereign either with money or with a sparrowhawk as part of their yearly feudal levy.[26]

One can speak of the Baltic as an international centre of the falcon trade because of its crucial geographical position. Trade associates made a deal after the second half of the thirteenth century in Lübeck, Germany, to send ten gyrfalcons from there, via Nuremberg and Venice, to Alexandria.[27] This fact reveals how German trade associations, not unlike the Burgundian ones, used specific routes through their connections and fellow merchants (for instance the Fondaco dei Tedeschi, or German merchants' headquarters, in Venice, which existed from the early thirteenth century) to deliver hawks for trading purposes as far as Alexandria.

However, beyond the huge distances involved in finding and trading hawks, rulers were, pragmatically enough, also interested in sourcing hawks on a smaller scale, closer to their own permanent residence. This is clear in a letter of about 748 from King Ethelbert II of Kent (700–762) to Boniface: 'Acquire these birds [falcons] and send them to us since very few of this kind are found in our region of Kent . . . that are so quick of Mind.'[28] Thus, even at this early stage there is the idea of collecting falcons with particular faculties that could not be found within one's own region. The search for falcons was as important in the micro scale as it was on the macro scale.

In a letter by Abd Al Aziz Ben Al Qabturnh, the secretary of the already mentioned al-Mutawakkil (822–861), the tenth Abbasid caliph, one reads the following striking testimony:

> Most excellent King, whose forefathers were falconers of the very highest distinction! You have adorned my neck with jewels beyond price, and chained them together like pearls upon a string. Adorn now my hand with a falcon. Honour me with a bird of translucent wings, whose plumage has been smoothed by the northern winds. How proud I will be when I venture forth with him at the break of day, my hand sending forth a bound and captive bird to seize a bird that freely flies.[29]

The caliph's powerful heritage becomes clear not only in political terms but also through falconry, since his ancestors are defined as falconers (and we are in the ninth century); both aspects are hence exposed as interwoven elements. The highest reward for the secretary is to ask the caliph to give him a falcon as a gift, and especially one from the north. In this way, the secretary can also have a connection to the very heritage of his own master. In this context, a falcon from the north could suggest a gyrfalcon. Certain relations are established here within one and the same court, and not even between equals, since these are forged within a clear-cut hierarchy. The falcon is classified regarding its precious value even above other luxurious objects ('jewels beyond price').

Bertha (863–925), the daughter of Lothair II of Lotharingia and the mother of Hugh of Italy, gave seven falcons and seven sparrowhawks as gifts to an embassy of the Abbasid caliph al-Muktafi in the year 906, a gesture proving that female rulers also partook in the ritual of falcon gift-giving.[30] This also reveals that, beyond trade, transcultural diplomatic relations were established through falcon gifts as early as the beginning of the tenth century, and very possibly even earlier.

In the ninth century, in a different part of the world – within the huge Chinese imperium during the Tang dynasty – it is documented how twelve falcons were sent from an imperial legate in Shandong to the emperor Xianzong, but were subsequently returned. This gesture of not accepting the gift, also an essential part of gift exchange, should reveal the sovereign's incorruptibility, even if, or precisely because, it was known that he passionately pursued falconry and other forms of hunting.[31] This counter-example simultaneously proves the prevalence of the practice of falcon gifts employed for diplomatic reasons around the globe.

Falcons as private gifts beyond family bonds is another crucial part of the story: for instance, Archbishop Boniface sent King Æthelbald of Mercia (r. 716–57) two falcons and a hawk as 'a token of our true love and devoted friendship'. Thus the symbol of a hawk as a tangible kind of bond appears as early as the eighth century.[32] Gift-giving also addressed informal relationships, related to the positive nature of a hawk as a token of love, in the spirit of the *Codex Manesse* miniatures.

Images of ambassadors, diplomatic receptions and gift-giving that explicitly involve hawks or falconry in general are less prevalent in medieval visual culture. The limited visibility of the phenomenon does not really do justice to the historical frequency with which the use of hawks for diplomatic and trade purposes occurred, as if there were a gap between the cultural practice of falcon gifting and the visualization of the phenomenon. Here we will not ask why this is the case, because there is nevertheless enough visual evidence to prove the presence and use of hawks during diplomatic encounters involving disputes, embassies and even gifts. We will instead trace some of these aspects through concrete visual examples.

A striking image from the twelfth century, in a relief on a baptismal font (brought from Tournai, today in Belgium) at Winchester Cathedral, depicts the story of St Nicholas and the dowries (illus. 63).[33] The poor elderly nobleman is depicted sitting on the ground, holding the hand, in gratitude, of the saint who rescued his daughters from poverty and prostitution through a secret gift of gold. The father simultaneously holds the hand of his first daughter, probably giving her the dowry in the form of the gold balls, or sacks of coins, that he received from the saint. The first daughter gestures with her hand towards her third sister, who carries a hawk on her fist. This motion is a reference to the financial security that has enabled one of the daughters to acquire a hawk and therefore facilitated marriage to the man standing beside her, who also carries a hawk as an indication of his noble status. The other possibility is that the hunting bird was given to her by her husband. In this sense, the hawk is, in the first possibility, an implicit gift (purchased as a social elevator using the dowry money), while in the second case it is an explicit one.

The second example dates from around 1290–1330 and derives from the *Roman de Laurin*, a French romance from the

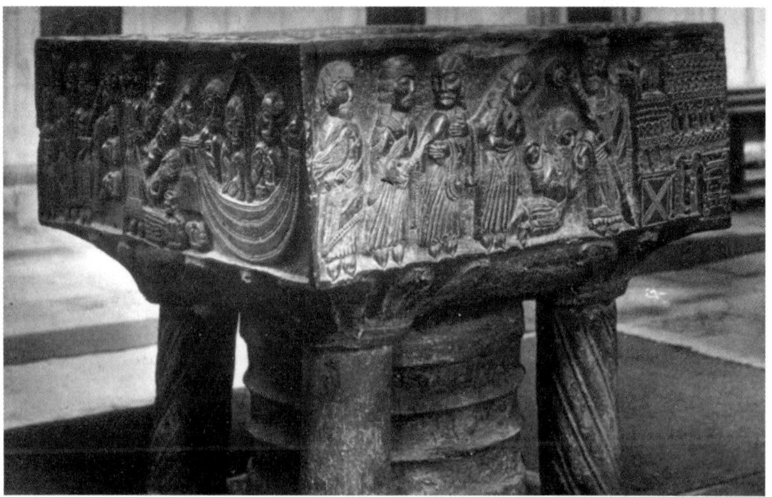

63 Scene showing St Nicholas being thanked for his gifts of gold, relief on south face of baptismal font, Winchester Cathedral, 12th century, black marble (photograph 1891).

end of the thirteenth century. The main character, the knight Laurin, is carrying a message to the emperor of Rome while carrying a hawk (illus. 64). Laurin is accompanied by a male figure who is shown holding a large spear, as if he were Laurin's guard. Judging from the gestures of the two main figures (Laurin and the emperor), the hawk is certainly not the main reason for the embassy. However, it emphasizes its nature and even the content of the message and hence the eventual outcome of the mission, which could potentially be peaceful but may also be belligerent – a possibility underlined, beyond the hawk, by the spear.[34] The visual narrative order unfolds against the standard mode of depiction from left to right. Three mounted figures, among them the figure with the spear and Laurin carrying his hawk and, notably, a sword, are depicted in the landscape having left their castle, on their way to deliver their message to the emperor. Here the attributes of spear, hawk and sword, carried by Laurin, are not only demonstrations of prestige but may act, if needed, as weapons.

In an illumination from a medieval manuscript of the life of Alexander the Great, the so-called *Roman d'Alexandre*, the Macedonian king is depicted receiving a gift from the Amazons, who were initially his enemies but later became his allies (illus. 65).[35] The image dates from around 1300–1350. The woman next to the Amazon, who is shown in the act of offering a golden ring as a gift, is holding a hawk that is eating from its quarry. This motif embodies the inherently aggressive nature of the wild bird and is related, at least to a certain extent, to the well-known subject of power and manning. The Amazons were as wild as their own hawks, but they could be peaceful as well if they were treated correctly. The ring was sent by the queen of the Amazons as an act of goodwill and acceptance to become an ally of the mighty king.[36] A certain warning is, however, embodied through the hawk, underlining not only her own wild nature but also that

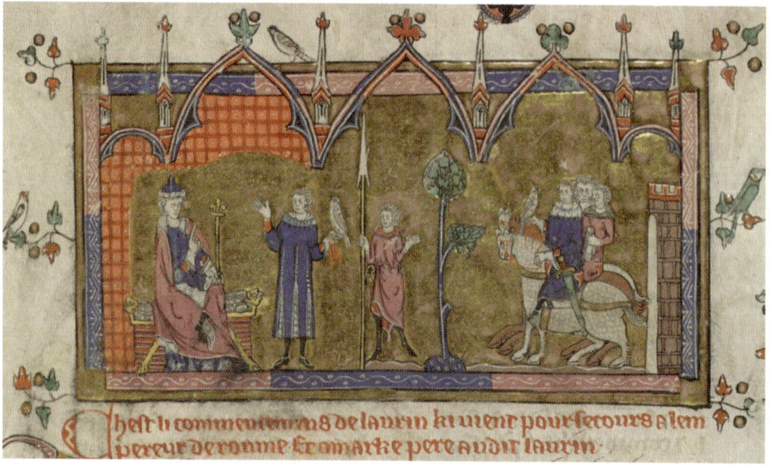

64 Laurin bringing an embassy to the emperor of Rome, miniature from the *Roman de Laurin*, c. 1290–1330.

of the human carrier. Here, again, the hawk is an attribute and not the main vehicle of exchange.

We have observed in a miniature from a Burgundian variant of Frederick II's *De arte venandi cum avibus* manuscript the kneeling figure, possibly Frederick's own son, presenting a hawk to the emperor (perhaps as a gift) (illus. 3). Here, the beholder's full attention is directed towards the hawk, which acts as a vehicle between the two figures, be it an official transaction or even a private exchange within the same court between family members. The emperor's passion, as manifested in text and image in his book, is underlined through the very presentation of the hooded hawk, which functions in effect as an introduction to this French translation of his treatise. Let us not forget here that Frederick was not only one of the most famous collectors of hawks but responsible for gathering falconers from all over the medieval world. Around fifty falconers are documented to have been active at his court.[37] This number is almost insignificant in comparison to Kublai Khan (1215–1294), who, according to Marco Polo (*c.* 1254–1324) and after a sixteenth-century translation of the *Travels of Marco Polo*, possessed 'ten thousande Faulcons, five thousande Gerfaulcons [or] other kinde of Hawkes a great Number, which are very singular and good . . . for every one of them hath fastened unto hys Belles a Scutcheon of gold, wherin is written the name of hys Mayster'.[38]

Nonetheless, one still has to arrive at the early modern period to find artefacts related entirely, in visual terms, to the hawk itself as an agent of diplomatic exchange and negotiation. For instance, a print by the Flemish artist Aegidius Sadeler, dated 1605, is a circulating image par excellence, for it bears inscriptions in Farsi and Latin (illus. 66). The Persian ambassador to Prague, Mechti

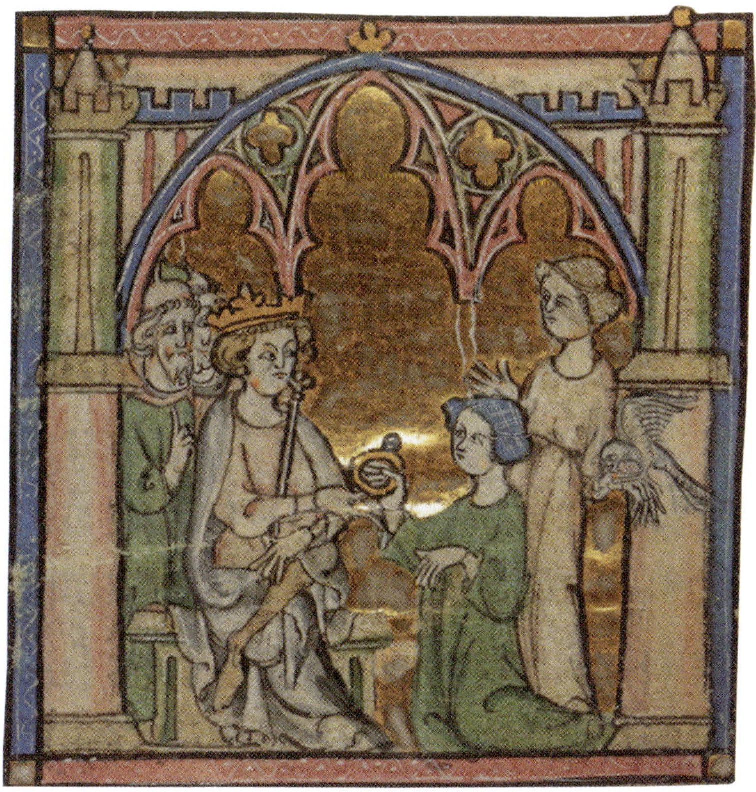

65 Alexander the Great receiving a gift sent by the Amazon queen, miniature from the *Roman d'Alexandre*, c. 1300–1350.

Kuli Beg, is depicted *ad vivum*, as the inscription tells us – meaning from life – visiting the court of Emperor Rudolf II and carrying a hawk, possibly as a gift.[39] The hawk, wearing around her neck a *jangoli* or *halsband* (used almost exclusively in the East, for instance in Persia or the Indian Subcontinent, to lower a hawk's head for aerodynamic reasons before casting her directly at quarry), functions on the one hand as a symbol of the Orient and on the other

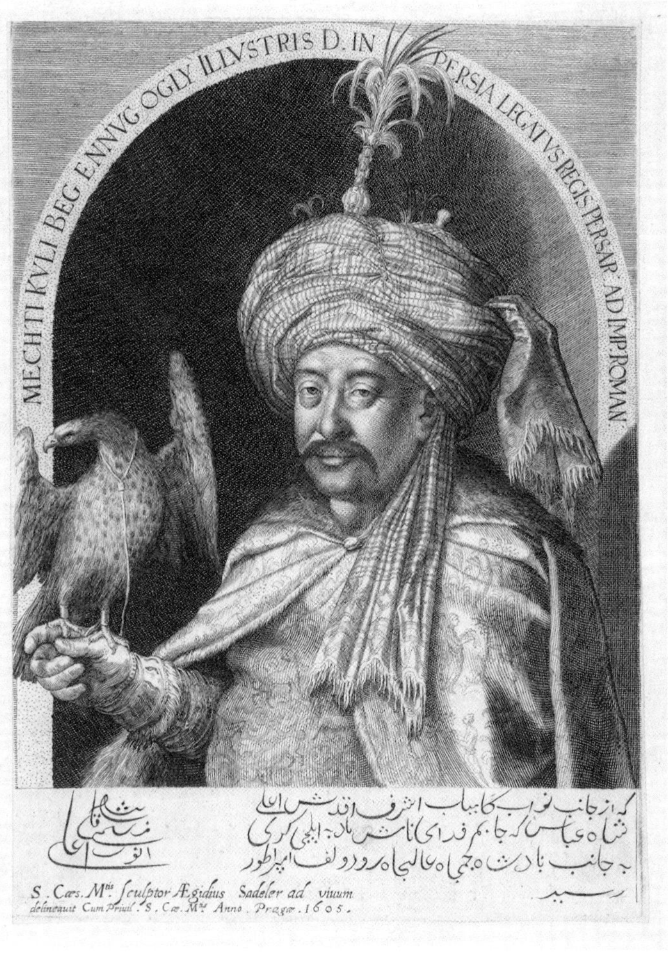

66 Aegidius Sadeler, *Mechti Kuli Beg with Hawk*, 1605, etching.

as a means to initiate mutual diplomatic relations. The animal is not introduced as something foreign, since the technique of falconry was commonly shared in Habsburg Prague as in Persian Isfahan, even if with different cultural symbolism.

The ambassador carrying the hawk speaks not only to the movable medium of images printed on paper but to the movable nature of the content (the hawk) depicted in such images, which was meant for an international audience, not only a Persian or a Habsburg one. It is, in other words, a transcultural image in motion. Forged through the art of falconry, the relations between the two empires and their alliance against the Ottoman Empire were visually conveyed. The print by Sadeler encapsulates the aforementioned thesis: the hawk's aggressive but also obedient nature underlines at once the seriousness of the alliance and its fragility. The print, in matters of medium and content, is a paradigmatic example of visual diplomacy.

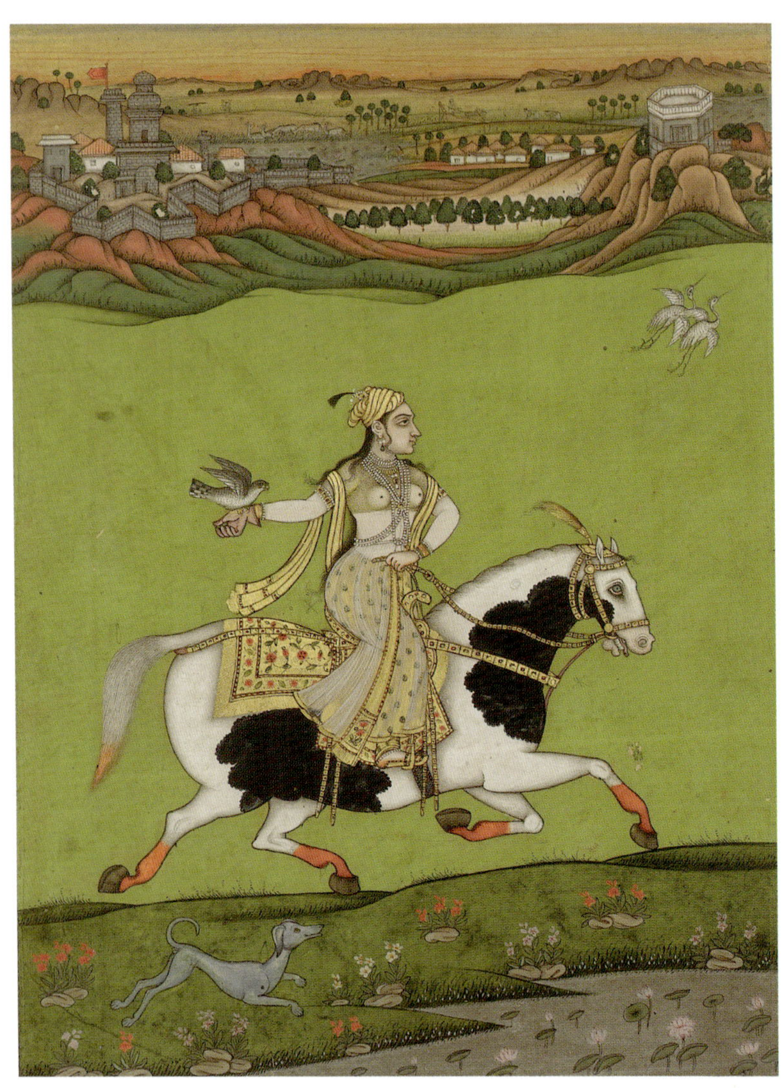

67 Deccan School, *Chand Bibi Hawking*, 18th century, gouache and ink.

CODA

Falconry's Visual Legacy

The engraving by Aegidius Sadeler discussed at the end of the previous chapter is an exemplary demonstration of the visual legacy and power of falconry in the longue durée of history. In other words, while the various aspects and connotations of falconry discussed here were actively at work during the Middle Ages, we should rather think of falconry's ongoing legacy as one of global survival, with distinctly different and asymmetric manifestations, not unlike the practice's transcultural beginnings.

Concepts such as the 'Middle Ages' or the 'Renaissance' are operative terms useful for navigating in time, especially if one considers our own historical distance from those epochs. The problem of defining when a phenomenon begins and when it ends is certainly a complicated one, deeply rooted in methodological and historiographical disputes, some of them continuing today. For example, the fifteenth century encapsulates both the Renaissance and the (Late) Middle Ages (particularly north of the Alps). Let us think of the coexistence of Late Gothic and Renaissance elements in Sandro Botticelli's later work, to name just one famous example.[1]

Many ideas introduced in the previous sections reappear in the early modern period and after, whereas other issues take more concrete shape or are broadened, in particular those concerning the agents of falconry. It is, however, of less interest to show here what has changed in falconry, and more pertinent to reveal how the survival of certain commonplaces took different shapes, especially in regard to falconry's visual power.

One of the main concerns pursued so far is that falconry is also a metaphor for rulership, implicitly connected to the notion of the *cura publica* ('public care', or the common good). An emblem from the collection of Johannes Sambucus (János Zsámboky), the sixteenth-century Hungarian humanist, explicitly establishes this idea in image and word (illus. 68). In the emblem, dating from 1564 and dedicated to the Italian republican humanist Pietro Vettori, we see a nobleman, his left hand resting on a long sword and his right hand holding a lure. In the air, his falcon chases three birds, while a servant standing to his

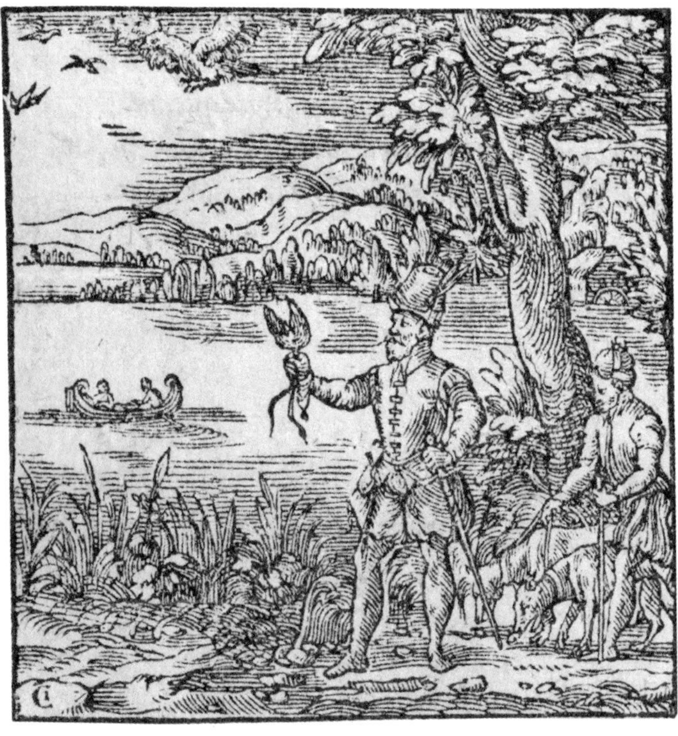

68 'Cura publica', from Johannes Sambucus, *Emblemata*, 4th edn (1576).

right holds two dogs on a leash. The nobleman's virtue, of course, lies in his handling of the hawk and such devices as the lure. The emblem thematizes the relations between falconry, political power and the state. As the *subscriptio* below the image explains, a true ruler, like the falcon, ought to serve the common good:

> I, the falcon . . . [am] totally devoted to hunting. Since long, Nature has attributed this capacity [to me], so that I can serve my masters in the air and gladden them with the prey. No hunger ruins my mind . . . May those [to] whom the public administration leaves no rest, show that they care for the common good rather than for themselves.[2]

Cura publica and the mutual *cura* (care) of master and falcon are clearly interchangeable virtues.

As we have already observed, women, mostly from the aristocracy, engaged heavily in falconry.[3] They used hawks as representational vehicles of power not only in Europe but, for instance, in the Indian subcontinent – a perhaps surprising fact, at least to Western eyes. Chand Bibi, the female Muslim regent of Bijapur (r. 1580–90) and later Ahmednagar (r. 1596–9), in one of the Deccan sultanates, is depicted in several pictures dating from the eighteenth century in which we see her going out hawking and carrying a hawk on her fist (illus. 67).[4] She moves, like an Amazon, through a cultivated land. Ultimately, she was destined to lose her life and kingdom to the mighty Mughal forces of Akbar, but her name became a symbol of resistance against the new empire, and she remained as untamed as her hawks. The image operates with all the classical, one might even say global, iconography of mounted sovereigns hawking. Around 1700, when the Mughal Empire started to decline, Bibi became a popular subject in the Deccan school of painting. A powerful symbol of resistance, her image truly became a circulating form of disobedience.

Certain cultural techniques that the ruler had to learn were passed on from father to son or, as in Bibi's case, from father to daughter. This applied not only to riding a horse, dancing or drawing but, as observed in the case of Philip the Handsome (illus. 30) and his son Charles v, to falconry. The training took years and if stages were skipped, things could go terribly wrong. To take a contemporary example, in 2015 Donald Trump posed for a photo during his presidential campaign. Sitting in his office, he posed holding a bald eagle, symbol of American power, by the name of Uncle Sam. The bird immediately lunged for his famous dyed golden hair. Though Trump later boasted that he had not felt afraid, this was not quite the *cura publica* pictured in Sambucus's emblem.[5]

However, it is not only similarities between falconry in the Middle Ages and the early modern period that are at issue here: there are also major differences. Though commoners had already practised falconry for some time, they began, starting in the late sixteenth century but primarily in the seventeenth century, to be portrayed as falconers and to acquire images connected to hawking.[6] This self-fashioning disposition could be called an 'as if' aristocratic habit, since the regent class imitated the habits of the aristocrats. Social changes and the lack of a powerful aristocracy in the Netherlands did play a crucial part in this process.

During the seventeenth century, Dutch paintings of everyday scenes, still-lifes and landscapes increasingly gained their independence as artistic genres and were frequently produced for a majority that clearly did not belong to the aristocracy. Among those new genres, and certainly also portraits, falconry images were painted in huge numbers – a fascinating example of pictorial mass-mobility and a material manifestation of falconry's visual agency.

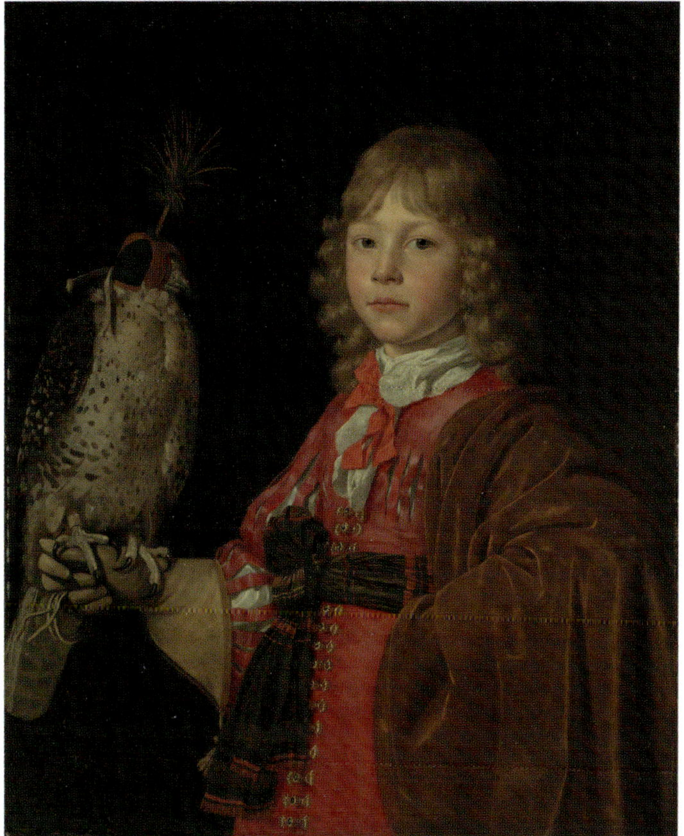

69 Wallerant Vaillant, *Boy with a Falcon*, c. 1643–77, oil on canvas.

Owing to the pedagogical nature of falconry, a number of these images depict children with hawks. Such portraits derive from seventeenth-century upper-class Dutch families with no necessary connection to the aristocracy. A painting by Wallerant Vaillant (1623–1677), for instance, shows a boy in a fancy garment bearing a hooded falcon of great size on his right hand in a confident manner, underlined through his so-called 'Renaissance elbow' pose, with his left hand on his waist, a gesture signalling self-possession (illus. 69).[7] Did the Dutch regents and merchants like to foster analogies between a monarch's rule of his territory and their own capacities as local or regional regents and merchants ruling their companies? Risk-taking in business (as the child is part of a regent family) is juxtaposed with the contingent nature of the hawk and the falconer's supposed mastery of her. *Cura publica* is transformed into a *cura oeconomica*.

However, particularly in the Netherlands, we also witness the aesthetic autonomy of falconry furniture, something already observed in fifteenth-century playing cards or even in the margins of Frederick II's magnum opus. Such an observation speaks not only to the inherent visual power of falconry furniture but to its pictorial fetishization. In dozens of still-lifes, the hood, pictured among lures and falconry bags, is shown in a certain hierarchical, vertical position in relationship to the quarry, even in cases where the hawk itself is absent. The hood implies a meta-political iconography: it is a *pars pro toto*, a self-referential index possessing pictorial agency. What we see is the result of a process: the hawk targets her quarry after her hood is removed. The work of Willem van Aelst (1627–1683), a master in the genre of still-life paintings with game, deftly reveals this hierarchical relation of hood to quarry (illus. 70).[8] The verticality of the hoods upon the dead birds in his *Still-life with Game and Hunting Gear* (1660) underlines their implicit power. The interplay between artificiality and naturalness, between the hawk's absence and the manifestation of its presence through the hood, addresses the core question of simulation (an illusion that alludes to reality) and dissimulation (knowing it is an illusion but behaving as if it is not) for both falconry and imagery.

The Roman senator and author Petronius, as early as the first century AD, referred to the bird catcher as an *artifex*, meaning an artist or craftsperson, and Frederick II also wrote of the 'art' of making birds fly.[9] An artist is like a falconer in that he or she pursues his or her art in a constant dialogue with the image, as the falconer does with the hawk; the critical difference, however, is that the animal has its own will and vitality, which the work of art only suggestively possesses. The hawk's activity and the human–animal interaction in falconry have certain structural resemblances to the way artists work with materials that have an intrinsic agency. To explore their affordances, as well as letting one be guided through them, creates a re-enactment between artist, image and beholder (the subject). This could be said equally for the trinity falconer–hawk–beholder. Last but not least, the landscape is the canvas upon which the art of falconry unfolds, and its topography, as well as the elements, may influence and rapidly change the flights and movements of the *dramatis personae*.

One should perhaps not be surprised, then, that artists have also depicted themselves as falconers, or rather staged themselves as such. However, this tendency only commenced relatively late, starting in the eighteenth century. In James Northcote's *Self Portrait as a Falconer* (1823), a finely clad male figure shown in profile appears in a semi-darkened room (illus. 71).[10] With an elevated arm, he is pointing in the direction of two perches, on each of which a hawk is depicted. One is in motion with open wings and looks towards the man. The other, hooded on the perch, is captured in stillness. A dog accompanies the man and observes the active hawk, which wears jesses and is emphasized through light. The light corresponds with the painting's chiaroscuro values and hence to the question of darkness and light, a question that the hawks are also raising through *kinesis* (motion) and *stasis* (immobility) as well as seeing (the unhooded hawk) and not seeing (wearing the hood as a second skin; its colour partly resembles the hawk's feathers). The gaze of the person who wears a falconer's glove, and seems to own the two hawks, is absorbed. At the same time, the man's gesture is in motion,

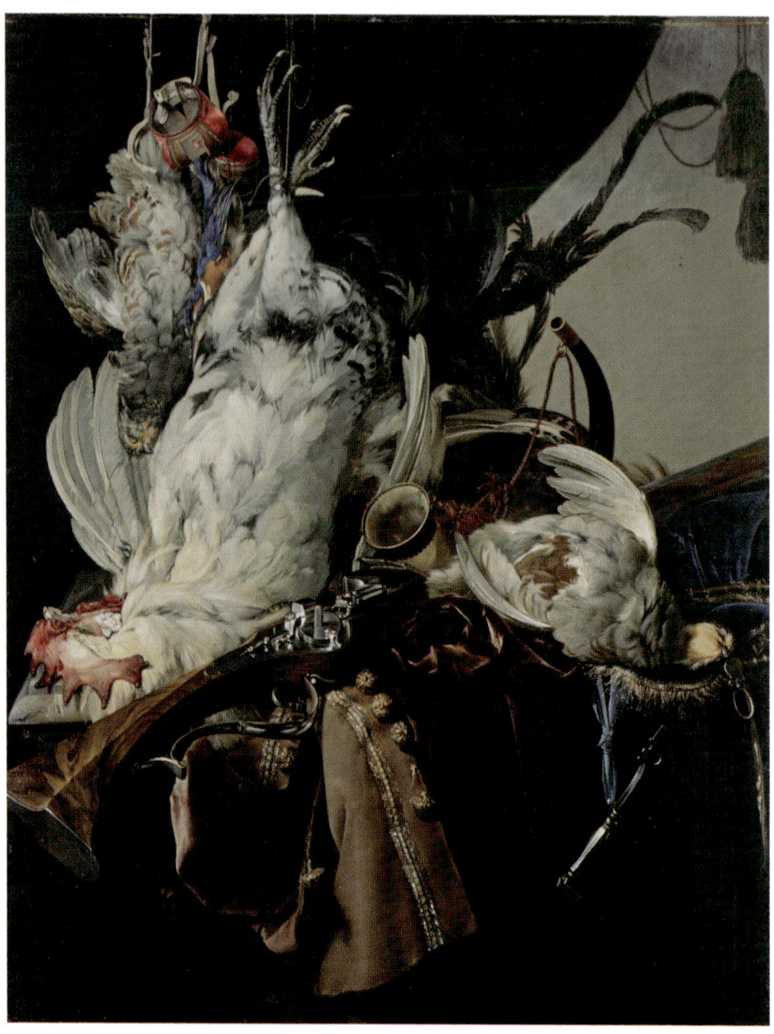

70 Willem van Aelst, *Still-life with Game and Hunting Gear*, 1660, oil on canvas.

whereas his left hand rests on a chair, as if mirroring both the activity of one hawk and the passivity of the other. The male figure is an artist: Northcote has painted himself here as a falconer. One of the basic assumptions of the interaction between falcon and falconer, between image and image-maker, is that vision is a crucial way of perceiving and creating the world. The painting demonstrates how the art of falconry and the art of painting have striking structural resemblances.

Two radically different legacies of medieval falconry in the twentieth century concerning politically oriented iconology, one in Hitler's Germany and the other in the United Arab Emirates

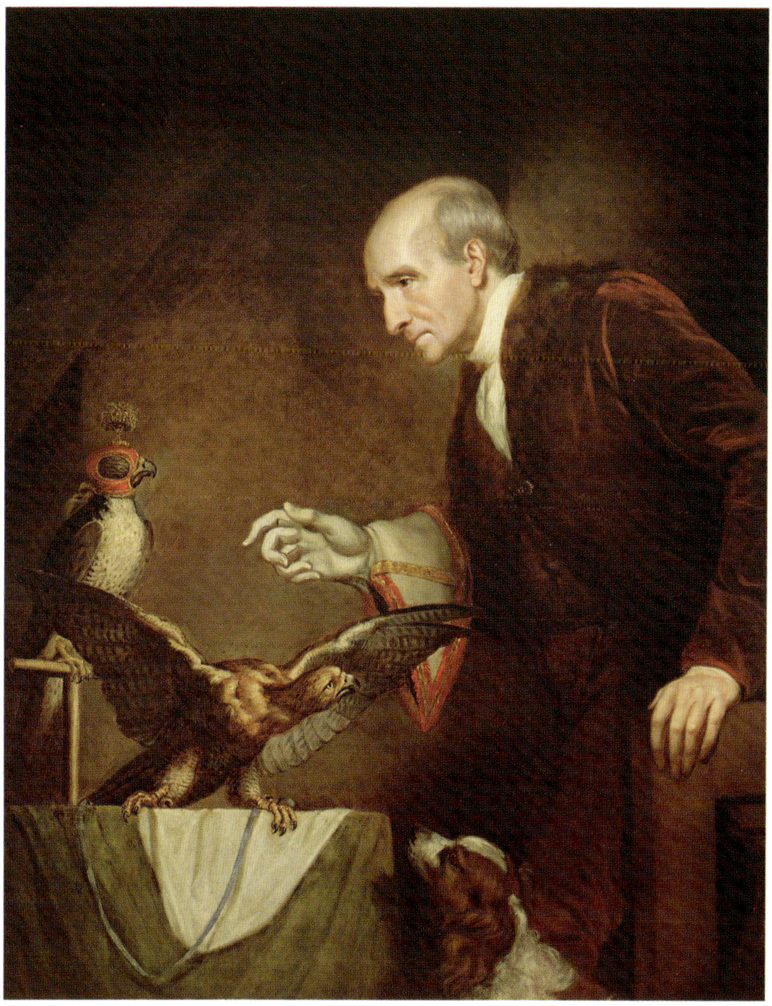

71 James Northcote, *Self Portrait as a Falconer*, 1823, oil on canvas.

during the founding of that state, will be briefly discussed to bring the discussion to a close. In both cases, Frederick II forms the thread of different kinds of ways that the medieval is received in the twentieth century; in the one case as a supposedly uninterrupted Germanic legacy, the Third Reich, and in the other as a transcultural practice that the Germanic emperor imported to Europe from the Arab world.

Falconry during the Third Reich had a powerful visual and aesthetic import, following a period when the practice, at least on a representational level, seemed largely to have been in hibernation in Europe since the late nineteenth century.[11] The relative popularity of falconry in Hitler's Germany was primarily connected to the relationship between two men: Renz Waller (1895–1979) and Hermann Göring (1893–1946).

Renz Waller was a falconer and founding member of the Deutscher Falkenorden (DFO), the national falconers' association, as well as a painter, writer and, in a certain sense, curator.[12] In this way he connects several aspects that are crucial to our story. Waller was president of the DFO not only during the National Socialist era but afterwards, from 1932 to 1957. He curated the falconry section of the Internationale Jagdausstellung (International Hunting Exhibition) held in Berlin in 1937, conceived and organized by Göring, an enthusiastic hunter and the regime's Reichsjägermeister, or Reich Master of the Hunt. Waller has also participated with his own works, depicting either hawks or portraits of falconers who had important positions in the Nazi regime.

Waller, himself a member of the National Socialists, wrote one of the most important books (both within and outside the German-speaking world) on the practice of falconry during the first half of the twentieth century, where he made no verbal mention of any predilection on the part of Hitler's regime for his own practice of falconry or vice versa, although this was perhaps conveyed through his visual arguments, including reproductions of his own works. They appeared in the book without any commentary, as if they were mere neutral illustrations of the practice.[13] In other words, the reactivation of both images and practices with a political and even a Germanic racial legitimization took place with falconry.

Waller designed the DFO's official logo, which is still in use today: a falcon appears in strict profile, facing to the left, in a tondo format and with no further indications concerning falconry (apart from the inscription 'Deutscher Falkenorden', or German Order of Falconry) (illus. 72). Through the use of sharp and raw graphic lines, the falconer-artist formed an equivalent to the harshness and strength of the falcon, also demonstrating an affinity with Nazi aesthetics through certain expressionistic allusions. During the Nazi regime, the badge was accompanied by two swastikas because the DFO was supported by high-ranking Nazis, including many prominent members of the SS and particularly Göring. The latter even posed for a Waller painting as a modern St Hubert, with a falcon on his fist that Waller bequeathed him as a gift. Without Göring's political influence and power, falconry would not have been institutionalized as a propaganda weapon of the regime. He even supported a polar expedition to bring gyrfalcons, the Nordic symbol par excellence, to Germany, as if continuing the already described medieval trade in those luxurious animals. The project did not end well, however, as many of the gyrfalcons died.

The apparent passion of the Nazis for falconry cannot be understood without the party's ideological employment of Frederick II and his Germanic legacy, readjusted as a continuous line of evolution leading to the Third Reich. The catalogue of the 1937 International Hunting Exhibition featured on its cover an Aryan bodybuilder reminiscent of sculptures by state-affiliated artists Arno Breker (1900–1991) or Josef Thorak

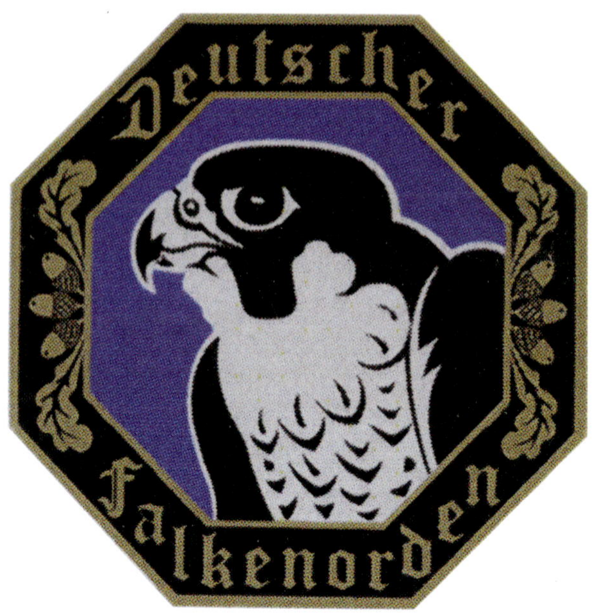

72 Contemporary Deutscher Falkenorden (German Order of Falconry) badge designed by Renz Waller.

(1889–1952) (illus. 73). The sharp-lined, crystalline body of the man carries a hawk and is framed by antlers as heraldic supports, acting as a kind of Germanic tattoo or even hunting trophy.

The falconry section of the exhibition made certain geographical excursions, with displays of falconry equipment from the Indian subcontinent and Arabia as well as, not by coincidence, the collection of the Japanese emperor.[14] The notion of transcultural falconry around the time of Frederick II was visualized with objects deriving either from Indo-Aryan countries or from contemporary allies of the Third Reich like Japan. The importation of certain falconry techniques to Europe by Frederick II was constructed as a visual Germanic legacy supporting the political present.

The example of falconry in the United Arab Emirates, pre-eminent as a practice in the newly founded independent state, is more a case of survival. As a precious heritage and a symbol of power, falconry expresses the economic influence of the UAE on a symbolic level. While it does explicitly occupy a place of memory in the national imagination, the celebration of falconry is not merely oriented towards the past. It has an active potential in forging contemporary Emirati visual culture. This becomes obvious in the volume *Falconry as a Sport: Our Arab Heritage*,

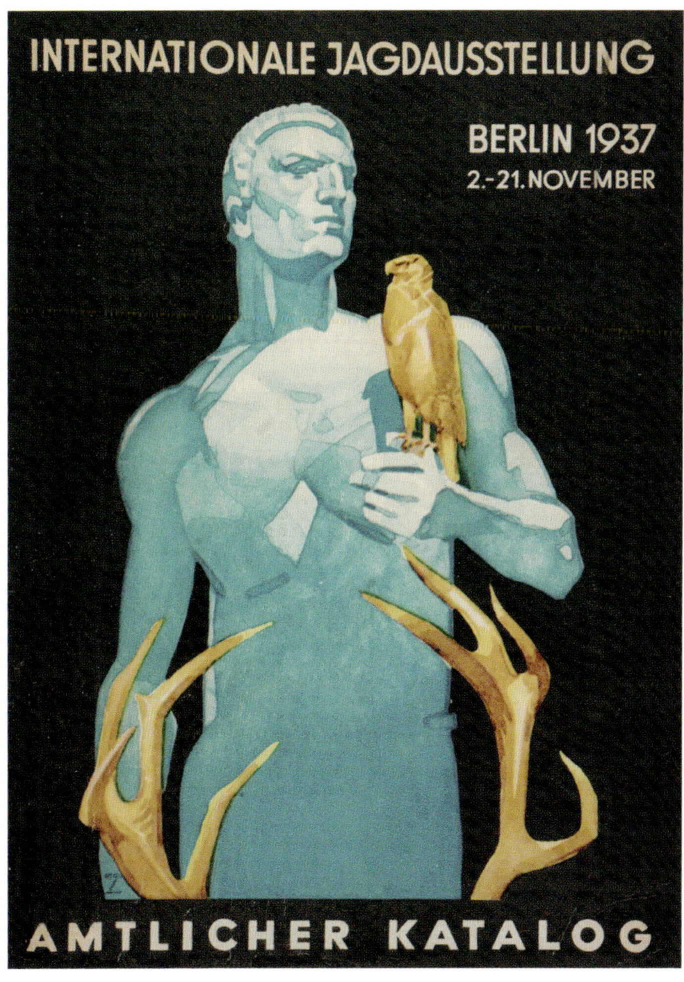

73 Cover of the catalogue from the Internationale Jagdausstellung, 1937.

which was published for the First Falconry Festival in 1976 (in which Renz Waller participated), five years after the founding of the UAE (illus. 74).[15]

Celebrating falconry was a way for the young state to create an identifying figure and make itself known internationally through the organization of a major event. Thus, the festival created visibility for the new state after its declaration of independence from the British in 1971. The falcon was an ideal identifying image, a symbol that would function not only within but outside the borders of the newly established state.

Falconry as a Sport reminds one of Frederick II's *De arte venandi cum avibus*, since Sheikh Zayed bin Sultan Al Nahyan (1918–2004), first president of the UAE and a passionate falconer, was also the author of the book. Just like Frederick, Sheikh Zayed refers explicitly to the analogies between hawking and handling the affairs of state, not least in the sense of a *cura publica*:

> Despite the heavy demands of my task in building up our young state I resolved to meet this request [of writing this book] . . . Some wise kings and rulers have been criticised for their attachment to the hunt on the grounds that it distracts them from affairs of State. They reply that they derive great benefits from their indulgence in it. Not least of these is the knowledge acquired about the state of the land, its progress, development and prosperity, or otherwise.[16]

Falconry reinforces a sense of physical and spiritual community, regardless of the social status of the participants. This aspect is again emphasized by Zayed:

> Another very important factor which led me to prefer falconry was its more sociable aspect. A hunting

> expedition with falcons brings together a group of men . . . The group may include a king, a governor, a prince or a prominent merchant or, again, just an ordinary man who has a house and a family to support, but a love of sport, friendship and a desire for the chase brings them all together . . . Each one feels a sense of release and well-being in both body and soul.[17]

This statement reminds one again of Frederick II. Indeed, Zayed placed himself deliberately within that tradition. Personal practice and communal experience were of central importance for both rulers. Furthermore, Zayed's idea of such a communal experience during falconry expeditions seems to echo Frederick's notion of falconry as a social leveller; as the Holy Roman Emperor wrote:

> The pursuit of falconry enables nobles and rulers worried by the cares of state to find relief in the pleasures of the hunt. The poor, as well as the less noble, may earn some of the necessities of life; and both classes will find in bird life attractive manifestations of the processes of nature.[18]

Both sovereigns shared the idea that falconry is a practice that combines state action, hunting, sport and art. One might therefore argue that not only were Frederick II's falconry practices of interest to Zayed, but they were also essential to the consecration of his image as the falconer-sovereign par excellence, based on a Western visual vocabulary. Zayed, however, did not explicitly mention Frederick because, in his eyes, the latter drew inspiration from falconry practices that he considered to be genuinely Arabic. In this sense, unlike the Germanic emperor, who also transferred knowledge through images, the Emirati royal did not need an intermediary, since falconry is

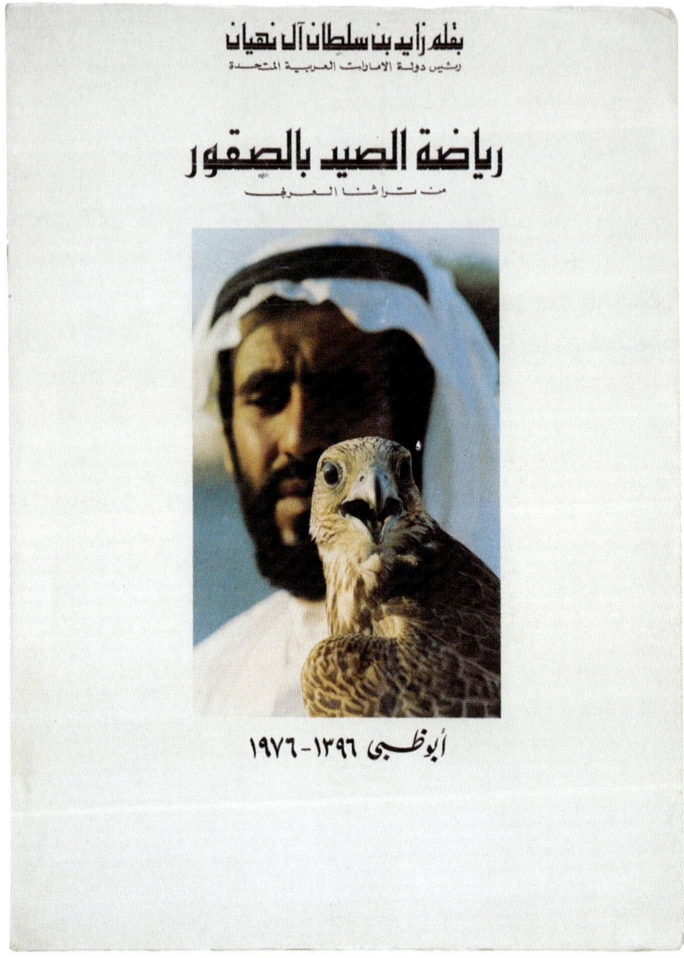

74 Arabic cover of Zayed bin Sultan Al Nahyan, *Falconry as a Sport: Our Arab Heritage* (1976).

part of an uninterrupted Arab heritage. The falcon as a cultural symbol has an astonishing visual agency and is, in itself, a locus of vivid memories.

Although during the early modern period we observe a substantial quantitative and qualitative increase in falconry's visual presence, with the Dutch Republic and England in the fore, from the eighteenth century onwards, and particularly after the French

Revolution, a gradual decline in falconry as a hunting practice is visible, at least among the Western European traditions that have formed the core of the present study.

Falconry as a transcultural practice has undergone major visual transformations, finding representation in miniatures, printmaking, painting and applied arts and, more recently, new media such as photography, film, the Internet and even objects such as drones. While Western film and TV media have visually reflected falcon subject-matter in different ways, it has often created a productive conflict between form and content; between Western traditions, in terms of image and form, and Arabic ones: the subject and the content. Through the evolution of falconry imagery in different media, a unified world has also been visually created that acknowledges local traditions.[19] This visual world exists today thanks to the power and legacy of falconry unleashed during the transcultural Middle Ages.

REFERENCES

Introduction

1 For the notion of agency, see David Freedberg, *The Power of Images: Studies in the History and Theory of Response* (Chicago, IL, 1989); Alfred Gell, *Art and Agency: An Anthropological Theory* (Oxford, 1998); Horst Bredekamp, *Theorie des Bildakts: Frankfurter Adorno Vorlesungen 2007* (Berlin, 2010); Caroline van Eck, *Art, Agency and Living Presence: From the Animated Image to the Excessive Object* (Berlin and Boston, MA, 2015). There are fundamental differences between these books, but this is not a subject for the present context. The Select Bibliography features titles related to the subject, with a focus on English literature as well as recent studies.

2 On the study of falconry's visual representation, see most recently the impressive two volumes of *Raptor on the Fist: Falconry, its Imagery and Similar Motifs throughout the Millennia on a Global Scale*, ed. Oliver Grimm in cooperation with Karl-Heinz Gersmann and Anne-Lise Tropato (Kiel and Hamburg, 2020). For a first attempt to bring together visual culture with falconry, see Yannis Hadjinicolaou, ed., *Visual Engagements: Image Practices and Falconry* (Berlin and Boston, MA, 2020).

3 Helen Macdonald, *Falcon* (London, 2006).

4 John Cummins, *The Hound and the Hawk: The Art of Medieval Hunting* (London, 1988), p. 219; Frederick II, *The Art of Falconry: Being the 'De arte venandi cum avibus' of Frederick II of Hohenstaufen*, ed. Casey A. Wood and F. Marjorie Fyfe (Stanford, CA, 1943), p. 3. The translation of Frederick is the only English edition from 1943. The text is quoted without any corrections.

5 The global impact of falconry today is documented in brilliant photographs in Hossein Amirsadeghi, ed., *Sky Hunters: The Passion of Falconry* (London, 2008).

6 José Manuel Fradejas Rueda, *Literatura cetreta de la Edad media y el Renacimiento español* (London, 1998), p. 8; Baudouin van den Abeele, 'Medieval Latin and Vernacular Treatises on Falconry (11th–16th C.): Tradition, Contents and Historical Interest', in *Raptor and Human: Falconry and Bird Symbolism throughout the*

Millennia on a Global Scale, ed. Karl-Heinz Gersmann and Oliver Grimm (Kiel and Hamburg, 2018), p. 1278.

7 See Frederick II, *The Art of Falconry / Von der Kunst mit Vögeln zu jagen: Das Falkenbuch Friedrichs II. – Kulturgeschichte und Ornithologie*, ed. Mamoun Fansa and Carsten Ritzau, exh. cat., Landesmuseum für Natur und Mensch, Osnabrück (Mainz, 2007); Martina Giese, 'The "De Arte venandi cum avibus" of Emperor Frederick II', in *Raptor and Human*, ed. Gersmann and Grimm, pp. 1459–69.

8 Frederick II, *The Art of Falconry*, pp. 3–4; Robin S. Oggins, *The Kings and Their Hawks: Falconry in Medieval England* (New Haven, CT, 2004), p. 5.

9 Baudouin van den Abeele, *Texte et image dans les manuscrits de chasse médiévaux* (Paris, 2013), pp. 37–8.

10 For a compelling argument about the transnational circulation of ideas and things that is not anchored only in the West, see Michael Edwardes, *East–West Passage: The Travel of Ideas, Arts and Inventions between Asia and the Western World* (London, 1971).

11 'Falconry' is the generic term for the sport and encompasses the phenomenon as a whole, while 'hawking' may be considered synonymous with the actual hunting purpose. Thus, even with falcons, the pursuit of quarry in English has always been called hawking, as in grouse hawking with peregrine falcons. I will therefore be using those terms interchangeably. The same goes for the words 'falcons' and 'hawks'. The genus *Falco* includes falcons and kestrels and although hawks are technically a different family, the word 'hawk' is used in falconry equally.

12 Daniela Boccassini, 'Falconry as Cognitive Dynamics: Self-Training, Imagination and the Recovery of the Feminine', in *Falconry in the Mediterranean Context during the Pre-Modern Era*, ed. Charles Burnett and Baudouin van den Abeele (Geneva, 2021), p. 65.

13 Of special importance here is Martin Warnke, 'Politische Ikonographie', in *Die Lesbarkeit der Kunst: Zur Geistes-Gegenwart der Ikonologie*, ed. Andreas Beyer (Berlin, 1992), pp. 23–8; Uwe Fleckner, Martin Warnke and Hendrik Ziegler, eds, *Handbuch der politischen Ikonographie*, 2 vols (Munich, 2011).

1 Global Beginnings

1 See recently Karl-Heinz Gersmann and Oliver Grimm, 'Introduction, Discussion and Summary – Raptor and Human:

Falconry and Bird Symbolism throughout the Millennia on a Global Scale', in *Raptor and Human: Falconry and Bird Symbolism throughout the Millennia on a Global Scale*, ed. Karl-Heinz Gersmann and Oliver Grimm (Kiel and Hamburg, 2018), pp. 18–25.

2 Lisa Anna Medrow, 'Falkenjagd in Arabien im 8.-13. Jahrhundert', in *Von der Kunst mit Vögeln zu jagen: Das Falkenbuch Friedrichs II. – Kulturgeschichte und Ornithologie*, ed. Mamoun Fansa and Carsten Ritzau, exh. cat., Landesmuseum für Natur und Mensch, Osnabrück (Mainz, 2007), pp. 14–17.

3 Hans Epstein, 'The Origin and Earliest History of Falconry', *Isis*, XXXIV/6 (1943), pp. 497–509; Kurt Lindner, *Beiträge zu Vogelfang und Falknerei im Altertum* (Berlin, 1973), p. 90. Augustine of Hippo indicates that Vandals in North Africa kept hawks and hounds.

4 Aristotle, *Historia animalium* IX, 36, 620b, Loeb Classical Library, www.loebclassics.com, accessed 21 November 2022. Aristotle's description seems to suggest humans working co-operatively with wild hawks. For this geographical area see Dilyana Boteva, 'Birds of Prey in the Visual Texts of Ancient Thrace and Dacia', in *Raptor on the Fist: Falconry, its Imagery and Similar Motifs throughout the Millennia on a Global Scale*, ed. Oliver Grimm in cooperation with Karl-Heinz Gersmann and Anne-Lise Tropato (Kiel and Hamburg, 2020), pp. 337–60.

5 For the Near and Middle East, see Henry Maguire, '"Signs and Symbols of Your Always Victorious Reign": The Political Ideology and Meaning of Falconry in Byzantium', in *Images of the Byzantine World: Visions, Messages and Meanings: Studies Presented to Leslie Brubaker*, ed. Angeliki Lymberopoulou (Farnham, 2011), p. 144; Epstein, 'The Origin and Earliest History of Falconry', p. 501. For China, see Leslie V. Wallace, 'Early Raptor and Falconry Imagery in China: Four Case Studies (10th Century BC until 8th Century AD)', in *Raptor on the Fist*, ed. Grimm, Gersmann and Tropato, pp. 569–86. For India, see Lindner, *Beiträge zu Vogelfang und Falknerei im Altertum*, p. 117; Thomas T. Allsen, *The Royal Hunt in Eurasian History* (Philadelphia, PA, 2006); Richard Francis Burton, *Falconry in the Valley of the Indus* (London, 1852). On Central Asia, see David A. Warburton, 'Birds of Prey and Religion: Aspects of the First 40,000 Years of Early Bird and Human Contact', in *Raptor on the Fist*, ed. Grimm, Gersmann and Tropato, pp. 85–110; Elisabeth von der Osten-Sacken, 'Decorative Raptors, Protective Raptors: Bird Talon Amulets and other Forms of Apotropaic Use of Birds of Prey in the Ancient Near East from the Epipaleolithic to the

Neo-Assyrian period (*c.* 20,000–500 BC)', in *Raptor on the Fist*, ed. Grimm, Gersmann and Tropato, pp. 287–325. Hawks played a significant role in Central Asian art as symbols of power substituting the divine in everyday life, and, more specifically, in religion or myth as political legitimation of the sovereign. An impressive figure of a hawk of some kind is known from the Gonur Depe necropolis in today's Turkmenistan. It dates from between the third and the middle of the second millennium BC. However, like in Egypt, there are no written records or artefacts documenting the pursuit of falconry around this period. See Matthias Wemhoff and Manfred Nawroth, eds, *Margiana: Ein Königreich der Bronzezeit in Turkmenistan*, exh. cat., Neues Museum Berlin (2018), pp. 144–5 and p. 207.

6 Warburton, 'Birds of Prey and Religion', p. 88.

7 Wallace, 'Early Raptor and Falconry Imagery in China', p. 571.

8 See, for instance, Epstein, 'The Origin and Earliest History of Falconry', p. 497.

9 Helen Macdonald, *Falcon* (London, 2006), p. 55.

10 On the power of images in antiquity and the self-representation of Roman sovereigns as Hercules: Paul Zanker, *The Power of Images in the Age of Augustus* (Ann Arbor, MI, 1988).

11 See Johannes Nolle, 'Birds of Prey on Greek and Roman Coins: Symbols of Superhuman Power, Manifestations of Gods, and Heaven's Messengers', in *Raptor on the Fist*, ed. Grimm, Gersmann and Tropato, pp. 387–401.

12 Brunno Overlaet, 'Late Pre-Islamic Raptor Imagery from South-East Arabia', in *Raptor on the Fist*, ed. Grimm, Gersmann and Tropato, pp. 349–446.

13 Austen Henry Layard, *Discoveries among the Ruins of Nineveh and Babylon* (London, 1853). See Joshua Hammer, *The Falcon Thief: A True Tale of Adventure, Treachery, and the Hunt for the Perfect Bird* (New York, 2020), p. 31.

14 Layard, *Discoveries among the Ruins*, p. 413.

15 Allsen, *The Royal Hunt in Eurasian History*, p. 58. See Karin Reiter, 'Falconry in the Ancient Orient? I. A Contribution to the History of Falconry', and 'II. The Sources', in *Raptor and Human*, ed. Gersmann and Grimm, pp. 1631–58.

16 Jenny Vorys Canby, 'Falconry (Hawking) in Hittite Lands', *Journal of Near Eastern Studies*, LXI/3 (2002), pp. 161–201.

17 See 'Forgotten Kingdoms: From the Hittite Empire to the Arameans', 2 May–12 August 2019, Louvre, www.louvre.fr, accessed 8 December 2022.

18 Canby, 'Falconry (Hawking) in Hittite Lands', pp. 167–8.

19 See Macdonald, *Falcon*, p. 84; Gersmann and Grimm, 'Introduction, Discussion and Summary', in *Raptor and Human*, ed. Gersmann and Grimm, pp. 18–25.

20 Macdonald, *Falcon*, p. 55.

21 During active falconry, hawks attack and take the quarry themselves. However, they could also be used passively to subdue other birds and animals by their presence alone – the implicit threat they posed to natural prey species – which would allow fowlers to take and/or kill them (with the use of nets, for instance). Lindner, *Beiträge zu Vogelfang und Falknerei im Altertum*, p. 156.

22 Thomas Allsen underlines the lesser importance of hunting in general among the Romans and Greeks. Allsen, *The Royal Hunt in Eurasian History*, pp. 15–16. See also G. Åkerström-Hougen, *The Calendar and Hunting Mosaics of the Villa of the Falconer in Argos: A Study in Early Byzantine Iconography* (Stockholm, 1974).

23 Daniela Boccassini, *Il volo della mente: Falconeria e sofia nel mondo mediterraneo: Islam, Federico II, Dante* (Ravenna, 2003), pp. 49–50.

24 See more recently José Manuel Fradejas Rueda, 'The Depiction of Falconry of Late Roman/Early Byzantine Mosaics', in *Raptor on the Fist*, ed. Grimm, Gersmann and Tropato, pp. 519–34.

25 Ibid., p. 522.

26 Florian Hurka, 'Falconry and Similar Forms of Hunting According to Ancient Greco-Roman Sources', in *Raptor and Human*, ed. Gersmann and Grimm, p. 693. This is practically repeated by Bishop Sidonius Apollinaris (AD 431–487).

27 Quoted after Epstein, 'The Origin and Earliest History of Falconry', p. 505.

28 Takayo Kaku, 'Ancient Japanese Falconry from an Archaeological Point of View with a Focus on the Early Period (5th to 7th Centuries AD)', in *Raptor and Human*, ed. Gersmann and Grimm, pp. 1919–36; Yuji Mizuno, 'A Symbol of Power: Japanese Falconry Images (8th to 17th Centuries)', in *Raptor on the Fist*, ed. Grimm, Gersmann and Tropato, pp. 969–86.

29 For Central Asia (Mongolia, possibly since the third millennium BC), see Ulambayar Erdenebat, 'A Contribution to the History of Mongolian Falconry', in *Raptor and Human*, ed. Gersmann and Grimm, pp. 587–602. For Korea, see Ho-tae Jeon, 'Falconry in Ancient Korea', in *Raptor and Human*, ed. Gersmann and Grimm, pp. 1891–1918.

30 Maguire, 'Signs and Symbols of Your Always Victorious Reign'.
31 Maria Bergamo, *Alessandro, il cavaliere, il Doge: Le placchette profane della Pala d'oro di San Marco* (Rome, 2022).
32 Andreas Külzer, 'Raptor and Falconry Images in the Byzantine Empire', in *Raptor on the Fist*, ed. Grimm, Gersmann and Tropato, pp. 535–55.
33 Medrow, 'Falkenjagd in Arabien im 8.-13. Jahrhundert', p. 15; Javier Ceballos, *Falconry: Celebrating a Living Heritage* (Dubai, 2009), pp. 146–7.
34 Eric J. Goldberg, *In the Manner of the Franks: Hunting, Kingship and Masculinity in Early Medieval Europe* (Philadelphia, PA, 2020), p. 151.
35 Epstein, 'The Origin and Earliest History of Falconry', pp. 506–7.
36 Anna Akasoy, 'The Influence of the Arabic Tradition of Falconry and Hunting on Western Europe', in *Islamic Crosspollinations: Interactions in the Medieval Middle East*, ed. James Montgomery, Anna Akasoy and Peter E. Pormann (Oxford, 2007), p. 54. See also Anna Akasoy, 'Falconry in Arabic Literature: From its Beginnings to the Mid-9th Century', in *Raptor and Human*, ed. Gersmann and Grimm, pp. 1769–91.
37 Dafydd Jenkins, 'Hawk and Hound: Hunting in the Laws of Court', in *The Welsh King and His Court*, ed. T. M. Charles-Edwards, Morfydd E. Owen and Paul Russell (Cardiff, 2000), pp. 262–4.
38 Akasoy, 'The Influence of the Arabic Tradition of Falconry'; Guglielmo de Giovanni Centelles, 'Astori, Sparvieri e Girifalchi nel Mediterraneo Medievale', in *Annali della pontificia insigne Accademia di Belle Arti e Lettere dei virtuosi al Pantheon*, XIV (2014), p. 117.

2 Human–Animal Interaction: Training and Tools

1 Frederick II, *The Art of Falconry: Being the 'De arte venandi cum avibus' of Frederick II of Hohenstaufen*, ed. Casey A. Wood and F. Marjorie Fyfe (Stanford, CA, 1943), p. 6.
2 Helen Macdonald, *H is for Hawk* (London, 2014), pp. 113–14 and p. 83. See more recently Herman Roodenburg, '"Still be Mindeful on You": Hints of Human–Falcon Empathy in Late Medieval and Early Modern Europe', in *Visual Engagements: Image Practices and Falconry*, ed. Yannis Hadjinicolaou (Berlin and Boston, MA, 2020), pp. 53–60.
3 In a seventeenth-century source we read the following: 'it is necessary for everyone who has charge of hawks to feel as much

affection for them and to take care of them as a nurse does for her child.' John Loft, ed., *The Mirror of Falconry by Pierre Harmont and The Falconry of Francois de Saincte Aulaire* (Louth, 2013), p. 23.

4 John Cummins, *The Hound and the Hawk: The Art of Medieval Hunting* (London, 1988), p. 202.

5 Quoted in Robin S. Oggins, *The Kings and Their Hawks: Falconry in Medieval England* (New Haven, CT, 2004), p. 25.

6 Baudouin van den Abeele, *Texte et image dans les manuscrits de chasse médiévaux* (Paris, 2013), p. 92.

7 Anna Akasoy, 'The Influence of the Arabic Tradition of Falconry and Hunting on Western Europe', in *Islamic Crosspollinations: Interactions in the Medieval Middle East*, ed. James Montgomery, Anna Akasoy and Peter E. Pormann (Oxford, 2007), pp. 57–8.

8 Cummins, *The Hound and the Hawk*, p. 2. Cristina Arrigoni Martelli, 'Flying High in Lombard Skies: Falconry in Sforza Milan', in *Falconry in the Mediterranean Context during the Pre-Modern Era*, ed. Charles Burnett and Baudouin van den Abeele (Geneva, 2021), pp. 39–59.

9 Giancarlo Malacarne, *Lords of the Sky: Falconry in Mantua at the Time of the Gonzagas* (Bologna, 2011), p. 32.

10 Helen Macdonald, *Falcon* (London, 2006), p. 23.

11 Akasoy, 'The Influence of the Arabic Tradition of Falconry', p. 47.

12 Rachel Parikh, '"The King's Boon Companion": Falconry in Mughal Imperial Portraiture from Akbar to Azam Shah, 1556–1707', in *Raptor on the Fist: Falconry, its Imagery and Similar Motifs throughout the Millennia on a Global Scale*, ed. Oliver Grimm in cooperation with Karl-Heinz Gersmann and Anne-Lise Tropato (Kiel and Hamburg, 2020), p. 904.

13 Frederick II, *The Art of Falconry*, p. 369. It is important to note here that 'waiting on' is a structure in which the agents of the flight – falcon, falconer, dogs and indeed the quarry – are all constantly moving between passivity and activity.

14 Renz Waller, *Der Falke ist mein Gesell: Ein Leben für Falk und Habicht* (Melsungen, 1973), p. 163. This cooperation (and indeed 'punishment') may also happen when dogs are used in hawking other than the waiting-on flight: for instance, pointers might be used to find and flush pheasants for goshawks.

15 See Bruno Latour, *Reassembling the Social: An Introduction to Actor-Network-Theory* (Oxford, 2007).

16 Markus Wild and Dominik Perler, eds, *Der Geist der Tiere: Philosophische Texte zu einer aktuellen Diskussion* (Frankfurt, 2005).

17 Macdonald, *Falcon*, p. 32.
18 Arthur MacGregor, *Animal Encounters: Human and Animal Interaction in Britain from the Norman Conquest to World War One* (London, 2012), p. 186.
19 Marcelle Pitt, *The Country Sportsman's Quotation Book: A Sporting Companion* (London, 1992), p. 55. Peter Hühn and Jens Kiefer, 'W. B. Yeats: The Second Coming', in Peter Hühn and Jens Kiefer, *The Narratological Analysis of Lyric Poetry* (Berlin, 2005), pp. 177–86.
20 Michael Tomasello, *A Natural History of Human Thinking* (Cambridge, MA, and London, 2014).
21 Ibid., p. ix.
22 Terence Clark and Muawiya Derhalli, *Al-Mansur's Book on Hunting* (Warminster, 2001), p. 110.
23 Frederick II, *The Art of Falconry*, p. 248.
24 Timothy B. Husband, *The World in Play: Luxury Cards, 1430–1540* (New York, 2016), p. 26.
25 Kurt Lindner, *Beiträge zu Vogelfang und Falknerei im Altertum* (Berlin, 1973), p. 115. Janet Nelson spoke of the virtue of collaboration in relation to the royal hunt as being a political lesson. Quoted in Thomas T. Allsen, *The Royal Hunt in Eurasian History* (Philadelphia, PA, 2006), p. 201.
26 Frederick II, *The Art of Falconry*, p. 6.
27 Michael Menzel, 'Die Jagd als Naturkunst: Zum Falkenbuch Kaiser Friedrichs II', in *Natur im Mittelalter: Konzeptionen, Erfahrungen, Wirkungen*, ed. Peter Dilg (Berlin, 2003), pp. 355–7.
28 Thomas Nagel, 'What Is it Like to Be a Bat?', *Philosophical Review*, LXXXIII/4 (October 1974), pp. 435–50.
29 Quoted in Malacarne, *Lords of the Sky*, p. 239. See Olaf B. Rader, *Friedrich II: Der Sizilianer auf dem Kaiserthron, Eine Biographie* (Munich, 2010), pp. 308–9; Christine Kleiter and Gerhard Wolf, 'The Falcon, the Eagle and the Owl: Raptors' and Falconers' Gaze between Practice, Theory and Art(s)', in *Visual Engagements*, ed. Hadjinicolaou, p. 187.
30 Frederick II, *The Art of Falconry*, p. 151.
31 Aristotle, *De anima*, II, 2,413b.
32 Frederick II, *The Art of Falconry*, p. 61. Baudouin van den Abeele, *La Fauconnerie au Moyen Âge: Connaissance, affaitage et médecine des oiseaux de chasse d'apres les traités latins* (Paris, 1994), pp. 200–202.
33 Frederick II, *The Art of Falconry*, p. 171.

34 Ibid.

35 Quoted in Anna Akasoy, 'The "Founding Fathers" of Falconry According to Medieval Arabic Literature', in *Falconry in the Mediterranean Context*, ed. Burnett and Van den Abeele, p. 35.

36 Frederick II, *The Art of Falconry*, p. 243.

37 See recent general surveys with falconry examples: Alison Langdon, ed., *Animal Languages in the Middle Ages: Representations of Interspecies Communication* (London, 2019).

38 Frederick II, *The Art of Falconry*, pp. 243–4.

39 A further acoustic trace for the falconer were the hawk's bells, worn generally on the legs or tail.

40 Quoted in Charles Burnett, 'Master Theodore, Frederick II's Philosopher', in *Federico II e le nuove culture: Atti del XXXI Convegno storico internationale, Todi, 9–12 ottobre 1994, Spoleto, Centro Italiano di Studi sull'alto Medioevo* (Spoleto, 1995), pp. 276–7.

41 Daniela Boccassini, 'Falconry as Royal *Delectatio*: Understanding the Art of Taming and its Philosophical Foundations in 12th- and 13th-Century Europe', in *Raptor and Human: Falconry and Bird Symbolism throughout the Millennia on a Global Scale*, ed. Karl-Heinz Gersmann and Oliver Grimm (Kiel and Hamburg, 2018), p. 377. See Adelard of Bath, *Conversations with His Nephew: On the Same and the Different – Questions on Natural Science and on Birds*, ed. Charles Burnett et al. (Cambridge, 1998), pp. 238–41.

42 Hoods were also used on, for instance, trained cheetahs.

43 See Frederick II, *The Art of Falconry*, p. 208; Oggins, *The Kings and Their Hawks*, p. 26.

44 James West Nelson, *Hoods, Hooding and Hoodmaking* (Sheridan, WY, 2016).

45 MacGregor, *Animal Encounters*, p. 182; Thor Hanson, *Feathers: The Evolution of a Natural Miracle* (New York, 2011). See Monika Wagner, 'Leather and Feather: Material Interactions in the Art of Falconry', in *Visual Engagements*, ed. Hadjinicolaou, pp. 108–23.

46 Malacarne, *Lords of the Sky*, p. 112.

47 Frederick II, *The Art of Falconry*, pp. 139–40; Michael Lewis and Ian Richardson, *Inscribed Vervels: A Corpus and Discussion of Late Medieval and Renaissance Hawking Rings Found in Britain* (Oxford, 2019), p. 1.

48 Oggins, *The Kings and Their Hawks*, p. 111; Lewis and Richardson, *Inscribed Vervels*, p. 2.

49 See for instance Richard Almond, 'Hunting from the Fist: Looking at Hawking and Falconry in Late Medieval England (1000–1500)

through Art History', in *Raptor and Human*, ed. Gersmann and Grimm, pp. 1125–6.

50 Horst Bredekamp, *Image Acts: A Systematic Approach to Visual Agency*, trans. Elizabeth Clegg (Berlin and Boston, MA, 2018), pp. 37–63. Various objects from the Middle Ages bear inscriptions in the first person singular and are discussed in terms of visual agency.

51 See Cummins, *The Hound and the Hawk*, p. 188.

52 Frederick II, *The Art of Falconry*, pp. 225 and 227.

53 Ibid., pp. 237 and 242.

54 Even the jesses and the leash had an autonomous, visual quality, like in the translation of *De arte venandi cum avibus* from Lorraine that belonged to John the Fearless around 1310. See Baudouin van den Abeele, 'Horns, Falcon Hoods, Books and Tapestries: Hunting Culture in the 1420 Inventory of John the Fearless Duke of Burgundy', in *Animals in Text and Textile: Storytelling in the Medieval World*, Riggisberger Berichte 23, ed. Evelin Wetter and Kathryn Starkey (2019), p. 246. Van den Abeele does not take the aspect of visual autonomy into account.

55 Herwarth Rottgen, 'Das Ambraser Hofjagdspiel', in *Jahrbuch der Kunsthistorischen Sammlungen in Wien*, LVII (1961), pp. 39–68.

56 See Detlef Hoffmann, *Kultur und Kunstgeschichte der Spielkarte* (Marburg, 1995), pp. 41–2. See also Wilfried Seipel, ed., *Herrlich Wild: Höfische Jagd in Tirol*, exh. cat., Kunsthistorisches Museum Vienna (2004), p. 140; Husband, *The World in Play*.

57 See Roodenburg, '"Still be Mindeful on You"', pp. 53–60.

58 Annette Hoffmann, 'Peacock Feathers and Falconry in the Book of Hours of Engelbert of Nassau', in *Images Take Flight: Feather Art in Mexico and Europe, 1400–1700*, ed. Alessandra Russo, Gerhard Wolf and Diane Fane (Munich, 2015), pp. 156–77.

59 Hans Ulrich Gumbrecht, *In Praise of Athletic Beauty* (Cambridge, MA, 2006).

60 David Freedberg and Vittorio Gallese, 'Motion, Emotion and Empathy in Aesthetic Experience', *Trends in Cognitive Science*, XI/5 (2007), pp. 37–61.

61 Macdonald, *H is for Hawk*, p. 109.

3 Power and Aristocracy

1 See for instance Salvatore Settis, Walter Cupperi and Jadranka Bentini, eds, *The Palazzo Schifanoia in Ferrara* (Modena, 2008).

2 Quoted in John Cummins, *The Hound and the Hawk: The Art of Medieval Hunting* (London, 1988), p. 208. See also Pedro López de Ayala, *Traité de fauconnerie et d'autres oiseaux de vol*, ed. Michel Garcia (Geneva, 2018).

3 Vera Henkelmann, 'The Falcon and its Significance in Depictions of Courtly Love on Late Medieval Mirror Cases (14th Century) from Western European Workshops', in *Raptor on the Fist: Falconry, its Imagery and Similar Motifs throughout the Millennia on a Global Scale*, ed. Oliver Grimm in cooperation with Karl-Heinz Gersmann and Anne-Lise Tropato (Kiel and Hamburg, 2020), pp. 763–95.

4 Quoted in Baudouin van den Abeele, 'Falconry in Old French Literature', in *Raptor and Human: Falconry and Bird Symbolism throughout the Millennia on a Global Scale*, ed. Karl-Heinz Gersmann and Oliver Grimm (Kiel and Hamburg, 2018), p. 1519.

5 Wilfried Seipel, ed., *Herrlich Wild: Höfische Jagd in Tirol*, exh. cat., Kunsthistorisches Museum Vienna (2004), p. 96.

6 Clifford Geertz, *Negara: The Theater State in Nineteenth Century Bali* (Princeton, NJ, 1980); see also Peter Burke, *The Fabrication of Louis XIV* (New Haven, CT, and London, 1992), p. 7.

7 Martin Warnke, *Political Landscape: The Art History of Nature* (London, 1994).

8 Lothar Voetz, *Der Codex Manesse: Die berühmteste Liederhandschrift des Mittelalters* (Darmstadt, 2018), p. 112. For the English translation see 'Der Von Kürenberg', https://en.wikipedia.org, accessed 21 November 2022.

9 See Ralf Bleile, 'The Rider with a Bird on His Arm: On the Interpretation of the "Rider with Falcon" Motif, Taking the Examples of the Bayeux Tapestry and the Seal of King Canute IV of Denmark', in *Raptor on the Fist*, ed. Grimm, Gersmann and Tropato, pp. 715–38.

10 Olga Karaskova-Henry, 'Mary of Burgundy (1457–1482): Lady with a Hawk', in *Raptor on the Fist*, ed. Grimm, Gersmann and Tropato, pp. 819–34.

11 Dorothea Walz, 'Falkenjagd – Falkensymbolik', in *Codex Manesse*, ed. Elmar Mittler and Wilfried Werner, exh. cat., Heidelberg University Library (1988), p. 365. Around the seal one reads: '*S[igillum] Sophie filie Sancte Elizabet duccisse Brabancie*' (This is the seal of Sophie daughter of Saint Elisabeth Duchess of Brabant).

12 Peter Burke, *The Fortunes of the Courtier: European Reception of Castiglione's 'Cortegiano'* (Cambridge, 1995).

13 On the importance of hunting and falconry in Philip the Handsome's court, see Christoph Niedermann, *Das Jagdwesen am Hoffe Herzog Philipp des Guten von Burgund* (Brussels, 1995).

14 Helen Macdonald, *Falcon* (London, 2006), p. 101.

15 Frederick II, *The Art of Falconry: Being the 'De arte venandi cum avibus' of Frederick II of Hohenstaufen*, ed. Casey A. Wood and F. Marjorie Fyfe (Stanford, CA, 1943), p. 151.

16 See Johan Huizinga, *Homo Ludens: A Study of the Play-Element in Culture* (Boston, MA, 1955); Roger Caillois, *Man, Play and Games*, trans. Meyer Barash (Urbana and Chicago, IL, 2001).

17 Sara Ayres, 'A Mirror for the Prince? Anne of Denmark in Hunting Costume with Her Dogs (1617) by Paul van Somer', *Journal of Historians of Netherlandish Art*, XII/2 (2020), pp. 9–13.

18 Richard Almond, *Medieval Hunting* (Stroud, 2003), pp. 143–66.

19 Quoted in Niedermann, *Das Jagdwesen*, p. 315.

20 Anna Maria D'Achille, 'Qualche riflessione sul Falconiere nel Museo dell'Opera del Duomo di Ravello', *Arte Medievale*, I, ser. 4, VII (2017), p. 143.

21 Barbara Schlieben, 'Wissen am alfonsinischen Hof: Der kastilische Moamin als Beispiel für höfisches Wissen', in *Kulturtransfer und Hofgesellschaft im Mittelalter: Wissenskultur am sizilianischen und kastilischen Hof im 13. Jahrhundert*, ed. Johannes Fried and Gundula Grebner (Berlin, 2008), p. 335.

22 Ibid., p. 336.

23 Niccolò Machiavelli, *Il Principe / Der Fürst*, ed. Philipp Rippel (Stuttgart, 2007), pp. 134–5.

24 Al-Bazyar, *Das Falken und Hundebuch des Kalifen al-Mutawakkil*, ed. Anna Akasoy and Stefan Georges (Berlin, 2005), pp. 35–6. The editors of the treatise ask how it is possible to understand the relationship between hunting, philosophy and sovereignty, when precisely this point was elaborated, as already seen, in several cases in word and image.

25 Terence Clark and Muawiya Derhalli, *Al-Mansur's Book on Hunting* (Warminster, 2001), p. 2.

26 Henry Maguire, '"Signs and Symbols of Your Always Victorious Reign": The Political Ideology and Meaning of Falconry in Byzantium', in *Images of the Byzantine World: Visions, Messages and Meanings: Studies Presented to Leslie Brubaker*, ed. Angeliki Lymberopoulou (Farnham, 2011), p. 141.

27 Macdonald, *Falcon*, pp. 52–3.

28 Quoted in David Horobin, 'The Pen and the Peregrine: Literary Influences on the Development of British Falconry (8th Century to the Present)', in *Raptor and Human*, ed. Gersmann and Grimm, p. 1066.

29 British Museum's Harleian Library, MS 2340.

30 Ibid., p. 1068. Similar links also appear in the Persian *Conference of the Birds* (c. 1177).

31 Michael Menzel, 'Die Jagd als Naturkunst: Zum Falkenbuch Kaiser Friedrichs II.', in *Von der Kunst mit Vögeln zu jagen: Das Falkenbuch Friedrichs II. – Kulturgeschichte und Ornithologie*, ed. Mamoun Fansa and Carsten Ritzau, exh. cat., Landesmuseum für Natur und Mensch, Osnabrück (Mainz, 2007), p. 130.

32 Thomas T. Allsen, *The Royal Hunt in Eurasian History* (Philadelphia, PA, 2006), p. 8. See in general Werner Rösener, 'Der König als Jäger: Antike Einflüsse auf die herrschaftliche Jagd im Mittelalter', in *Die Jagd der Eliten in der Erinnerungskulturen von der Antike bis in die Frühe Neuzeit*, ed. Wolfram Martini (Göttingen, 2000), pp. 15–37.

33 Baudouin van den Abeele, 'Le Faucon sur la main: Un parcours iconographique médiéval', in *La chasse au Moyen Âge: Société, traités, symbols*, ed. Agostino Paravicini Bagliani and Baudouin van den Abeele (Florence, 2000), pp. 97–109.

34 Ernst Kantorowicz, *The King's Two Bodies: A Study in Medieval Political Theology* (Princeton, NJ, 1957).

35 It is no coincidence that in personifications of the air one finds many references to falconry.

36 Warnke, *Political Landscape*, chapter 'Hills and Castles', pp. 39–52.

37 See Tanja Michalsky, 'Gaining Insight through a Bird's Eye View: On the Chorography of Naples in the Early Modern Era', in *Visual Engagements: Image Practices and Falconry*, ed. Yannis Hadjinicolaou (Berlin and Boston, MA, 2020), pp. 272–6.

38 Andreas F. Beitin, 'Imagination, Elevation, Battlefield Automation: From the Elevated View to Battle Drones', in *Mapping Spaces: Networks of Knowledge in 17th Century Landscape Painting*, ed. Ulrike Gehring and Peter Weibel, exh. cat., ZKM Karlsruhe (Munich, 2014), p. 461. See also Jeanne Haffner, *The View from Above: The Science of Social Space* (Cambridge, MA, 2013).

39 Giancarlo Malacarne, *Lords of the Sky: Falconry in Mantua at the Time of the Gonzagas* (Bologna, 2011), p. 155.

40 M. Minovi, ed., *Nowruznama Pseudo-Khayyam* (Tehran, 1933), p. 56, quoted in Touraj Daryaee and Soodabeh Malekzadeh,

'Falcons and Falconry in Pre-Modern Persia', in *Raptor and Human*, ed. Gersmann and Grimm, p. 1805.
41 See Matthew Knox Averett, 'Becoming Giorgio Cornaro: Titian's *Portrait of a Man with a Falcon*', *Zeitschrift für Kunstgeschichte*, LXXIV/4 (2011), p. 561.
42 Baldassare Castiglione, *The Book of the Courtier* (Garden City, NY, 1959), p. 319.
43 See for instance Deirdre Jackson, *Lion* (London, 2010).
44 Maguire, 'Signs and Symbols of Your Always Victorious Reign', p. 140.
45 Hossein Amirsadeghi, ed., *Sky Hunters: The Passion of Falconry* (London, 2008), p. 39.
46 Quoted in Anna Akasoy, 'The Influence of the Arabic Tradition of Falconry and Hunting on Western Europe', in *Islamic Crosspollinations: Interactions in the Medieval Middle East*, ed. James Montgomery, Anna Akasoy and Peter E. Pormann (Oxford, 2007), p. 53.
47 Ibid., p. 51.
48 On rituals: Barbara Stollberg-Rilinger, *Rituale* (Frankfurt, 2019); Pierre Bourdieu, *Language and Symbolic Power* (Oxford, 1992).
49 S. M. Oberhelman, *The Oneirocriticon of Achmet* (Lubbock, 1991), p. 239. Maguire, 'Signs and Symbols of Your Always Victorious Reign', p. 141. Achmet, who claims to be the dream interpreter of Mamun, the caliph of Babylon, explains that the treatise 'was written to provide his master with a convenient . . . compendium of dream symbols, with their various interpretative meanings, so that his master could prognosticate future events'. Oberhelman, *The Oneirocriticon of Achmet*, p. 11.
50 Maguire, 'Signs and Symbols of Your Always Victorious Reign', p. 141.
51 Quoted in Giorgio Agamben, *Herrschaft und Herrlichkeit: Zur theologischen Genealogie von Ökonomie und Regierung* (Berlin, 2010), pp. 89–91.
52 Ibid., p. 90.
53 For this idea in general see Louis Marin, *The Portrait of the King* (Minneapolis, MN, 1988), whose prime example, however, is Louis XIV.
54 Alfred P. Smyth, *The Medieval Life of King Alfred the Great: A Translation and Commentary on the Text Attributed to Asser* (Basingstoke, 2002), p. 34. See Robin S. Oggins, *The Kings and Their Hawks: Falconry in Medieval England* (New Haven, CT, 2004),

p. 40; Martina Giese, 'Evidence of Falconry on the European Continent and in England, with an Emphasis on the 5th to 9th Centuries: Historiography, Hagiography and Letters', in *Raptor and Human*, ed. Gersmann and Grimm, p. 1478.

55 Linda Koch, 'Power, Prophecy, and Dynastic Succession in Early Medici Florence: The Falcon Impresa of Piero di Cosimo de' Medici', *Zeitschrift für Kunstgeschichte*, LXXIII/4 (2010), p. 512.

56 Quoted in Oggins, *The Kings and Their Hawks*, p. 110.

57 Katharina Fietze, *Im Gefolge Dianas: Frauen und höfische Jagd im Mittelalter (1200–1500)* (Cologne, Vienna and Weimar, 2005), p. 70.

58 Cummins, *The Hound and the Hawk*, p. 222.

59 Jochen Sander, *Die Magie der Dinge: Stillebenmalerei 1500–1800*, exh. cat., Städel Museum, Frankfurt, and Kunstmuseum Basel (Ostfildern, 2008), p. 220.

60 Quoted in Oggins, *The Kings and Their Hawks*, p. 73.

61 Quoted ibid., p. 83.

62 Cadge carriers (often termed 'cadgers') were people who held the frames known as 'cadges', on which multiple hawks could be carried to or in the field by one person.

63 Cummins, *The Hound and the Hawk*, p. 2.

64 Quoted ibid., p. 202.

65 Malacarne, *Lords of the Sky*, p. 14.

66 Frederick II, *The Art of Falconry*, p. 150.

67 Ibid., pp. 150–51.

68 Horst Bredekamp, *Der schwimmende Souverän: Karl der Große und die Bildpolitik des Körpers. Eine Studie zum schematischen Bildakt* (Berlin, 2014), pp. 26–42.

69 Frederick II, *The Art of Falconry*, p. 151.

70 Malacarne, *Lords of the Sky*, p. 14.

71 Frederick II, *The Art of Falconry*, p. 6. The differentiation between common hunting and falconry occurs also in treatises such as *The Bokys of Haukyng and Huntynge*, Book of St Albans, 15th C.

72 Ibid., p. 152.

73 Ibid., p. 141.

74 See Andreas Beyer, 'Bildnis und Territorium', in *Sprezzatura: Geschichte und Geschichtserzählung zwischen Fakt und Fiktion*, ed. Johannes von Müller, Camillo von Müller and Lukas Burkart (Göttingen, 2016), p. 31. Beyer underlines that it is not about the government of a single person, but rather of a communal council.

75 Herfried Münkler, *Politische Bilder: Politik der Metaphern* (Frankfurt, 1994), p. 60.

76 The motto reads: '*senza paura ognúom franco camini, e lavorando semini ciascuno, mentre che tal comuno. Manterra questa donna.*' ('Let everyone go about without fear, and let everyone sow, while this lady rules the land, for she has taken the power from all the guilty.') See Max Seidel, *Dolce Vita: Ambrogio Lorenzettis Porträt des Sieneser Staates* (Basel, 1999), p. 45. The relation to the city and hence to justice makes the fresco's communal function clear. It is a mirror image corresponding to the habit of every Sienese citizen. Nicolai Rubinstein, 'Political Ideas in Sienese Art: The Frescoes by Ambrogio Lorenzetti and Taddeo di Bartolo in the Palazzo Publico', *Journal of the Warburg and Courtauld Institutes*, XXI/3–4 (1958), p. 184; Quentin Skinner, 'Ambrogio Lorenzetti's *Buon Governo* Frescoes: Two Old Questions, Two New Answers', *Journal of the Warburg and Courtauld Institutes*, LXII (1999), pp. 1–28.
77 See Hans Belting, 'Das Bild als Text: Wandmalerei und Literatur im Zeitalter Dantes', in *Malerei und Stadtkultur in der Dantezeit*, pp. 37–9. The connection to the falconers is not made.
78 Anna Rapp Buri and Monica Stucky-Schürer, *Der Flachsland Teppich: Wilde Leute auf der Hirschjagd, Ein Basler Wirkteppich um 1468* (Basel, 1989).
79 Ibid., p. 8.
80 Quoted ibid., p. 12.
81 Ibid., pp. 18–25. The tapestry was a commission for his wedding with Barbara von Breitenlandenberg. Does this allude to a commentary on their new life?
82 Peasants did hunt to survive as an effect of the population's growth, as medieval historian Georges Duby argued. See Allsen, *The Royal Hunt in Eurasian History*, p. 5.
83 Baudouin van den Abeele, 'The Hooded Falcon as an Allegory of Hope (15th–17th Century)', in *Visual Engagements*, ed. Hadjinicolaou, p. 128.
84 Linda Woolley, *Medieval Life and Leisure in the Devonshire Hunting Tapestries* (London, 2002).
85 Larry Feinberg, 'Fra Bartolomeo's Nativity: A Rediscovered High Renaissance Masterpiece', *Art Institute of Chicago Museum Studies*, XXXII/2 (2006), p. 38.
86 Frederick II, *The Art of Falconry*, p. 4. See also Oggins, *The Kings and Their Hawks*, p. 127.

4 East and West Dimensions

1 Christine Göttler and Mia Mochizuki, eds, *The Nomadic Object: The Challenge of World for Early Modern Religious Art* (Leiden and Boston, MA, 2017); Andreas Beyer, Horst Bredekamp, Uwe Fleckner and Gerhard Wolf, eds, *Bilderfahrzeuge. Aby Warburgs Vermächtnis und die Zukunft der Ikonologie* (Berlin, 2018).

2 John Cummins, *The Hound and the Hawk: The Art of Medieval Hunting* (London, 1988), p. 197.

3 Dagmar Oldenthal, *Kaiser Friedrich der Zweite: Über die Kunst mit Vögeln zu jagen* (Frankfurt, 1964), p. 143.

4 Karl Heinz Rueß, ed., *Das Staunen der Welt: Kaiser Friedrich II. von Hohenstaufen, 1194–1250* (Göppingen, 1996), p. 21.

5 See Barbara Drake Boehm, 'A Brilliant Resurrection: Enamel Shrines for Relics in Limoges and Cologne, 1100–1230', in *Treasures of Heaven: Saints, Relics and Devotion in Medieval Europe*, ed. Martina Bagnoli et al., exh. cat., British Museum, London (2011), pp. 149–61.

6 Birgit Blass Simmen, '*Laetentur coeli* oder die byzantinische Hälfte des Himmels: Die *Anbetung der Könige* von Antonio Vivarini und Giovanni d'Alemagna in der Gemäldegalerie in Berlin', *Zeitschrift für Kunstgeschichte*, LXXII (2009), p. 454.

7 J. Russell Sale, 'Birds of a Feather: The Medici Adoration Tondo in Washington', *Burlington Magazine*, CXLIX/1246 (2007), p. 7.

8 Lisa Jardine and Jerry Brotton, *Global Interests: Renaissance Art between East and West* (London, 2000), pp. 43–6; Franco Cardini, *The Chapel of the Magi in Palazzo Medici* (Florence, 2006), pp. 30–31.

9 Simmen, '*Laetentur coeli* oder die byzantinische Hälfte des Himmels', p. 468.

10 Stavros Lazaris, 'Hunting in Byzantium: A Case Study in Falconry', in *Falconry in the Mediterranean Context during the Pre-Modern Era*, ed. Charles Burnett and Baudouin van den Abeele (Geneva, 2021), pp. 261–76.

11 Cardini, *The Chapel of the Magi in Palazzo Medici*, pp. 39 and 82.

12 Linda A. Koch, 'Power, Prophecy and Dynastic Succession in Early Medici Florence: The Falcon Impresa of Piero di Cosimo de' Medici', *Zeitschrift für Kunstgeschichte*, LXXIII/4 (2010), pp. 507–38.

13 Laurence B. Kanter and Pia Palladino, eds, *Fra Angelico*, exh. cat, Metropolitan Museum of Art, New York (New Haven, CT, and London, 2005), p. 278.

14 See for instance Margit Kern, 'Introduction: Transcultural Imaginations of the Sacred: Changing Perceptions of Alterity

in Processes for Transcultural Negotiations', in *Transcultural Imaginations of the Sacred*, ed. Margit Kern and Klaus Krüger (Paderborn, 2019), pp. 19–33.

15 On the term 'hybridity' see the classic study by Homi K. Bhabha, *The Location of Culture* (New York, 1994).

16 For this aspect see the intriguing study by Victor I. Stoichita, *Darker Shades: The Racial Other in Early Modern Art* (London, 2019).

17 Stephen Greenblatt, *Cultural Mobility: A Manifesto* (Cambridge, 2009), p. 16.

18 Hans Belting, *Florence and Baghdad: Renaissance Art and Arab Science* (Cambridge, MA, 2011).

19 See here William Greenwood and Lucien de Guise, eds, *Inspired by the East: How the Islamic World Influenced Western Art*, exh. cat., British Museum, London (2019). See also Montgomery Watt, *The Influence of Islam on Medieval Europe* (Edinburgh, 1972).

20 Anne Goldgar, *Tulipmania: Money, Honor, and Knowledge in the Dutch Golden Age* (Chicago, IL, and London, 2007).

21 See for instance Burnett and Van den Abeele, eds, *Falconry in the Mediterranean Context*.

22 Michael Edwardes, *East–West Passage: The Travel of Ideas, Arts and Inventions between Asia and the Western World* (London, 1971), pp. 88–9.

23 Giovanni Boccaccio, *The Decameron*, trans. J. M. Rigg, vol. II, www.gutenberg.org (2004), pp. 164–5.

24 Ibid.

25 Ibid., p. 165.

26 Ibid., p. 167.

27 Kanter and Palladino, eds, *Fra Angelico*, p. 116. We must mention here that the painting was part of the predella, made up of five different pictures.

28 Ibid.

29 Ibid., p. 278.

30 Al-Bazyar, *Das Falken und Hundebuch des Kalifen al-Mutawakkil*, ed. Anna Akasoy and Stefan Georges (Berlin, 2005), p. 35.

31 Stefan Georges, *Das zweite Falkenbuch Kaiser Friedrichs II* (Berlin, 2008), p. 25.

32 Anna Akasoy, 'The Influence of the Arabic Tradition of Falconry and Hunting on Western Europe', in *Islamic Crosspollinations: Interactions in the Medieval Middle East*, ed. James Montgomery, Anna Akasoy and Peter E. Pormann (Oxford, 2007), p. 54.

33 See Verena Daibner, 'The Falcon and the Ruler: Birds of Prey in the Iconography of Nobility and Leadership in the Art of the Central Arabic Lands from the 1st to 9th Century AH/7th to 15th Century AD', in *Raptor on the Fist: Falconry, its Imagery and Similar Motifs Throughout the Millennia on a Global Scale*, ed. Oliver Grimm in cooperation with Karl-Heinz Gersmann and Anne-Lise Tropato (Kiel and Hamburg, 2020), p. 605.

34 Jean Taralon, *Les Trésors des églises de France* (Paris, 1966), pp. 264–5. Compare Ariane Dor, 'The Suaire de Saint Lazare at Autun: The Story of the Shroud; or, How a Hispano-Moresque Silk became a Relic', in *The Chasuble of Thomas Becket: A Biography*, ed. Avinoam Shalem (Munich, 2017), pp. 126–39. See also Miriam Ali-de-Unzaga, 'Revisiting Andalusi-Umayyad Caliphat Material Culture: The Multiple Biographies of the Embroidery Housed in Oña, Burgos', in *The Chasuble of Thomas Becket*, ed. Shalem, pp. 110–25.

35 Dirk Booms and Peter Higgs, eds, *Sicily: Culture and Conquest*, exh. cat., British Museum, London (2016).

36 The sculpture's provenance can only be traced up to the 1950s, though the restoration report makes it clear it is not a copy. As a high percentage of tin was found, the work cannot originate from an area north of the Alps but rather from the south (Restoration Report, Archive, Bode Museum, Berlin).

37 Almut von Gladiß, *Glanz und Substanz: Metallarbeiten in der Sammlung des Museums für Islamische Kunst* (8. bis 17. Jahrhundert) (Berlin, 2012), p. 23; Gerhard Wolf, *Die Vase und der Schemel: Ding, Bild oder eine Kunstgeschichte der Gefässe* (Dortmund, 2019), pp. 147–61.

38 Von Gladiß, *Glanz und Substanz*, pp. 22–5. Water-dispensing automata derived from aquamanile, which also had the form of birds.

39 Leor Jacobi, 'On the Mighty Hand of the Lord: Medieval Falconry Intrudes upon the Biblical Narrative', in *Raptor on the Fist*, ed. Grimm, Gersmann and Tropato, p. 881.

40 Katrin Kogman-Appel criticized the assumption of a dominant Islamic impact on the miniature; she acknowledged however the existence of Islamic traces, even if the dominant ones are Christian/Jewish, according to her. Katrin Kogman-Appel, *Jewish Book Art between Islam and Christianity: The Decoration of Hebrew Bibles in Medieval Spain* (Leiden, 2004), p. 95.

5 Chivalry, Warfare, Religion

1 See, for this issue, Horst Bredekamp, 'Falconry as a Variant of the Image Act', in *Visual Engagements: Image Practices and Falconry*, ed. Yannis Hadjinicolaou (Berlin and Boston, MA, 2020), pp. 196–212.
2 Giorgio Vasari, *The Lives of the Painters, Sculptors and Architects*, trans. A. B. Hinds, 4 vols (London, 1970), vol. II, pp. 21–2.
3 Franz-Joachim Verspohl, *Michelangelo Buonarroti und Niccolò Machiavelli: Der David, die Piazza, die Republik* (Göttingen, 2003).
4 Herfried Münkler, *Die Begründung des politischen Denkens der Neuzeit aus der Krise der Republik Florenz* (Frankfurt, 2004).
5 See for instance Caroline Campbell, ed., *Love and Marriage in Renaissance Florence: The Courtauld Wedding Chests*, exh. cat., Courtauld Institute of Art, London (2009).
6 Albert the Great, *On Animals: A Medieval Summa Zoologica*, trans. Kenneth F. Kitchell Jr and Irven M. Resnick (Baltimore, MD, 1999), quoted in Robin S. Oggins, *The Kings and Their Hawks: Falconry in Medieval England* (New Haven, CT, 2004), p. 11. See Irven M. Resnick and Kenneth F. Kitchell Jr, *Albertus Magnus and the World of Nature* (London, 2022).
7 Xenophon and Arrianos, *Jagd und Jagdhunde*, ed. Niklas Holzberg and Bernhard Zimmermann (Berlin and Boston, MA, 2018), pp. 27–30.
8 Thomas T. Allsen, *The Royal Hunt in Eurasian History* (Philadelphia, PA, 2006), p. 209.
9 Helen Macdonald, *Falcon* (London, 2006), p. 148. See G. P. Dementiev, *The Gyrfalcon* (Moscow, 1960).
10 Quoted in John Cummins, *The Hound and the Hawk: The Art of Medieval Hunting* (London, 1988), p. 4.
11 Baudouin van den Abeele, 'Falconry in Old French Literature', in *Raptor and Human: Falconry and Bird Symbolism throughout the Millennia on a Global Scale*, ed. Karl-Heinz Gersmann and Oliver Grimm (Kiel and Hamburg, 2018), p. 1529.
12 See 'Falconry', *Guto's Wales*, www.gutorglyn.net/gutoswales/diddordebau-hela-adar.php, accessed 14 November 2022.
13 *Das Staunen der Welt: Das Morgenland und Friedrich II (1194–1250)*, exh. cat., ed. Staatliche Museen zu Berlin Preußischer Kulturbesitz (Berlin, 1995), p. 21.
14 Terence Clark and Muawiya Derhalli, *Al-Mansur's Book on Hunting* (Warminster, 2001), pp. 2–3.
15 Allsen, *The Royal Hunt in Eurasian History*, p. 82.

16 Antonella Sciancalepore, 'Hawks and Knights: (De)constructing Knightly Identity through Animals in French Chivalric Literature (12th–13th Century)', *Reinardus: Yearbook of the International Reynard Society*, XXIX (2017), pp. 120–41. See also Cummins, *The Hound and the Hawk*, p. 190.

17 Sciancalepore, 'Hawks and Knights', p. 122.

18 Van den Abeele, 'Falconry in Old French Literature', p. 1527.

19 W. W. Skeat, ed., *The Complete Works of Geoffrey Chaucer* (Oxford, 1951), pp. 502–3; David Horobin, *Falconry in Literature: The Symbolism of Falconry in English Literature from Chaucer to Marvell* (Surrey, British Columbia, 2004), p. 71.

20 Harald Wolter-von dem Knesebeck, 'Aspekte der höfischen Jagd und ihrer Kritik in Bildzeugnissen des Hochmittelalters', in *Jagd und höfische Kultur im Mittelalter*, ed. Werner Rösener (Göttingen, 1997), pp. 506–7. See also Heinz Peters, 'Miles Christianus oder Falke und Taube', in *Festschrift für Otto von Simson zum 65. Geburtstag*, ed. Lucius Grisebach and Konrad Renger (Frankfurt, Berlin and Vienna, 1977), pp. 54–5.

21 Peters, 'Miles Christianus oder Falke und Taube', p. 56. It is striking that Peters does not make the connection to the pope as falconer, as we shall see later.

22 James Elkins, *The Object Stares Back: On the Nature of Seeing* (San Diego, CA, New York and London, 1997), pp. 11 and 21; Klaus Krüger, 'Art is Aiming for the Eye: Gazes as Arrows in the Early Modern Era', in *Visual Engagements*, ed. Hadjinicolaou, pp. 214–38.

23 Helen Macdonald, *Falcon* (London, 2006), pp. 150–51. See the specific sequence (3:10–4:00) in 'A Canterbury Tale 1944 Part 1', www.youtube.com, accessed 8 November 2022.

24 'The outcome of the fight is uncertain' is the *subscriptio* of an emblem by Joachim Camerarius (1599) that represents the contest between a falcon and a heron.

25 Homer, *The Iliad*, trans. Samuel Butler, Book 22, www.literaturepage.com, accessed 17 November 2022.

26 See for instance Craig Clunas, *Art in China* (Oxford, 2009), pp. 63–4.

27 Francis Klingender, *Animals in Art and Thought: To the End of the Middle Ages* (London, 1971), pp. 410–13.

28 Linda Koch, 'Power, Prophecy, and Dynastic Succession in Early Medici Florence: The Falcon Impresa of Piero di Cosimo de' Medici', *Zeitschrift für Kunstgeschichte*, LXXIII/4 (2010), p. 524. Concerning Dante and falconry see Daniela Boccassini, *Il volo della*

mente: Falconeria e sofia nel mondo mediterraneo: Islam, Federico II, Dante (Ravenna, 2003); Christine Kleiter and Gerhard Wolf, 'The Falcon, the Eagle and the Owl: Raptors' and Falconers' Gaze between Practice, Theory and Art(s)', in *Visual Engagements*, ed. Hadjinicolaou, pp. 184–94.

29 Johan Huizinga, *The Waning of the Middle Ages: A Study of the Forms of Life, Thought, and Art in France and the Netherlands in the Fourteenth and Fifteenth Centuries* (London, 1987), pp. 87–8.

30 Quoted in Dan Jones, *The Plantagenets: The Kings Who Made England* (London, 2012), p. 455.

31 See Bruno Meißner, *Assyrische Jagden: Auf Grund alter Berichte und Darstellungen geschildert (AO 3,2)* (Leipzig, 1911), 5.14. Compare in general, Zainab Bahrani, *Rituals of War: The Body and Violence in Mesopotamia* (New York, 2008).

32 Holm Bevers, ed., *Meister E. S.: Ein Oberrheinischer Kupferstecher der Spätgotik*, exh. cat., Staatliche Graphische Sammlung, Munich (1986).

33 Ibid., pp. 76–7.

34 Erasmus, *Moriae Encomium; or, A Panegyrick upon Folly*, trans. White Kennett (London, 1709), p. 74.

35 Christian Müller, ed., *Hans Holbein d.J.: Die Jahre in Basel, 1515–1532*, exh. cat., Kunstmuseum Basel (Munich, 2006), p. 150.

36 Pilar Silva Maroto, ed., *Bosch: The 5th Centenary Exhibition*, exh. cat., Museo Nacional del Prado, Madrid (2016), pp. 302–12. The Bosch motif reminds us of the detail of a convex mirror from a painting by Petrus Christus in New York (Metropolitan Museum of Art, 1449). The reflection of an aristocrat appears on the mirror together with that of his servant, who holds a hawk as a prestigious object. They go towards a goldsmith's shop, in which a wealthy couple is already being served. In other words, luxury, money and falconry are elements belonging to the same kind of status and habitus. See Maryan W. Ainsworth and Keith Christiansen, eds, *From Van Eyck to Bruegel: Early Netherlandish Painting in the Metropolitan Museum of Art*, exh. cat., Metropolitan Museum of Art, New York (1998), pp. 150–53. In certain *vanitas* iconography, one might find death confronting a falconer. See Huigen Leeflang, Erik Hinterding and Harrie Knol, eds, *The Lure of Falconry / De Verlokkingen van de Valkerij*, exh. cat., Rijksmuseum, Amsterdam (2012), p. 48. In the subject of the three living and the three dead princes, even the profane sovereigns are not spared from death, another important aspect of the 'Dance of Death' as a subject.

Several images dating from the end of the thirteenth century onwards depict the three living princes carrying hawks. For this particular iconography, see Anne-Lise Tropato, 'Man, Death and Birds of Prey: Images of an Encounter (Christian Occident, 13th–15th Centuries)', in *Raptor on the Fist: Falconry, its Imagery and Similar Motifs throughout the Millennia on a Global Scale*, ed. Oliver Grimm in cooperation with Karl-Heinz Gersmann and Anne-Lise Tropato (Kiel and Hamburg, 2020), pp. 797–818.

37 Cummins, *The Hound and the Hawk*, pp. 210–11.

38 Kathleen Kulp-Hill, ed. and trans., *Songs of Holy Mary of Alfonso x, The Wise: A Translation of the 'Cantigas de Santa Maria'* (Tempe, AZ, 2000), p. 59.

39 Oggins, *The Kings and Their Hawks*, p. 105.

40 See Lothar Voetz, *Der Codex Manesse: Die berühmteste Liederhandschrift des Mittelalters* (Darmstadt, 2017).

41 Baudouin van den Abeele, *La Fauconnerie dans les lettres françaises du XIIe au XIVe siècle* (Leuven, 1990), pp. 174–86.

42 Quoted in Katharina Fietze, *Im Gefolge Dianas: Frauen und höfische Jagd im Mittelalter (1200–1500)* (Cologne, Vienna and Weimar, 2005), p. 85.

43 Cummins, *The Hound and the Hawk*, p. 208.

44 Elkins, *The Object Stares Back*, p. 21.

45 Jerome Delhaye, 'Falconry as a Symbol of Peace in 13th–16th Century Western European Art', in *Raptor on the Fist*, ed. Grimm, Gersmann and Tropato, p. 840. Van den Abeele, *La Fauconnerie dans les lettres françaises*, p. 38.

46 Beate Kellner, *Spiel der Liebe im Minnesang* (Paderborn, 2018), pp. 260–62.

47 Quoted in Oggins, *The Kings and Their Hawks*, p. 62.

48 Quoted ibid.

49 José Manuel Fradejas Rueda, ed., *Evangelista's 'Libro de cetrería': A Fifteenth-Century Satire of Falconry Books* (London, 1992), pp. xxviii–xxx; Thomas Szab, 'Die Kritik der Jagd – Von der Antike zum Mittelalter', in *Jagd und höfische Kultur im Mittelalter*, ed. Rösener, pp. 167–229.

50 Fradejas Rueda, ed., *Evangelista's 'Libro de cetrería'*, pp. xxviii–xxx; Michael Hammer, 'Evangelista's *Libro de cetrería* as Social Satire', in *La Corónica: A Journal of Medieval Hispanic Languages, Literatures and Cultures*, XXXVIII/1 (2008), pp. 247–58.

51 Quoted in Oggins, *The Kings and Their Hawks*, p. 121.

52 Johannes Fried, *Kaiser Friedrich II als Jäger oder ein zweites Falkenbuch Kaiser Friedrichs II?* (Göttingen, 1996), p. 121.

53 Michael Menzel, 'Die Jagd als Naturkunst: Zum Falkenbuch Kaiser Friedrichs II', in *Natur im Mittelalter: Konzeptionen, Erfahrungen, Wirkungen*, ed. Peter Dilg (Berlin, 2003), p. 358. This is a similar critique to the one addressed to Ludwig XIII concerning hawking and Ludwig XIV concerning hunting in general.

54 Carl Arnold Willemsen, *Das Falkenbuch Kaiser Friedrichs II* (Munich, 1999), p. 251; Lisa Anna Medrow, 'Falkenjagd in Arabien im 8.-13. Jahrhundert', in *Von der Kunst mit Vögeln zu jagen: Das Falkenbuch Friedrichs II. – Kulturgeschichte und Ornithologie*, ed. Mamoun Fansa and Carsten Ritzau, exh. cat., Landesmuseum für Natur und Mensch, Osnabrück (Mainz, 2007), p. 18.

55 Menzel, 'Die Jagd als Naturkunst', pp. 357–8.

56 Christian Antoine de Chamerlat, *Falconry and Art* (Paris, 1987), p. 88; Oggins, *The Kings and Their Hawks*, p. 121.

57 Robert Seidenader, *Kulturgeschichte der Falknerei mit besonderer Berücksichtigung von Bayern: Von Augustinus bis Kurfürst Maximilian I*, vol. I (Munich, 2007), p. 205.

58 Chamerlat, *Falconry and Art*, p. 113.

59 Andreas Beyer, 'Papstbildnis', in *Handbuch der politischen Ikonographie*, ed. Uwe Fleckner, Martin Warnke and Hendrik Ziegler, vol. II (Munich, 2011), pp. 197–203.

60 Jörg Traeger, *Der reitende Papst: Ein Beitrag zur Ikonographie des Papsttums* (Munich, 1970).

61 Ibid., p. 87. Clemens V did not go as Bishop of Bordeaux to Rome but to Avignon.

62 Ibid.

63 Michael McCormick, 'Profectio', in *The Oxford Dictionary of Byzantium*, ed. Alexander P. Kazhdan (Oxford, 2005), www.oxfordreference.com, accessed 10 March 2021.

64 See Bruno Galland, *Les Papes d'Avignon et la maison de Savoie: (1309–1409)* (Rome, 1998).

65 Traeger, *Der reitende Papst*, p. 85.

66 Georges Didi-Huberman, *The Eye of History: When Images Take Positions*, trans. Shane B. Lillis (Cambridge, MA, 2018).

67 Traeger, *Der reitende Papst*, p. 85.

68 Ibid., p. 86.

69 Von dem Knesebeck, *Aspekte der höfischen Jagd*, p. 523.

70 Among many other cases, in the choir of St Hippolyte at Poligny there is a statue with a nobleman holding a hawk, dated around

1400. See Philipp Steinkamp, 'Vogel', in *Der Naumburger Meister. Bildhauer und Architekt im Europa der Kathedralen*, ed. Hartmut Krohm et al., exh. cat., Dom and Schlösschen-Stadtmuseum Hohe Lilie, Naumburg (Petersberg, 2011), p. 946. The author of the entry avoids characterizing the animal as a kestrel. More recently the bird has been identified as a pigeon. See Jacqueline E. Jung, 'In Praise of the Pigeon: Interpretive Adventures in Naumburg Cathedral', in *How Do Images Work? Strategies of Visual Communication in Medieval Art*, ed. Christine Beier et al. (Turnhout, 2021), pp. 149–64.

71 Heinrich Pfeiffer, 'Gemalte Theologie in der Sixtinischen Kapelle: Teil 1. Die Szenen des alten und neuen Testamentes ausgeführt unter Sixtus IV', *Archivum Historiae Pontificiae*, XXVIII (1990), p. 147. I do not want to comment upon the quite rigid symbolical reading of Pfeiffer, who believes that the Devil is the partridge, whereas the falcon embodies goodness.

72 A.E.H. Swaen, *De Valk in de Ikonographie* (Amsterdam, 1926), p. 34.

73 Ibid.

74 Richard Offner, 'The Barberini Panels and Their Painters', in *Medieval Studies in Memory of A. Kingsley Porter*, ed. Wilhelm Koehler (Cambridge, MA, 1939), pp. 205–53.

75 Mario Gaglione, *Sculture minori del Trecento conservate in Santa Chiara a Napoli ed altri studi* (Naples, 1995), pp. 35–43; Nicolas Bock, *Kunst am Hofe der Anjou-Durazzo: Der Bildhauer Antonio Baboccio (1351–c. 1423)* (Munich, 2001), pp. 280–308.

76 Tanja Michalsky, *Memoria und Repräsentation: Die Grabmäler des Königshauses Anjou in Italien* (Göttingen, 2000), pp. 310–24. See also Baudouin van den Abeele, 'Falconry at the Aragonese Court of Naples (15th Century)', *International Journal of Falconry*, VII/1 (2020), pp. 58–61. Van den Abeele does not mention the tomb monuments.

77 San Giuliano l'Ospitaliere, also a former knight, is depicted in the sixteenth century as a falconer, simultaneously carrying his sword (for instance in the work *Giuliano l'Ospitaliere* by Perino del Vaga, oil on canvas, at the Galleria Colonna, Rome).

78 Huizinga, *The Waning of the Middle Ages*, pp. 91–3. See Wim Huyskens, *De vrije vogelflucht. Kunst en valkerij: Motief, portret, gedicht* (Zutphen, 1992), pp. 26–42.

6 Diplomacy and Gifts

1 See Mark Hegener and Nadir Weber, eds, *Animals and Courts: Europe, c. 1200–1800* (Berlin and Boston, MA, 2020).
2 Thomas T. Allsen, *The Royal Hunt in Eurasian History* (Philadelphia, PA, 2006), p. 243.
3 Concerning a different historical context, see Claudia Swan, 'Dutch Diplomacy and Trade in *Rariteyten*: Episodes in the History of Material Culture of the Dutch Republic', in *Global Gifts: The Material Culture of Diplomacy in Early Modern Eurasia*, ed. Zoltán Biedermann, Anne Gerritsen and Giorgio Riello (Cambridge, 2018), p. 197.
4 Nadir Weber, 'Lebende Geschenke: Tiere als Medien der frühneuzeitlichen Außenbeziehungen', in *Medien der Außenbeziehungen von der Antike bis zu der Gegenwart*, ed. Peter Hoeres and Anuschka Tischer (Cologne, Weimar and Vienna, 2017), pp. 166–7.
5 See, for the issue of debt, Nathalie Karagiannis, 'Debt, Time, Creation: An Introduction', *Social Science Information*, LVIII/3 (2019), pp. 393–402.
6 Marcel Mauss, *The Gift: Form and Reason for Exchange in Archaic Societies* (New York and London, 1990), p. 39.
7 Ibid., p. 41.
8 Ibid.
9 John Cummins, *The Hound and the Hawk: The Art of Medieval Hunting* (London, 1988), p. 196.
10 Costas M. Constantinou, 'Diplomacy', in *Visual Global Politics*, ed. Roland Bleiker (London and New York, 2018), p. 104.
11 Helen Macdonald, *Falcon* (London, 2006), p. 67.
12 Henry Maguire, '"Signs and Symbols of Your Always Victorious Reign": The Political Ideology and Meaning of Falconry in Byzantium', in *Images of the Byzantine World: Visions, Messages and Meanings: Studies Presented to Leslie Brubaker*, ed. Angeliki Lymberopoulou (Farnham, 2011), p. 135; Macdonald, *Falcon*, p. 27.
13 Arthur MacGregor, *Animal Encounters: Human and Animal Interaction in Britain from the Norman Conquest to World War One* (London, 2012), p. 179.
14 Robin S. Oggins, *The Kings and Their Hawks: Falconry in Medieval England* (New Haven, CT, 2004), p. 12; Sigurdur Aegisson, *Icelandic Trade with Gyrfalcons: From Medieval Times to the Modern Era* (Siglufjörður, 2015); Ragnar Orten Lie, 'Falconry, Falcon-Catching and the Role of Birds of Prey in Trade as Alliance Gifts in Norway (800–1800 AD) with an Emphasis on Norwegian and Later Foreign

Participants in Falcon-Catching', in *Raptor and Human: Falconry and Bird Symbolism throughout the Millennia on a Global Scale*, ed. Karl-Heinz Gersmann and Oliver Grimm (Kiel and Hamburg, 2018), pp. 727–86.

15 Javier Ceballos, *Falconry: Celebrating a Living Heritage* (Dubai, 2009), p. 149; Wilfried Seipel, ed., *Herrlich Wild: Höfische Jagd in Tirol*, exh. cat., Kunsthistorisches Museum, Vienna (2004), p. 135.

16 Christian Antoine de Chamerlat, *Falconry and Art* (Paris, 1987), p. 116.

17 Joshua Hammer, *The Falcon Thief: A True Tale of Adventure, Treachery, and the Hunt for the Perfect Bird* (New York, 2020), p. 142.

18 Christoph Niedermann, *Das Jagdwesen am Hoffe Herzog Philipp des Guten von Burgund* (Brussels, 1995), pp. 54–8. Crucial remarks concerning trapping in the Middle Ages are included in the French treatise of 1379 *Le Livre du roy Modus et de la royne Ratio*.

19 Pero López de Ayala, *Libro de la caça de las aves*, ed. John Cummins (London, 1986), pp. 88–9.

20 Niedermann, *Das Jagdwesen*, p. 56; Thierry Buquet, 'The Gyrfalcon in the Middle Ages: An Exotic Bird of Prey (Western Europe and Near East)', in *Falconry in the Mediterranean Context during the Pre-Modern Era*, ed. Charles Burnett and Baudouin van den Abeele (Geneva, 2021), pp. 79–98.

21 Allsen, *The Royal Hunt in Eurasian History*, p. 251.

22 Linda Komaroff, ed., *Gifts of the Sultan: The Arts of Giving at the Islamic Courts*, exh. cat., Los Angeles County Museum of Art (New Haven, CT, 2011), p. 42.

23 Niedermann, *Das Jagdwesen*, pp. 321–2.

24 Chamerlat, *Falconry and Art*, p. 70.

25 Quoted in MacGregor, *Animal Encounters*, p. 179.

26 Niedermann, *Das Jagdwesen*, p. 322.

27 Johannes Fried, *Kaiser Friedrich II als Jäger oder ein zweites Falkenbuch Kaiser Friedrichs II?* (Göttingen, 1996), p. 123. See also Baudouin van den Abeele, *Au Moyen Âge: Conaissance, affaitage et médecine des oiseaux de chasse d'apres les traités latins* (Paris, 1994), pp. 82–6.

28 Eric J. Goldberg, *In the Manner of the Franks: Hunting, Kingship and Masculinity in Early Medieval Europe* (Philadelphia, PA, 2020), p. 153. See also Martina Giese, 'Evidence of Falconry on the European Continent and in England, with an Emphasis on the 5th to 9th Centuries: Historiography, Hagiography and Letters', in *Raptor and Human*, ed. Gersmann and Grimm, p. 1477, and David Horobin, 'The Pen and the Peregrine: Literary Influences

on the Development of British Falconry (8th Century to the Present)', in *Raptor and Human*, ed. Gersmann and Grimm, p. 1056.

29 Ceballos, *Falconry*, p. 88.

30 Stefan Georges, *Das zweite Falkenbuch Kaiser Friedrichs II* (Berlin, 2008), p. 26.

31 Edward H. Schafer, 'Falconry in Tang Times', *T'oung Pao*, XLVI/3–5 (1958), p. 304.

32 Goldberg, *In the Manner of the Franks*, p. 153.

33 Oggins, *The Kings and Their Hawks*, p. 113.

34 Jerome Delhaye, 'Falconry as a Symbol of Peace in 13th–16th Century Western European Art', in *Raptor on the Fist: Falconry, its Imagery and Similar Motifs throughout the Millennia on a Global Scale*, ed. Oliver Grimm in cooperation with Karl-Heinz Gersmann and Anne-Lise Tropato (Kiel and Hamburg, 2020), p. 841. In this context it is rather about the already mentioned dialectical nature of falconry fluctuating between peaceful and aggressive activity.

35 See in general concerning Alexander's visual reception: Nicos Hadjinicolaou, ed., *Alexander the Great in European Art*, exh. cat., Teloglion Fine Arts Foundation, Thessaloniki (1997).

36 Delhaye, 'Falconry as a Symbol of Peace', p. 841.

37 Fried, *Friedrich II als Jäger*, p. 132.

38 Quoted in David Horobin, *Falconry in Literature: The Symbolism of Falconry in English Literature from Chaucer to Marvell* (Surrey, British Columbia, 2004), p. 28.

39 See Keelan Overton, 'Ambassadors and Their Gifts', in *Gifts of the Sultan*, ed. Komaroff, p. 140; Gary Schwartz, 'Terms of Reception: Europeans and Persians and Each Other's Art', in *Mediating Netherlandish Art and Material Culture in Asia*, ed. Thomas da Costa Kaufmann and Michael North (Amsterdam, 2014), p. 46.

Coda: Falconry's Visual Legacy

1 How terms like 'medieval' are used in regard to non-European art is a further methodological problem.

2 Joannes Sambucus, *Emblemata* (Antwerp, 1564), ed. Bibliotheca Hungarica Antiqua XI (Budapest, 1982), pp. 218–19. Translation: French Emblems at Glasgow, www.emblems.arts.gla.ac.uk, accessed 19 May 2021. Compare A.S.Q. Visser, *Joannes Sambucus and the Learned Image: The Use of the Emblem in Late-Renaissance Humanism* (Leiden and Boston, MA, 2005), pp. 6–9.

3 See Sara Petrosillo, *Hawking Women: Falconry, Gender and Control in Medieval Literary Culture* (Columbus, OH, 2022).

4 See the recent article with a brief mention of Bibi, without the above-mentioned aspect: Rachel Parikh, '"The King's Boon Companion": Falconry in Mughal Imperial Portraiture from Akbar to Azam Shah, 1556–1707', in *Raptor on the Fist: Falconry, its Imagery and Similar Motifs throughout the Millennia on a Global Scale*, ed. Oliver Grimm in cooperation with Karl-Heinz Gersmann and Anne-Lise Tropato (Kiel and Hamburg, 2020), p. 936.

5 See Associated Press, 'Raw: Bald Eagle Attacks Trump during Photoshoot', www.youtube.com, 10 December 2015. During his Fox interview after the shoot, Trump stated: 'This bird is seriously dangerous but beautiful.' Quoted in Tierney McAfee, *People*, www.people.com, 30 March 2016.

6 Concerning portraiture in seventeenth-century Netherlands, see Jan Baptist Bedaux and Rudi Ekkart, eds, *Pride and Joy: Children's Portraits in the Netherlands, 1500–1700*, exh. cat., Frans Hals Museum, Haarlem (New York, 2001).

7 Joaneath Spicer, 'The Renaissance Elbow', in *A Cultural History of Gesture: From Antiquity to the Present Day*, ed. Jan Bremmer and Herman Roodenburg (Cambridge, 1991), pp. 84–128.

8 Tanya Paul et al., eds, *Elegance and Refinement: The Still-Life Paintings of Willem van Aelst*, exh. cat., National Gallery of Art, Washington, DC (New York, 2012).

9 Kurt Lindner, *Beiträge zu Vogelfang und Falknerei im Altertum* (Berlin, 1973), p. 90.

10 Mark Ledbury, ed., *James Northcote, History Painting, and the Fables*, exh. cat., Yale Center for British Art, New Haven, CT (New Haven, CT, and London, 2014). See Yannis Hadjinicolaou, 'Visual Encounters: Falconry as Image Practice', in *Visual Engagements: Image Practices and Falconry*, ed. Yannis Hadjinicolaou (Berlin and Boston, MA, 2020), pp. 3–7.

11 Thomas T. Allsen, *The Royal Hunt in Eurasian History* (Philadelphia, PA, 2006), p. 11.

12 Hugo Richter, *Renz Waller: Maler, Falkner, Schriftsteller* (Düsseldorf, 1985).

13 Renz Waller, *Der wilde Falk ist mein Gesell* (Neudamm, 1937).

14 Peter N. Klüh, *Die Falknerei im Nationalsozialismus* (Darmstadt, 2017), p. 128.

15 This groundbreaking event, the first of its kind, was originally entitled the International Conference on Falconry and

Conservation, and so this appears on the programme's cover. However, it is now recognized as the first of the international Festivals of Falconry.

16 Zayed Bin Sultan Al Nahyan, *Falconry as a Sport: Our Arab Heritage* (Abu Dhabi, 1976), pp. 8 and 16.

17 Ibid., pp. 8–9.

18 Frederick II, *The Art of Falconry: Being the 'De arte venandi cum avibus' of Frederick II of Hohenstaufen*, ed. Casey A. Wood and F. Marjorie Fyfe (Stanford, CA, 1943), p. 4.

19 See on this subject Yannis Hadjinicolaou, 'Kinetic Symbol: Falconry as Image Vehicle in the United Arab Emirates', in *All Things Arabia: Arabian Identity and Material Culture*, ed. Ileana Baird and Hülya Yağcioğlu (Leiden and Boston, MA, 2021), pp. 127–42.

SELECT BIBLIOGRAPHY

Akasoy, Anna, 'The Influence of the Arabic Tradition of Falconry and Hunting on Western Europe', in *Islamic Crosspollinations: Interactions in the Medieval Middle East*, ed. James Montgomery, Anna Akasoy and Peter E. Pormann (Oxford, 2007)

Allsen, Thomas T., *The Royal Hunt in Eurasian History* (Philadelphia, PA, 2006)

Almond, Richard, *Medieval Hunting* (Stroud, 2003)

Amirsadeghi, Hossein, ed., *Sky Hunters: The Passion of Falconry* (London, 2008)

Belting, Hans, *Florence and Baghdad: Renaissance Art and Arab Science* (Cambridge, MA, 2011)

Boccassini, Daniela, *Il volo della mente: Falconeria e sofia nel mondo mediterraneo: Islam, Federico II, Dante* (Ravenna, 2003)

Bourdieu, Pierre, *Language and Symbolic Power*, trans. Gino Raymond and Matthew Adamson (Oxford, 1991)

Bredekamp, Horst, *Image Acts: A Systematic Approach to Visual Agency*, trans. Elizabeth Clegg (Berlin and Boston, MA, 2018)

Burnett, Charles, and Baudouin van den Abeele, eds, *Falconry in the Mediterranean Context During the Pre-Modern Era* (Geneva, 2021)

Ceballos, Javier, *Falconry: Celebrating a Living Heritage* (Dubai, 2009)

Chamerlat, Christian Antoine de, *Falconry and Art* (Paris, 1987)

Clark, Terence, and Muawiya Derhalli, eds, *Al-Mansur's Book on Hunting* (Warminster, 2001)

Cockram, Sarah, and Andrew Wells, eds, *Interspecies Interactions: Animals and Humans between the Middle Ages and Modernity* (London, 2017)

Cummins, John, *The Hound and the Hawk: The Art of Medieval Hunting* (London, 1988)

Didi-Huberman, Georges, *The Eye of History: When Images Take Positions*, trans. Shane B. Lillis (Cambridge, MA, 2018)

Eck, Caroline van, *Art, Agency and Living Presence: From the Animated Image to the Excessive Object* (Berlin and Boston, MA, 2015)

Edwardes, Michael, *East–West Passage: The Travel of Ideas, Arts and Inventions between Asia and the Western World* (London, 1971)

Fleckner, Uwe, Martin Warnke and Hendrik Ziegler, eds, *Handbuch der politischen Ikonographie*, 2 vols (Munich, 2011)

Fradejas Rueda, José Manuel, ed., *Evangelista's 'Libro de cetrería': A Fifteenth-Century Satire of Falconry Books* (London, 1992)

Frederick II, *The Art of Falconry: Being the 'De arte venandi cum avibus' of Frederick II of Hohenstaufen*, ed. Casey A. Wood and F. Marjorie Fyfe (Stanford, CA, 1943)

Freedberg, David, *The Power of Images: Studies in the History and Theory of Response* (Chicago, IL, 1989)

Fried, Johannes and Gundula Grebner, eds, *Kulturtransfer und Hofgesellschaft im Mittelalter. Wissenskultur am sizilianischen und kastilischen Hof im 13. Jahrhundert* (Berlin, 2008)

Gersmann, Karl-Heinz, and Oliver Grimm, eds, *Raptor and Human: Falconry and Bird Symbolism throughout the Millennia on a Global Scale* (Kiel and Hamburg, 2018)

Goldberg, Eric J., *In the Manner of the Franks: Hunting, Kingship, and Masculinity in Early Medieval Europe* (Philadelphia, PA, 2020)

Greenblatt, Stephen, *Cultural Mobility: A Manifesto* (Cambridge, 2009)

Grimm, Oliver, in cooperation with Karl-Heinz Gersmann and Anne-Lise Tropato, eds, *Raptor on the Fist: Falconry, its Imagery and Similar Motifs throughout the Millenia on a Global Scale* (Kiel and Hamburg, 2020)

Gumbrecht, Hans Ulrich, *In Praise of Athletic Beauty* (Cambridge, MA, 2006)

Hadjinicolaou, Yannis, ed., *Visual Engagements: Image Practices and Falconry* (Berlin and Boston, MA, 2020)

Hegener, Mark, and Nadir Weber, eds, *Animals and Courts: Europe, c. 1200–1800* (Berlin and Boston, MA, 2020)

Horobin, David, *Falconry in Literature: The Symbolism of Falconry in English Literature from Chaucer to Marvell* (Surrey, British Columbia, 2004)

Huizinga, Johan, *The Waning of the Middle Ages: A Study of the Forms of Life, Thought, and Art in France and the Netherlands in the Fourteenth and Fifteenth Centuries* (London, 1987)

Husband, Timothy B., *The World in Play: Luxury Cards, 1430–1540* (New York, 2016)

Jardine, Lisa, and Jerry Brotton, *Global Interests: Renaissance Art between East and West* (London, 2000)

Kantorowicz, Ernst, *The King's Two Bodies: A Study in Medieval Political Theology* (Princeton, NJ, 1957)

Kogman-Appel, Katrin, *Jewish Book Art between Islam and Christianity: The Decoration of Hebrew Bibles in Medieval Spain* (Leiden, 2004)

Latour, Bruno, *Reassembling the Social: An Introduction to Actor-Network-Theory* (Oxford, 2007)

Layard, Austen Henry, *Discoveries among the Ruins of Nineveh and Babylon* (London, 1853)
Leeflang, Huigen, Erik Hinterding and Harrie Knol, eds, *The Lure of Falconry / De Verlokkingen van de Valkerij*, exh. cat., Rijksmuseum, Amsterdam (2012)
Lindner, Kurt, *Beiträge zu Vogelfang und Falknerei im Altertum* (Berlin, 1973)
López de Ayala, Pero, *Libro de la caça de las aves*, ed. John Cummins (London, 1986)
Macdonald, Helen, *Falcon* (London, 2006)
—, *H is for Hawk* (London, 2014)
MacGregor, Arthur, *Animal Encounters: Human and Animal Interaction in Britain from the Norman Conquest to World War One* (London, 2012)
Maguire, Henry, '"Signs and Symbols of Your Always Victorious Reign": The Political Ideology and Meaning of Falconry in Byzantium', in *Images of the Byzantine World: Visions, Messages and Meanings: Studies Presented to Leslie Brubaker*, ed. Angeliki Lymberopoulou (Farnham, 2011)
Marin, Louis, *The Portrait of the King* (Minneapolis, MN, 1988)
Nagel, Thomas, 'What Is it Like to Be a Bat?', *Philosophical Review*, LXXXIII/4 (October 1974), pp. 435–50
Niedermann, Christoph, *Das Jagdwesen am Hofe Herzog Philipp des Guten von Burgund* (Brussels, 1995)
Oggins, Robin S., *The Kings and Their Hawks: Falconry in Medieval England* (New Haven, CT, 2004)
Russo, Alessandra, Gerhard Wolf and Diana Fane, eds., *Images Take Flight: Feather Art in Mexico and Europe, 1400–1700* (Munich, 2015)
Swaen, A.E.H., *De Valk in de Iconographie* (Amsterdam, 1926)
Van den Abeele, Baudouin, *La Fauconnerie au Moyen Âge: Conaissance, affaitage et médecine des oiseaux de chasse d'apres les traités latins* (Paris, 1994)
Van den Abeele, Baudouin, *Texte et image dans les manuscrits de chasse médiévaux* (Paris, 2013)
Warnke, Martin, *Political Landscape: The Art History of Nature* (London, 1994)
Watt, Montgomery, *The Influence of Islam on Medieval Europe* (Edinburgh, 1972)
Woolley, Linda, *Medieval Life and Leisure in the Devonshire Hunting Tapestries* (London, 2002)
Zayed Bin Sultan Al Nahyan, *Falconry as a Sport: Our Arab Heritage* (Abu Dhabi, 1976)

ACKNOWLEDGEMENTS

I would like to thank the many people who, in the course of my research, discussed, posed questions or brought specific information to my attention: Baudouin van den Abeele, Horst Bredekamp, Adrian Bremenkamp, Reindert Falkenburg, José Manuel Fradejas Rueda, Lukas Huppertz, Deirdre Jackson, Stuart Moss, Neville Rowley, Barbara Schellewald, Monika Wagner and the late Martin Warnke. Nicos Hadjinicolaou and Herman Roodenburg provided many critical insights.

During my time as a research fellow at New York University Abu Dhabi (2017–18) I had the great opportunity of conducting research in one of the cradles of falconry; Reindert Falkenburg, Martin Klimke and Alex Sandu were wonderful hosts during a highly stimulating time.

A grant from New York University Abu Dhabi (Humanities Research Fellowship programme) enabled me to brush up my manuscript with the indispensable assistance of David Horobin, who helped with his practical and scholarly knowledge on falconry to improve the text. Another editing of the text was kindly provided by Anastasia Caramanis.

The international research project 'Bilderfahrzeuge: Aby Warburg's Legacy and the Future of Iconology', with colleagues in London (Warburg Institute), Berlin (Humboldt University), New Delhi (Max Weber Stiftung) and, last but not least, Hamburg (Warburg Haus/University of Hamburg), was an inspiring ground for conducting research. I wish to particularly thank Andreas Beyer, Horst Bredekamp, Uwe Fleckner, Bill Sherman and Gerhard Wolf for their support.

I would like to express my gratitude to the institute of art history (University of Bonn) and more specifically to Birgit Ulrike Münch for funding the copyrights of some reproductions. Deirdre Jackson is to be thanked for her proposal to publish the book in the series, as is Michael Leaman for his interest. Alex Ciobanu helped in a number of ways, especially concerning the images. I would also like to thank Emma Devlin, Dhanya Ramesh and Aimee Selby for their careful final editing.

Last but not least, Anja's immense support is what made it possible for me to complete the manuscript and enable it to 'walk' by itself, at the same time as Nikolas was learning to do the same.

PHOTO ACKNOWLEDGEMENTS

The author and publishers wish to express their thanks to the sources listed below for illustrative material and/or permission to reproduce it. Some locations of artworks are also given below, in the interest of brevity:

Alte Pinakothek, Munich: 18; Art Institute of Chicago: 5; Bayeux Museum: 28; Biblioteca Apostolica Vaticana, Vatican City (Pal. lat. 1071): 2 (fol. 1v), 8 (fol. 82v); Bibliothèque de Genève (MS fr. 170, fol. 1r), CC BY-NC 4.0: 1, 3; Bodleian Library, University of Oxford (MS Douce 219, fol. 55v), CC BY-NC 4.0: 23; British Library, London (MS Or 2737, fol. 69r): 47; The British Museum, London: 19, 51, 57; Christ Church, University of Oxford (MS 92, fol. 1r): 14; collection of the author: 72 (photo Jean-Luc Ikelle-Matiba), 73, 74; photo G. Dagli Orti/De Agostini via Getty Images (Musée du Louvre, Paris): 4; The David Collection, Copenhagen: 42; Gallerie degli Uffizi, Florence: 38; Gemäldegalerie, Staatliche Museen zu Berlin/Jörg P. Anders: 70; Gunma Prefectural Museum of History, Takasaki: 10; John Heseltine/Alamy Stock Photo: 11; Historisches Museum Basel: 35; Institut für Geschichte, Karl-Franzens-Universität Graz (CC BY-NC-SA 4.0): 29; The J. Paul Getty Museum, Los Angeles: 60; Koninklijke Bibliotheek van België, Brussels: 64 (MS 9433–34, fol. 97r), 65 (MS 11040, fol. 46v); Kunsthistorisches Museum, Vienna, photos © KHM-Museumsverband: 17, 20, 21 (CC BY-NC-SA 4.0); Kunstmuseum Basel: 52; Kupferstichkabinett, Staatliche Museen zu Berlin, photo bpk/Kupferstichkabinett, SMB/Dietmar Katz: 16; Lindenau-Museum, Altenburg: 41; Louvre Abu Dhabi (LAD 2009.025), photo © Department of Culture and Tourism – Abu Dhabi/photo Thierry Ollivier: 37; The Metropolitan Museum of Art, New York: 27, 59, 69; Museé Condé, Chantilly (MS 368/1375, fol. 1v): 24; © Musée Rolin, Autun: 44; Museo Nacional del Prado, Madrid: 53; Museo Nazionale del Bargello, Florence: 31; The National Gallery, London: 49, 50; National Gallery of Art, Washington, DC: 32, 43; private collection: 13, 67; photo Antonio Quattrone/Electa/Mondadori Portfolio via Getty Images: 61; Real Biblioteca del Monasterio de San Lorenzo de El Escorial (MS T-I-1, fol. 64r), courtesy Patrimonio Nacional: 54; Rijksmuseum, Amsterdam: 22, 66; © Royal Albert Memorial Museum/Bridgeman Images: 71; from Joannes Sambucus, *Emblemata et aliquot nummi antiqui operis Ioan*, 4th edn (Antwerp, 1576), photo Universitätsbibliothek Basel: 68;

The State Hermitage Museum, Saint Petersburg: 46, 62; Stiftsbibliothek Heiligenkreuz (Cod. 226, fol. 129v): 48; Universitätsbibliothek Heidelberg: 15 (Cod. Pal. germ. 300, fol. 141r), 55 (Cod. Pal. germ. 848, fol. 249v); courtesy University of St Andrews Libraries and Museums: 63; Victoria and Albert Museum, London: 36; Wikimedia Commons: 9 (photo Dick Osseman, CC BY-SA 4.0), 30 (photo Siren-Com, public domain; Musée de la Chasse et de la Nature, Paris), 45 (photo Miguel Hermoso Cuesta, CC BY-SA 4.0; Skulpturensammlung und Museum für Byzantinische Kunst, SMB), 56 (photo Jean-Marc Rosier/www.rosier.pro, CC BY-SA 3.0).

INDEX

Illustration numbers are indicated by *italics*

Abbasid Caliphate 74, 163–4
Abd al Aziz Ben Al Qabturnh 163
Abd al-Rahman 41
Abu Nuwas 49
Achilles 130
Achmet of Basra 82
Adelard of Bath 50
Adenes Le Roi 126
Adonis 32
Aelst, Willem van 178, *70*
Æthelbald of Mercia 165
Ahmednagar 175
Akbar 175
Al-Andalus 115–16
Albertus Magnus 125
Alexander III, pope 143
Alexander the Great 21, 167, 169, *65*
Alexandria 163
Alexios I 30
Al-Fakhri 127
Alfonso X of Castile 137–8
Alfonso XI of Castile 126
Alfred the Great 83
Al-Ghitrif 81
Allah 46–7, 116
al-Malik al-Kamil 110
Almería 113
al-Muktafi 164
al-Mutawakkil 75, 163
Altstetten, Konrad von 141, *55*
Amazon 167
Ambras 59
Anatolia 22
Anglesey 126
Arabia 15, 19, 21–2, 50–52, 81, 106–7, 109, 111, 182, 184, 187–9
Aragon 139
Argos 22, 26, *6*, *7*
Aristotle 14, 19, 48, 55, 87
Armenia 15
Arras 95
Asia 15, 22, 106–7, 161–2
Asser 83
Assisi 155, *61*
Assyria 21–2, 115, 132
aquamanile 116, *46*
Aquarius 29
Avignon 145, 148, *56*
Ayala, Pedro López de 34, 65–6, 72, 86, 161

Babylon 21
Baghdad 41, 106
Balkans 161
Balthazar 102
Baltic Sea 160, 163
Balzo, Raimondo del 152, *60*
Barclay, Alexander 150
Basel 92–3, *21*, *35*
Bavo, St 156, *62*
Bayeux Tapestry 70, *28*
Becket, Thomas 140
Bedouin 89
Belgium 165

bell 89, 100, 169
Belting, Hans 106–7
Berlin 182
Bertha 164
Bertini, Seguace dei 153
Bethlehem 99
Bijapur 175
bittern 126
Black Sea 161
Boccaccio 108
Boke of Seynt Albans 76
Boniface 165
Book of Bird Hunting 34, 66, 72, 86, 161
Book of Nature, The 44, 15
Born, Bertran de 143
Bosch, Hieronymus 136, 53
Bosporus 80
Botticelli, Sandro 173
Bourdieu, Pierre 82
Brabant 94, 126, 161, 163
Brandt, Sebastian 150
Breker, Arno 183
Britain 129, 186
Bruges 1, 3
Burgundy 11, 14, 115, 161–2, 168
Byzantium 8, 19, 29, 76, 80–81, 101–3, 111–13, 125

camel 111
Canterbury 140
Canterbury Tales 127, 129
Cantigas de Santa Maria 137, 139–40, 149, 54
carneria 11, 26, 36, 42
Castiglione, Baldassare 80
Castile 116, 47
Central Asia 14, 20, 29, 82, 159
Chand Bibi 175–6, 67
Chantilly 64, 132
Charlemagne 31, 88
Charles v 72, 161, 176
Charles vi of France 96
Chaucer, Geoffrey 76, 127–9
Cheseman, Robert 136
China 20, 75, 107, 111, 130, 164
Christ 30, 99, 102, 131, 137
Claris and Laris 141
Clement v, pope 146, 148, 57
Clement vi, pope 145
Codex Manesse 140–41, 143, 165, 55
Cologne 161
Colosseum 130
Constantine the Great 111, 131, 148
Constantinople 75, 80, 103, 131
Cossa, Francesco del 66–7
crane 57–8, 126, 132
Crevalcore, Antonio de 18
crow 132

Damietta 110
Dancus Rex 16
Dante 131
Daphnopates, Theodore 80
David 122–4, 50
De animalibus 125–6
De arte venandi cum avibus 7, 10–11, 15, 24, 44, 52, 88, 168, 186, 2, 3, 8, 16
De avibus 128
Deccan 175, 67
Denys, Bishop of Senlis 144–5
Der von Kürenberg 68, 140
dog 19, 23, 27, 30, 35, 37–8, 40, 47, 59, 73, 80–81, 83, 85, 93, 108, 122–4, 127–8, 137, 144, 175, 179, 31
dove 128, 130
duck 23, 38, 126, 7

Duke of Clarence 55
Dur-Sharrukin 21–2
Dürer, Albrecht 127

eagle 45–6, 77
Ecclesia 119, 147–9
Edward I 85
Edward III 38, 131, *14*
Edwardes, Michael 107
Egypt 20, 29, 108, 110, 116, 119
Ekkehard II 149
Engelbert II of Nassau 61, *22*, *23*
England 38, 55–6, 131, 160–62, 188, *14*
Erasmus of Rotterdam 134, 136–7, 143, *52*
Escorial 137
Esquiola, Mario 36
Este, Borso d' 65
Ethelbert of Kent 163
Europe 15, 19, 22, 27, 29–30, 51–2, 78, 89–90, 97, 103, 106–7, 116, 119, 160, 175, 182, 184, 189
Evangelista 143
ex voto 137, 139–40

Fabriano, Gentile da 99–102
Falcon Song 68–9
Ferrara 54, 65, 72, *25*, *26*
Fiore, Joachim of 148
Fisher King 85–6
Flachsland, Hans von 93
Flanders 161, *23*
Florence 99, 102–3, 106, 124, *39*, *40*
Fra Angelico 110, *41*, *43*, *57*
Fra Carnevale 56, 59
France 66, 68, 95, 131–2, 188
Francières, Jean de 35
Francis, St 110, *41*
Franks 30
Frederick II of Hohenstaufen 10–11, 14–15, 19, 24, 26, 31, 33, 36–8, 45–6, 48–50, 52, 55, 57–8, 67, 72, 74, 76–7, 81, 86–9, 96, 98–9, 119, 144, 168, 178, 182–4, 186–7, *1*, *2*, *3*, *8*, *16*
frog 45

Gallacianus 16
Geertz, Clifford 68
Germany 40, 44, 68, 97, 132, 140, 149–50, 161, 163, 181–4, 187
Ghirlandaio, Domenico 149
Giotto 92, *34*
glove 23, 29, 49, 93, 126, 179
Goliath 122–4, *50*
Göring, Hermann 182–3
goose 126, 131
goshawk 35, 76, 85, 111, 139
Gozzoli, Benozzo 102, 110, 113, *39*
Greece 19–20, 22, 26, 75, 101, 130, 147, *6*, *7*
Greenblatt, Stephen 106
Greenland 160
Gregory IX, pope 144
Gruuthuse, Louis de 15
Guo Xi 107
gyrfalcon 57, 160–62, 164, 169, 183

Haarlem 156
Habsburg dynasty 53, 57, 161, 171
Hagenau *15*
Han dynasty 20
Harold 70, *28*
Hauville, Gilbert de 85

Hector 130
Henry VIII 136
Hercules 77
Hereford 140
heron 59, 64–6, 131–3
Hippolytus 26–7
Hitler, Adolf 181–2
Hittite civilization 22
Holbein, Hans the Younger 134, 136, *52*
Holy Land 98, 110
Homer 130
hood 51–5, 74, 134, 137, 178–9
horse 15, 35, 37, 70, 92, 108, 146, 176
Horus 20, 134
Hubert, St 183
Hugh of Fouilloy 128, 152, *48*
Hugh of Italy 164
Huw Bulkeley of Beaumaris 126–7
Hywel Dda 31

Ibn al-Tiqtaqa 127
Iceland 160, 162
Iliad 130
Indian Subcontinent 20, 75, 111, 170, 175, 184
Iraq 37, 82, 117
Isfahan 171
Isis 20
Istanbul 80
Italy 51, 58, 73, 99–100, 103, 115–16, 122, *2*, *8*, *16*, *24*, *31*

James IV 84
Japan 29, 107, 184, *10*
Jerusalem 122
jesses 22, 55, 115, 179
John, king of England 160
Jordan 26
Joseph, Patriarch of Constantinople 103
Joshua 148
Julius Firmicus Maternus 27

Kantorowicz, Ernst 77
Kedripolis 19
Kent 163
kestrel 149, 58
Khayyam, Omar 37
Khazars 30
Khorsabad 22
Khurasan 81–2
Kitab al-Mutawakkil 74–5, 111
Korea 29
Kublai Khan 168

Lampugnano, Antonio de 64, *24*
lanner falcon 143
lark 126
Laurin 167, *64*
Layard, Austen Henry 21–2
Lazarus of Autun, St 113
leash 14, 23, 80, 93, 175
Leo X, pope 145
Leonardo 107
Les Livres du roy Modus et de la royne Ratio 72
Libro de cetrería 143
Limbourg brothers 96
Limoges 99, 102, *37*
Lincolnshire 162
Lindner, Kurt 42
lion 80, 130, 132–3
Lippi, Filippo 110, *43*
Lives of the Artists 123
Livre de fauconnerie 13
Lombard 31
Lombardy 36
London 107
Longchamp, Nigel de 144

Lorenzetti, Ambrogio 90, 92, 95, 121
Lorenzo il Magnifico 145
Lothair II of Lotharingia 164
Louis XII 15
Lübeck 163
lure 51–2, 56–9, 61–2, 66, 99, 102, 174, *20*, *21*
Luther, Martin 145

Macdonald, Helen 9, 33
Machiavelli, Niccolò 73
Madaba 26, *9*
Malta 161
Manasses, Constantine 75, 125, 131
Manfred 11, 26, 59, 168, *2*, *8*
Mantegna, Andrea 78
Mantua 36
Manuel I Komnenos 76
Marco Polo 168–9
Mark, St 29, 132, *11*, *12*, *51*
Mars 127, 130
Martin, St 153, *61*
Martini, Simone 153, *61*
Mary 137, 139, 152
Mary of Burgundy 70
Master E. S. 132
Master of the E-Series Tarocchi 79
Master of the Legend of the Magdalen 30
Master of Mary of Burgundy *23*
Master of the Princely Portraits *22*
Mauss, Marcel 159
Maximilian I 51, 53, 57, 127
Mechti Kuli Beg 169–70
Medici family 102, 111, 123, 145, *39*
Mediterranean 26, 32, 115–16
Megenberg, Konrad von *15*
Melchior 103
Ménagier de Paris 34
Mercury 29
merlin 72
Merovingian 30
Mértola 26
Mesopotamia 19, 22, 115, *4*
mews 84, 86, 150
Middle East 20, 52, 161
milan 64, 108
Milemete, Walter de *14*
Moamin 50, 64, 73, 138
Moses 116, 148
Mosul 22, 127
Mughal Empire 175
Muhammad ibn 'Abd Allah ibn 'Umar al-Bazyar 75

Naples 152, *60*
Naumburg 149, *58*
Near East 20
Nectanebo II 20
Netherlands 106, 161, 176–8, 188
Nevers, Jean de I 61–2
Nicholas, St 165, *63*
Nicopolis 161
Nike 77
Nineveh 21–2, *4*
North Africa 15, 19, 22, 160
Northcote, James 179–80, *71*
Norway 160–63
Nuremberg 163

Ordelafo Faliero *30*
Orpheus 131
Ottoman Empire 161, 171

Padua 34
Palaiologos, John VIII 103

Paris 22, 34, 72, 161
Parler School 61
parrot 116
partridge 38, 80
Paulinus of Pella 27
Pavia 108–9
perch 14, 34–5, 46, 115, 179
peregrine 76, 97
Persia 37, 75, 78, 82, 107, 111, 113, 169–71
Pesellino, Francesco 122, 123
Peter, St 147
Petronius 178
Phaedra 26–7
Pharaoh 116, 119, 47
pheasant 111, 149
Philip the Handsome 72, 176, 30
Phyllis 55
Piero di Cosimo de' Medici 103
Pisanello, Antonio 103
Plato 75
Portugal 26
Powell, Michael 129
Prague 61, 169, 171
Praise of Folly 134, 52
Pressburger, Emeric 129

Qabus-nama 81
Quest of the Holy Grail, The 82–3
Quran 46, 75

Raphael 127
Renart, Jean 128
Rhisiant Cyffin 126
Robert III of Artois 131
Roman de Alexandre 167
Roman Empire 19–20, 22, 26, 147
Roman de Laurin 166, 64
Roman de la Rose 66
Romans, Robin de 56
Romanos II 80
Rome 127, 147, 167, 64
Rothari 31
Rudolf II 170

Sadeler, Aegidius 169, 171–3, 66
Saladin 108–9
Sambucus, Johannes 174, 176
Saqqara 20
Seljuk Sultanate 37
senses 48–50
Sforza, Francesco 36
Sforza, house of 36, 64, 132
Shakespeare, William 140
Shandong 165
shark 45
Ship of Fools 150
Sicily 115
Siena 90, 121
Sint Jans, Geertgen tot 156, 62
snake 77, 81, 130
Sophie of Thuringia 70
Spain 34, 75, 113
sparrowhawk 66, 72–3, 126, 143
swan 132
Syria 22, 36, 116

Tang dynasty 164
Theodore of Antioch 144
Thorak, Josef 183
Thrace 19
Tomasello, Michael 41
Torello d'Istria 108–9
Tournai 165
Troja 130
Trump, Donald 176
Tughril 36
tulip 106–7

Tunisia 26, 161
Turkey 22, 111, 161

Umayyad Caliphate 75
United Arab Emirates 181, 184–7
Usama ibn Munqidh 36, 84, 127
Uta von Naumburg 149

Vaillant, Wallerant 177
Vandals 26
Vasari, Giorgio 123
Vatican 11, 26, 147
Venice 29, 132–3, 163, *11*, *12*
Venus 27, 32
vervel 51, 55–6
Vettori, Pietro 174
Vienna 51
Virgo 29
virgula 36, 50, 72
Visconti, Violante 55
Visigoths 30
Vows of the Heron, The 131

waiting on 37
Waller, Renz 40, 182–3, 186, *72*
Welsh 31
Winchester 165, *63*
Witz, Konrad 59

Xenophon 126
Xianzong 165

Yeats, William Butler 41
Yuan dynasty 130

Zayed bin Sultan Al Nahyan 186–7, *74*
Zeus 21, *77*
Zeuxis 61